A
Comparative Survey
of
Hindu, Christian and Jewish
Mysticism

Sri Garib Das Oriental Series No. 181

A Comparative Survey of Hindu, Christian and Jewish Mysticism

E.M. Abrahams

Sri Satguru Publications
A Division of
Indian Books Centre
Delhi - India

Published by :
SRI SATGURU PUBLICATIONS
Indological and Oriental Publishers
A Division of
INDIAN BOOKS CENTRE
40/5, Shakti Nagar,
Delhi-110007
(INDIA)

First Edition : Delhi, 1995

ISBN 81-7030-406-7

PRINTED IN INDIA

Dedicated with profound appreciation and deep love

To

Rachel, my wife and Reuben (my son), without whose help and patience this book would not have been published

Contents

Acknowledgements

I thank the University of Bombay for granting me permission to publish my thesis for Ph.D. degree (Philosophy) "Hindu, Christian and Kabbalistic Mysticism with special reference to Īśa, Kaṭha, Muṇḍaka and Kena, and "The Cloud of Unknowing". The thesis is being published in its original form with minor changes under the title "A Comparative Survey of Hindu, Christian and Jewish Mysticism".

I thank Dr. S.G. Mudgal who guided me throughout the preparation of my thesis for the degree of Ph.D of the University of Bombay. He also read and corrected the proofs of this book, placed diacritical marks and offered valuable advice from time to time.

I also thank Mr. S.S. Judah of Edinburg, U.K. for procuring books on Kabbalah and "The Cloud of Unknowing" as also arranging access to The Edinburgh Hebrew Congregation Library and Edinburgh City Libraries.

I am very grateful to Dr. K.K.A. Venkatachari for suggesting reference books from time to time. Dr. N.B. Pail, who taught me Sanskrit and Vedanta-Sara deserves special mention. He made valuable suggestions after perusing the Sanskrit portions of my thesis.

I thank the University of Bombay, Ananthacharya Indological Research Institute and Ruparel College Libraries for the various books and reference material they provided me during the course of my research.

I also thank Shri Sunil Gupta of Indian Books Centre, New Delhi who was very cordial, co-operative and patient. But for him, the book would not have been published in such a short period. Shri S.B. Rege designed the cover page. I thank him for it. I also thank, Mrs. E.R. Abrahams, my daughter-in-law, for helping me with the typing.

Bombay

August 1994

E.M. Abrahams

Foreword

I have gone through the Book 'A Comparative Survey of Hindu, Christian and Jewish Mysticism' by Dr. E.M. Abrahams. It is a scholarly and an erudite work. This book is a properly edited and revised version of his Doctoral Thesis.

The book is a comparative and evaluative study of Hindu, Christian and Jewish mysticism. Not much work is done in the field, though there are sketchy studies of any two of these schools and not all together. Again, the author has taken within his scope, not only the three schools of Vedanta, but has considered the four important Upaniṣads viz. Īśa, Kena, Kaṭha and Muṇḍaka. He has also rightly considered Buddhism. His study of these is thorough and his understanding very clear. He has then dealt with Christianity, with reference to the New Testament and the Christian Mystics. He has drawn on their works copiously. Being a practicing Jew himself, his study of Judaism and Kabbalah is thorough and gives a complete insight into these religious systems. The most important addition is the study of a great work. 'The Cloud of Unknowing' by an unknown author, who appears to be a Catholic Christian and who chose to remain anonymous, as the religious atmosphere of his days did not permit the freedom of expression he has shown in his work. As a matter of fact, the three middle Eastern religions were not very sympathetic to mysticism, though these religions produced great mystics.

Dr. Abrahams has rightly stated during the course of his studies that the quality of mystic/religious experiences, of all great mystics seems to be the same. But the apparent differences, which we find in their expression is due to their metaphysical and theological predilections and traditions.

There is a general saying that a Mystic alone can appreciate another Mystic properly. Dr. Abraham's work is a very good example of this statement.

It gives me pleasure to commend this scholarly book to both the Scholars and Commoners. Scholars will find it a very good source book and Commoners will find it highly interesting. This book will inspire them to study further, the other mystics and mystical religious systems, Both will find it illuminating.

All said and done, this is a mature work and can be read by all with great advantage.

Professor of Philosophy,
Ananthacharya Indological
Research Institute,
Bombay - 400 005.

S. G. MUDGAL.

Abbreviations

B.G.	...	Bhagavad Gītā.
Bṛ	...	Bṛhad Āraṇyaka Upaniṣad.
Chand.	...	Chāndogya Upaniṣad.
Īśa.	...	Īśa Upaniṣad.
Kaṭha.	...	Kaṭha Upaniṣad.
Mā.	...	Māṇḍūkya Upaniṣad.
Muṇḍ	...	Muṇḍaka Upaniṣad.

Introduction

We know only that which our senses perceive, has seemed to many people a matter of common sense. For such people, the perceptual world, the world that we perceive with our five senses, is the only world that exists. Simple as these statements appear to be, they have formed the basis of great metaphysical problems. How can we know, it is asked, that which is outside our experience? An obvious and a natural question. But then what do we mean by 'experience?' And why should the knowledge of our senses contain the whole of our experience? Even if experience is defined as sensuous knowledge, why should there not be other ways of knowing which transcend this form of experience?

On the other hand it is contended that the data given by the senses about reality are not valid as it is so strongly influenced by the nature of man and by his perceptual equipment and by his techniques of perception. The mystic believes that by means of special training he can so discipline, tune and train his total organism that it will be able to transcend these limitations and perceive reality more accurately.

To speak of mystics as having 'discipline' and there being research 'data', may strike some as seriously distorting the meaning of these words. This misapprehension is due to the tendency among us to associate words like 'research' with physics, etc. This is also due to the lack of information and knowledge on the part of the generality of people about the existence of records and interesting material describing the same phenomena, very often in identical words. The British philosopher C.D. Broad writing on this aspect says :

"To me the occurrence of mystical experience at all times and places, and the similarities between the statements of so many mystics all the world over seems to be a really significant fact. *Prima facie* it suggests that there is an aspect of reality with which these persons came in contact in their mystical experience, and which they afterwards strive and largely fail to describe in the language of daily life. I should say that this *prima facie* appearance of objectivity ought to be accepted at its face value."[1]

There is overwhelming consistency in the mystical reports. These have been admirably described by writers and philosophers, who themselves differ from one another in many other ways. William James, W.T. Stace, Bertrand Russell, Evelyn Underhill are a few instances. For those who care, first hand evidence lies at the core of the Upaniṣads and such other classics belonging to the major religious traditions of the world. These reports, as do the findings of physics, show that sensory data give at best a very limited picture of reality.

We mentioned the Upaniṣads deliberately. They constitute not only the scriptures but also are a veritable source of mysticism. Much before the depth psychology of today, the seers of India were led to explore the hidden zones of the unconscious : The ascetics and sages realised that it was not difficult to master man's physiological, social, cultural and religious conditionings. The difficulty lay in the area of the unconscious, from what the seers called *Saṃskāras* and the *Vāsanās*. The modern psychologist would call these the structures and the contents of the unconscious. But even here a significant difference exists between the depth psychology of today and the depth psychology of the seers and ascetics of ancient India. To the latter mere knowledge was not an end in itself. The key word was not "knowing" but "mastering." They were not interested in "knowing" the contents of the unconscious, as much as burning and rooting them out.

This book pertains to the mysticisms of Hinduism, Christianity and Judaism. If on our journey through these traditions we have strayed and touched upon philosophers like Kant, and Hume, it is because such references are inevitable. Ultimate reality, God, and Mysticism are inseparable. If we have attempted to consider the proofs offered for the existence of God, it is not because the mystic is concerned with proving God's existence. For the mystic the starting point is the existence of God.

There are several approaches to the study of Mysticism : physiological, psychological, theological and even literary. Levitation or occultism (ecstatic dancing etc.) would fall within the physiological study. We will mainly be concerned with the claims made by mystics that they had contact with Ultimate

Reality which transcends the empirical world. For this purpose we will study those portions of the Upaniṣads, the Bible, the Kabbalah, the Cloud of Unknowing, which carry the recorded experiences of the mystics. These records show that the mystics speak from the vantage point of knowledge which we, the non-mystics do not possess. Our study will, therefore, face several difficulties. There being no empirical testing method available, one would not be in a position to verify whether the mystic encountered a transcendent reality or that he had the experience of oneness with it.

It would be well to remember that when the mystic makes a claim that he has encountered Ultimate Reality or Brahman or God, he is *not* trying to prove that God exists. He does not want to put forward his encounter as evidence of the existence of God. It would be absurd to say that St. John of the Cross or St. Teresa or for that matter Śaṅkara, Rāmānuja, or Madhva tried to prove the existence of God or Brahman through their writings. What they tried to do was to direct humanity to the path of mysticism, through contemplative prayer, disciplines and meditation. In fact mystics like St. John of the Cross or the author of the Cloud of Unknowing were addressing not atheists or agnostics but believers. Mysticism, as evidence for the existence of a Reality, a One, which is transcendent in the sense that it is irreducible to the many, is relatively a modern phenomenon. One of the reasons for this is that the traditional arguments have met with widespread criticism and people who wanted arguments in support of the existence of God found religious experience to be very useful. Modern man has also realised that living faith can rest only on religious experience. This remark, of course, will be applicable more to the Western world than to the non-Western world. As we have raised the question of modern man, it will not be incorrect to say that growing knowledge of non-Western culture and the fact that mysticism has played a major role in oriental religion, has been responsible for turning the Western mind to mysticism. Therefore, it is clear that mysticism has not played an insignificant part in the meeting of the East and West. The two mystical traditions have, for this reason, to be studied together.

Generally speaking, if we exclude the materialistic schools of India, we find that the non-materialistic schools, both Vedic and non-Vedic, were preoccupied with the problem of salvation. The vicious circle of births and rebirths had to be broken, if man were to attain enlightenment. Enlightenment was just another name for mysticism. There existed no line of demarcation between philosophy and religion. The one spilled into the other and *vice versa*. Mysticism thus constituted the highest common denominator of religion and philosophy.

In the West religion and philosophy are separate. The mystic, more often than not, operates within the authority of religion. The Eastern seer sets as his goal the Ultimate Subject with which he attempts to identify. The Western mystic on the other hand wants to know about and relate himself to the object : Both do this through mysticism. The phenomenon of mysticism remains the same. Interpretations differ. They differ because the Western and Eastern mystic records them in a different fashion. Buddha refuses to discuss the reality of Brahman or Ātman, emphasising the sole reality of Nirvāṇa, the subjective state of mystical enlightenment, the major portion of Śaṅkara's philosophy is devoted to the discussion of Brahman. For Buddha to maintain that Ātman exists is a false view. To maintain that Ātman does not exist is also a false view. A stable substance is an unreality for Buddha. The upshot is that while one mystic attempts defining the Ultimate Reality, another does not. But *all* of them are none-the-less mystics. Similarly, the Eastern mystic can declare with impunity that he becomes in his mystical ecstasy what he has actually always been. Māyā stood between him and his real self. The Western mystic stops short. Were he to declare his potential divinity, he would be warned that his experience is related to a God who remains perennially transcendent and separate. The Christian mystic has the sword of cultural environment and Church hanging over him, ready to drop the moment he oversteps the authority of the church. Meister Eckhart who did feel that he had become divine came close to being tried at Avignon. Unfortunately for Pope John XXII, who had ordered his trial, Eckhart met with an untimely death.

So we see that essentially the mystical experience is the same. Its expression is tempered by the environment, religion and country in which the mystic is born. There is thus considerable scope for the comparison of the mysticism of Hindu, Christian and

Jewish traditions. For this purpose it is vital to examine whether there is a core of teaching running through the major religious traditions. Mystical traditions form the core of all major religious traditions. A doctrinal comparison between two religious traditions often sets the stage for a collision. Similarly, a comparison of ethics is also ruled out. In many respects ethics becomes relative. What for example is ethical for a Muslim is unethical for a Christian. Historical comparison is also unhelpful.

The God of Christianity, like the God of Judaism, acts in history. For the Hindu and Buddhist, such an idea would be unacceptable, for the simple reason that the Hindu and Buddhist see man in terms of an endless series of births and rebirths. An event in history is of no consequence to him.

In the psychology of religion what attract's the attention of the psychologist is not so much the doctrinal, ethical or historical aspects, but the mystical. The creative impulse in religion is provided by mysticism. The first thing that arrests the attention of the psychologist is that the mystical experience is an altered state of consciousness, which culminates in a state, described by the mystic, as union. A theist describes this state as a union with God, non-theist (e.g. a Buddhist) describes it in different terms. But what is significant is that both theist and non-theist agree on the importance of the experience, which they regard as a perception of some aspect of Reality. Mysticism for this reason has provided, as we said above, the creative impulse for all religious thought.

For those who have studied Hinduism even cursorily it will not be surprising to know that Hinduism is so all encompassing in its varieties of mystical experiences, that by itself alone it contains all the mystical experiences of all the major religious traditions of the world. Looked at dispassionately, Hinduism is a unique synthesis. This fact alone is sufficient to support the view that there is considerable scope for a comparative study of the major religious traditions of the world. In our case, however, we will restrict this study to a comparison between Hindu, Christian and Jewish traditions.

For the subject of this book we have chosen mysticism—Hindu, Christian and Jewish. It would not be incorrect to say simply mysticism unqualified, for in truth, pure mysticism being above and beyond all form and contingency is neither Eastern nor Western, neither Hindu, Christian nor Jewish, but universal. The exterior forms with which it is covered only serve the necessities of exposition, to express whatever is expressible. These forms may be Eastern or Western. Under the appearance of diversity there is always a basis of unity, atleast where true mysticism exists. The only difference is that, except in India, these doctrines are reserved for a relatively restricted and closed élite. To repeat, truth is one, and it is the same for all those who, by whatever way, have attained it.

It is possible to define mysticism as we understand it. But to define is to limit, and that with which we are concerned is, in itself truly and absolutely unlimited and cannot be confined in any formula. Therefore, though we have attempted a definition, in the ultimate analysis we leave the definition to the great mystics and writers on mysticism. The vast literature on mysticism eloquently speaks for itself. No doubt a study of the writings of the great mystics give us theoretical knowledge. Theoretical knowledge may be indirect and even symbolic, but it serves as a preparation and is, therefore, indispensable for true knowledge.

When we talk of knowledge, we do not mean knowledge in the sense in which Aristotle understood it as a knowledge of being *qua* being. He identified it with ontology. In other words, he took part for the whole. Mysticism demands that man go beyond himself. That is why in all true mysticism it is necessary to take into account the inexpressible. A human being is not a closed system like Leibnitz's monad—confined beyond remedy, in himself. If this were the case anything outside his own mode of existence would be unknown to him. When, therefore, the word 'knowledge' is used, especially by the Eastern mystic (particularly Hindu mystic), it means higher knowledge, metaphysics or even mysticism. For the mystic, knowledge carries its own benefits, unlike action which is momentary. We have tried to show that for mysticism (a general word we use for Nirvāṇa, Enlightenment, etc.) two things are necessary : Method and Wisdom. These are often described an husband and wife, eternally devoted to one another, never to be separated. For this reason method is masculine, wisdom, feminine. Those familiar with Buddhist iconographical symbolism will remember that method is always depicted as a male figure, wisdom as a female figure. The conjugal embrace of these two is often misinterpreted erotically, when actually the Buddhist calls it mystical marriage of wisdom and method.

The belief that method precedes wisdom is erroneous. Wisdom precedes method. In the study of the mystics we shall notice how true this is, for the simple reason that there has to be some kind of initial vision of the truth : you may call it a glimpse of wisdom, before a man is forced to change the direction of his life and seek God. This is termed "conversion." William James in his lecture on Conversion says :

"To be converted, to be regenerated, to receive grace, to experience religion, to gain an assurance, are so many phrases which denote the process, gradual or sudden, by which a self hitherto divided, and consciously wrong, inferior and unhappy, becomes unified and consciously right, superior and happy, in consequence of its firmer hold upon religious realities. This at least is what conversion signifies in general terms."[2]

Thus conversion implies grace, thanks to which one suddenly becomes aware of the futility of one's present state. This stirs in one an awareness, egging one on to reach a better and happier state. At this stage we ask ourselves : What must we do to reach our goal we discern in the distance ? This is in fact our prayer for method. We shall see in the mystical writings of mystics belonging to all traditions that wisdom and method go hand in hand as also wisdom is followed by method. Wisdom, in its abstract form, in an isolated form, will merely lead the mind into an intellectual blind alley, a dead end. It will end in pure philosophising. With the dawn of wisdom must come a concurrent means of active verifications. This is what is provided by mysticism. Tradition is responsible for maintaining a polar balance between theory and practice, between wisdom and its effective realisation by taking the help of appropriate spiritual means. We can say that wisdom is concerned with *knowing* and method with *being*. After all one can only know something by being that thing. The proverbial trap of the philosophers is to mistake a mental appreciation of knowledge, for knowledge. There can be no realisation till such time as being and knowing coincide. We have tried in the following chapters to apply this criterion to the various traditions and their respective mystics.

Śankara, Rāmānuja, Madhva, the Buddha, the author of the Cloud, the Seers of the Upaniṣads and the Kabbalists, all stand this test.

We have added an appendix (I) on Drugs. In the present drug scene, its use is straightaway ruled out of court. But it is well to remember that drugs have been used by the Seers with good effect. However, such benefits are so rare as to be almost non-existent. The American Indians, for example, used tobacco for sacramental rites. Today it has degenerated into a deadly luxury. Despite all this, a study of the Hindu Scriptures shows that, carried out under proper directions, this kind of physical or psychological adjunct to meditation and contemplation can have great uses, provided the indispensable link with a traditional wisdom is maintained from start to finish. Aldous Huxley's prophetic words still ring in our ears :

"In one way or another, the world's ecclesiastical authorities will have to come to terms with the new mind changers. They may come to terms with them negatively, by refusing to have anything to do with them . . . on the other hand, they may choose to come to terms with the mind changers in some positive way."[3]

The reaction to the negative attitude will be the development of a psychological phenomenon, potentially of great spiritual value "outside the pale of organised religion." In the event of the latter, it is anybody's guess how or what shape the positive reaction will take.[4]

The attack on Huxley for his radical views is now history. In fact many critics were of the view that Huxley's greatest output preceded his experimentation with drugs. Thereafter he tended to write about drugs, not to create with them. Huxley, for that matter all those who experimented with drugs, never denied their deliterious effects. But what Huxley tried to emphasise is that someday religion "from being an activity mainly concerned with symbols will be transformed into an activity concerned mainly with experience and intuition—an everyday mysticism."[5] Will this transformation come about through conventional religion or through psychedelics ? This is a thousand dollar question which defies an answer at the present juncture.

IMPORTANCE OF MYSTICISM

Religion and mysticism are related to each other. As we said before it is not possible to give a satisfactory definition of mysticism. The case is not very different with religion. J.B. Pratt proposes the following definition of religion :

"Religion is the serious and social attitude of individuals or communities toward the power or powers which they conceive as having ultimate control over their interests and destinies."[6]

Without going into the merits of the definition we ask what does it really mean to be religious ? Does it have any inner connection with tradition or institution ? Can religion be identical with ethics or psychology ? In the event of our abandoning the realm of the transcendent, will religion still remain religion ? Will religion still be religion if we cease to hope for an ultimate deliverance ? We will not be so foolhardy as to answer all these questions. However, we make bold to say that all religions, one way or the other, focus on deliverance. It should be borne in mind that when we use the word 'deliverance' we do not mean deliverance in the ordinary sense of the word, the ending merely of a particular dissatisfaction. What we mean is deliverance which has cosmic implications. If we forget for a moment that the word 'salvation' has a Christian flavour or overtone, we could use it in place of 'deliverance,' because the word 'salvation' allows of being used in a much broader sense.

In the following chapters we have discussed at length how the mysticisms of the various religious traditions of the world help us to achieve salvation. This is not taken to mean that salvation is conceived of as something lying in wait in the future or at the end of the mystical voyage. In fact in some traditions (like the Hindu Advaitic tradition for instance) it is spoken of as already achieved or already present only concealed and waiting to come to light.

The question then arises as to how 'salvation' and the notion of salvation apply to mysticism. The mystic sees and seeks the oneness of things, and in this sense he finds everything acceptable. He does not, therefore, desire to save himself, but to lose himself in an ultimate union, whether of love or knowledge. This is tantamount to saying that the mystic seeks to be saved from himself, from the finitude of his own existence and particularity of his ego. In the ultimate analysis the mystic can be said to be *self* centred. After all salvation is something that happens to an individual. Theravāda Buddhism, for example, has for its aim the straight forward pursuit of salvation. *Mahāyāna* rejects salvation, for the sake of helping others. But even in the latter the element of selfishness is not absent. When the *Mahāyānist* says that he would be more perfect if he were unselfish then what he is doing is to pursue unselfishness in a selfish manner. A purely unselfish act is non-existent. No matter how great the mystic, insofar as he seeks salvation, he is selfish. If we look at the great mystics dispassionately we discover that all of them had the inevitable streak of selfishness. Talking of philosophers, Aldous Huxley writes :

"The pure love of truth is always mingled to some extent with the need, consciously or unconsciously felt by even the noblest and the most intelligent philosophers, to justify a given form of personal or social behaviour, to rationalise the traditional prejudices of a given class or community."[7] This can be made applicable *mutatis mutandis* to the mystics.

While this streak runs through all mysticisms, it is glaringly present in Jewish mysticism. In no other mysticism does tradition play such an important role as in Jewish mysticism. But one thing should not be lost sight of : the word 'selfish' is not to be understood in the ordinary sense of the word. It would be too simplistic to label the great Śaṅkara or Rāmānuja or Moses, selfish. The word 'selfish' will have to be equated with the words 'need consciously or unconsciously felt'[8] referred to above by Huxley.

Despite this fact, however, the mysticism of the great mystics was never divorced from the ethical vision. A culture that divorces mysticism from the ethical vision is bound to be pervaded by narcissism. Today, mysticism has become an exportable commodity. Much of it has been exported to the West and the Americas. It is common knowledge that 'meditation' is freely marketed under all sorts of brand names. Apparently this is harmless. But what has transpired is that a culture has developed in the West wherein a 'search' for 'self' is 'taught'—a counterfeit mysticism that is completely divorced from the ethical vision. A culture that divorces mysticism from the ethical vision is bound to be pervaded by narcissism. In this mysticism is emptied of its spiritual content. It is psychologised. Meditation alone cannot be a method of self discovery. Neither in Buddhism, nor in Hinduism nor in Christianity is meditation a method of self discovery or self actualisation. In the East it is merely a step toward escaping illusion and ego, and toward seeing the world of impermanence and suffering for what it is. In Christianity meditation is one pole in the dialectic of action and repose, being and doing. The idea of meditation merely as inquiring into the self is rejected by both.

Love and Grace are the two vital constituents of mysticism. Even Buddhism, which is more agnostic than anything else, does not escape from these two elements. Despite its agnosticism Buddhism cannot get away from the concept of Grace. Our discussion on Buddhism attempts to bring this out. As for Christianity and Judaism, Love and Grace are the very foundation of their mysticism. Martin Buber, a great Jewish philosopher and mystic writes in his classic :

"The thou meets me through Grace—it is not found by seeking."[9] In both Christianity and Judaism the world and God are equally real but different. The relationship between them is one of love.

In our comparison of the mysticisms of the three traditions, Hindu and Buddhist, Christian and Jewish, an attempt has been made to show that there are several characteristics common to them. We are today in an age when the representative holy man is not the Buddha or Moses or Jesus, but a Gandhi, who passes over to the perspective of other religions, and then returns with new insight to his own. It is patent, for example—that a Christian, Jew or Muslim whose religion keeps him within the confines of his tradition, will have much to learn if he ventures into the highways and byways of Hinduism—a religion (in the broadest sense of the word) that encompasses all the traditions of other religions. Such a comparative study serves another useful purpose. A study of just one tradition, more often than not, leads to a quest for certainty. Such a quest is self-defeating. On the other hand the study of different traditions turns the quest into a voyage of discovery. On this voyage we discover that the difference between one religion and another is not religious but cultural.

It is well to remember at this juncture that culture and civilization are not synonymous. Civilization covers a special aspect of advanced culture. In this sense culture covers knowledge, belief, art, morals, law and so on. In other words, the word culture in its wider meaning covers man's capabilities and habits acquired by him as a member of society. In this sense it is a neutral term. But when taken in its philosophical sense, it refers to the spirit of man. It is humanity's effort to assert its inner and independent being. Human culture in this sense is a continuous movement towards a higher life. For our present purpose a discussion on these differences is not necessary and as such these considerations need not detain us here. But the point we are trying to make and which we have tried to make is that cultures being different, the religions and mystical traditions arising from them will also be different. If, however, in the higher reaches, mysticisms of the various traditions are similar, it is because everything, including culture, religious beliefs are left behind. To steam-roller all mysticisms into an entity would be too simplistic. It would be like saying that there can be a uniform world culture. For instances, Hinduism is essentially a mystical religion emphasising contemplation, self improvement and spiritual enlightenment. Judaism (even Islam) is prophetic religion emphasising love, brotherhood, etc.

Generally speaking our sensitivity to religion is highly developed. We cannot forget that we are Hindus or Muslims or Christians or Jews or Buddhists. It is for this reason that conversion is always a traumatic experience. It is a mistake to think that all religions are one. Such a view merely generates a sense of self deception, complacency, which is utterly unjustifiable. Similarly it is a mistake to think that all mysticisms are the same. The discussion in the following chapters will show that no two mysticisms can be on all fours. But we have also tried to show that learning the truth of other traditions can lead to respect and tolerance. Radhakrishnan in his "The Hindu View of Life" writes :

"Students of mysticism are impressed by the universality of mystic experience, though the difference in the formulations of it are by no means unimportant."[10] But he says, quoting Evelyn Underhill :

"Though mystical theologies of the East and the West differ widely—though the ideal of life which they hold out to the soul differ too—yet in the experience of the saint the conflict is seen to be transcended. When the love of God is reached, divergencies become impossible, for the soul has passed beyond the sphere of the manifold and is immersed in the one Reality."[11]

Thus, in mysticism and religion, we have to reconcile ourselves to apparent paradoxes.

REFERENCE

1. 'Religion, Philosophy and Psychical Research,' London, Routledge and Kegan Paul Ltd., 1953, p. 212.
2. The Varieties of Religious Experience, Gifford Lectures, The Modern Library, 1929, p. 186.
3. Collected Essays, Bantam Books, New York, 1960, p. 345.
4. Ibid, pp. 345-6.
5. Collected Essays, Bantam Books, New York, 1960, p. 346.
6. The Religious Consciousness, The MacMillan Company, 1951, New York, p. 2.
7. Ends and Means, Chatto and Windus, 1957, p. 272.
8. **Note**: There is, however, in Patañjalī, a different situation. Even the 'desire for salvation' or 'craving for or yearning for *mokṣa* is *vṛtti*. If *citta vṛtti Nirodha* is to be achieved, paradoxically the desire/craving/yearning for it must also be given up.
9. I and Thou, T. and T. Clark Edinburg, 1957, p. 11.
10. Blackie and Sons, Bombay, p. 26.
11. The Hindu View of Life, Radhakrishnan, Blackie and Sons, Bombay, p. 26.

    Quoted by Radhakrishnan from Introduction of Miss Underhill to the Autobiography of Devendranath Tagore, p. xi.

CHAPTER I

Introductory : General Considerations Regarding Mysticism

Man's sense of the sacred seems less apparent in our day. In the prevailing atmosphere of our civilization all trace of the sacred seems to be effaced by the critical and technological attitude : Living in a scientific age our thoughts are strongly coloured by scientific views. We also live in an age of disbelief. There has been a continuous erosion of belief in what Plato called universal values and a simultaneous strengthening of confidence in the reality of matter. We have come to regard the material world as the real world. So much so that words like "concrete" and "real" are used synonymously.

But science has also become a double edged weapon. On the one hand it has made our life well organised. On the other, it has created a disproportionate imbalance between "inner" and "outer" life. Its rapid advance has brought threats of nuclear war nearer home, with the result that man has become increasingly disillusioned by the inability of modern technology to stem the tides of war, crime, intolerance, poverty and pollution. Man is, therefore, impelled to seek new channels of achieving harmony. He has realised that a nonphysical element in his personality is of utmost significance in his quest for equilibrium in a world of apparent chaos. Consequently, science which once looked at things from the "outside" only, has discovered that there is an "inner" life which required to be delved into if some of the problems facing mankind are to be solved.

Contrary to Kipling's prophesy "never the twain shall meet," the East and West have met. Accelerated communication and travel have forged a closer transcultural link between Western empiricism and Eastern spirituality leading the way to the re-examination of ancient truths in the light of modern technology and psychology. In its search for solutions to psychosomatic problems the psychologist has stumbled upon experiences which come within the ambit of what is called 'Mysticism.' Amaury de Riencourt writes :

"At 5.30 on the morning of July 16, 1945, in a desert area known as the Jornada del Muerto in the Alamogordo air base, a stupendous white flash tore apart the sky, dazzling and blinding a small group of scientists ten thousand yards away. The enormously bright ball of fire grew steadily larger as if to wipe out the atmosphere and engulf the world, leading some terrified scientists into believing that they had lost control of man's first nuclear explosion. At this very moment, an apparently incongruous incident took place : Robert Oppenheimer, Director of the Los Alamos Scientific Laboratory and prime co-ordinator of the atomic experiment began to hum some stanzas he had read before when he was studying Sanskrit :

'If the splendour of a thousand Suns were to rise simultaneously in the sky, that would be like the splendour of that Mighty Being.'[1]

"No where in Western literature could he (Oppenheimer) have found an almost clinical description of mystical rapture that *also* fits the description of a nuclear explosion in the outer world."[2]

In mysticism we have an experience that is unique and consistently reported as qualitatively different from all other human experience. In spite of the tremendous power of the mystical experience to change personality, most psychologists have been almost without curiosity about the place of mysticism in personality. No doubt much of the neglect is due to the desire of psychologists to be considered scientists. Mysticism and mystical experience make a very elusive subject for the pursuit of scientific studies. Apart from suggestive speculations of Jungian oriented psychologists and some experimental psychologists like Abraham H. Maslow, there are few others who have propounded theories to explain mysticism and mystical experience. Maslow's theories of Peak Experience are noteworthy. However, some of the great psychotherapists were perfectly in accord with the ways of liberation while describing the aim of therapy as self-actualisation, (Maslow), creative selfhood (Adler), individuation (Jung), Eastern ways of liberation have influenced the great psychologists and psychotherapists. Psychotherapy is no more used to set right disordered, disrupted or confused personality. The unconscious factors behind these so called disorders have ceased to be merely psychological. Two short quotations from Alan W. Watts illustrate this point : He says—

"They (factors) lie in the whole pattern of his relationships with other people and, more particularly, in the social institutions by which these relationships are governed, the rules of communication employed by the culture, or group. These include the conventions of language and law, of ethics and aesthetics, of status, rule and identity, and of cosmology, philosophy, and religion. For this whole social complex is what provides the individual's conception of himself, his state of consciousness, his very feeling of existence.

"Seeing this, the pyschotherapist must realise that his science or art, is misnamed, for he is dealing with something far more extensive than a psyche and its private troubles. This is just what so many psychotherapists are recognising and what, at the same time, makes the *Eastern ways of liberation so pertinent to their work*. For they are dealing with people whose distress arises from what may be termed *Māyā*, to use the Hindu-Buddhist word whose exact meaning is not merely 'illusion' but the entire world-conception of a culture, considered as illusion in the strict etymological sense of a play (Latin *Ludere*). The aim of a way of liberation is not the destruction of *Māyā* but seeing it for what it is, or seeing through it."[3]

Though the parallel or equivalence between some Western psychologists like Jung and the Hindu Liberation ways will be accepted with some reservations, what is remarkable is the fact that these psychologists *felt* that such an equivalence *existed*. The extent to which Eastern insights and Eastern mysticism have influenced Western psychologists is evident from the following, quoted by Watts in his book referred to above. Watts writes thus before giving the quotation from Gardner Murphy's Book 'Personality—A Biosocial Approach to Origins and Structure.'

"The level at which Eastern thought and its insights may be of value to Western psychology has been admirably stated in Gardner Murphy, a psychologist who, incidentally, can hardly be suspected of the taint of Jung's mysticism." He (Murphy) writes :

"If, moreover, we are serious about understanding all we can of personality, its integration and disintegration, we must understand the meaning of depersonalisation, those experiences in which individual self awareness is abrogated and the individual melts into an awareness which is no longer anchored upon selfhood. Such experiences are described by Hinduism in terms of ultimate unification of the individual with the Ātman, the Super-Individual Entity which transcends both selfhood and materiality . . . ."

We shall have much to say on this problem of "depersonalisation" when discussing the mystical traditions of the various religions. Suffice to state that it is not a regression to the primitive or infantile type of awareness as is commonly misrepresented. There is no loss of ego strength. We get a true and correct perspective of the concepts of the ego when we view it within the tradition to which it belongs. A Hindu sect or mystic, for instance, would transcend the Ego Concept not by destroying it but by looking through it.

Any discussion of mysticism is handicapped by serious terminological difficulties. While in mystical literature it is commonplace to see words confused with things, symbols with realities, the most serious flaw is to be found in the fact that the actual experience is confused with the interpretation. What we read in the classical mystical literature is, therefore, not the mystical experience *per se* but the interpretations of it. Not that such interpretations are without value. In fact their value lies in the instructions the accounts left for anyone who should want to experience an experience similar to what the seers experienced. After all, the essentials of what the mystics experienced, died with them.

In view of the wide applicability acquired by the word 'mysticism,' it has not been easy to define it. We cannot do better than start at some point on the circumference of the subject by examining a few definitions given by the great scholars of mysticism. Evelyn Underhill writes :

"Broadly speaking, I understand it (mysticism) to be the expression of the innate tendency of the human spirit towards complete harmony with the transcendental order; whatever be the theological formula under which that order is understood. This tendency, in great mystics, gradually captures the whole field of consciousness; it dominates their life and, in the experience called 'Mystic Union,' attains its end. Whether that end be called the God of Christianity, The World Soul of Pantheism, the Absolute of Philosophy, the desire to attain it and the movement towards it—so long as this is a genuine life process and not intellectual speculation—is the proper subject of mysticism."[4]

mysticism defn

Nearer home, Prof. Dasgupta writes :

"Mysticism is not an intellectual theory; it is fundamentally an active, formative, creative, elevating and ennobling principle of life . . . . Mysticism means a spiritual grasp of the aims and problems of life in a much more real and ultimate manner than is possible to mere reason."[5]

Both the definitions quoted above are secular, some of the classical ones are, so to say, dressed in monistic robes. On divesting them of these robes we discover a residue which is universal, the same in all mystical traditions of the world. Even so, words like "Union," "Unity," "Identity" prove to be obstacles not to be easily got rid of. In the ultimate analysis "Mysticism" is to be viewed within a particular tradition. We will notice as we proceed that the Hindu theologian is the nearest to a viable definition of a mystic and of mysticism. This is perhaps due to an inexplicable historical development in Hindu theology which made mystical experience doctrinally crucial and necessary. What mysticism is *not* will become clear in the course of this book. At this stage it is sufficient to say that the term 'mystical' has a focus which is destroyed if we bring within its meaning, the superhuman, the supernatural, the occult and the drug induced ecstasis, subject to certain exceptions.

Mysticism as a separate subject is undoubtedly the product of the West. Hindu mysticism was always regarded as part of philosophy and religion. Hindu speculative philosophy has had an agelong preoccupation with definitions. The main theme of the

Upaniṣads centres round "Brahman" and "Ātman." "Tat tvam Asi," "Ayamātmā Brahma," "Aham Brahma Asmi" are an eloquent indication of how much the Upaniṣads are imbued with mysticism.

SELF

The *self* is central to mysticism. It occurs in all disciplines that take human nature as their primary subject, like literature, anthropology, psychology, philosophy. Descartes, writing early in the 17th century, began by doubting the existence of everything. But the very act of doubting persuaded him that atleast he must exist if nothing else does. He uttered the most famous sentence in philosophy. *Je pense donc je suis, Cogito ergo sum,* I think, therefore, I am. It was intended not as a syllogism but as an immediate experience, the clearest and the most distinct idea that we can ever have. It was indeed a revolution in philosophy that Descartes took as his starting point not external objects, supposedly known but the conscious self. We need not go into the Cartesian doubt by which he reached his *Cogito.* He merely began with scpticism in regard to the senses. However, Descartes' "thinking" is to be understood in the wide sense in which he used it. For him a thing that thinks is one that doubts, understands, conceives, affirms, denies, wills, imagines and feels. For him feeling, as it occurs in dreams, is a form of thinking. Thought constituted the very essence of the mind. It follows, therefore, that the mind must always think, even during deep sleep. In his Cogito, Descartes believed he had found the firm foundation on which he could build an absolutely reliable system of knowledge. Even though he could pretend he had no body, he could not possibly doubt that he was a substance whose whole essence consisted in thinking. "Thus the self, or rather the soul," he concluded, "by which I am what I am, is entirely distinct from the body, is indeed easier to know than the body, and would not cease to be what it is, even if there were no body."[6]

Knowledge of our own being we have by intuition, said Locke. We cannot doubt it. The self was self evident to itself. Its own existence required no proof. Locke coined 'self-consciousness' to describe this state of affairs.

With the coming of Hume, the self is practically thrown overboard. Though we may not fully agree with his views, it has to be admitted that his scepticism provided a necessary safeguard against credulity. The marriage between faith and reason which had characterised Western Christian thought since the second century was brought to an end. With regard to the self, he wrote in his Treatise of Human Nature, the idea of a permanent self or personal identity is a fiction of the imagination since it is "nothing but a bundle or collection of different perceptions, which succeed each other, with an inconceivable rapidity, and are in a perpetual flux, and movement."[7]

According to him memory held this bundle of perceptions together and gave it an illusion of being a self. This is quite strangely close to the Buddhist doctrine of *anattā* or non-self.

When Hume sought to reduce the self to a series of fleeting impressions and ideas with no real bond between them, he lost sight of the fact that there had to be someone or something ; after all one mental state does not merely recall another, it may recall it as *mine*. His argument that "I never can catch *myself*. . ." suffers from a peculiar but obvious form of self contradiction. In fact Hume does not deny that perceptions do combine to form minds though he is unable to explain how that happens. Obviously a scepticism that confessedly is abandoned in actual life must be wrong in theory, for practice is the final test of theory. But then it is not so simple as that. If the word "agnostic" had been coined at that time, Hume would have been called one. It does not perhaps follow from his argument that there is no simple self. It only means that we are not in a position to know whether there is or not. Hume's sceptical conclusions are, therefore, not to be brushed aside lightly. As Bertrand Russell has said that the certain sceptical conclusions to which Hume was led "are equally difficult to refute as to accept. The result was a challenge to philosophers, which, in my opinion, has still not been adequately met."[8]

Kant rejected Hume's scepticism. He stated as his grounds that there are limits to the capacity of pure reason to deal adequately with certain important areas of the human experience. To do this he denied knowledge to make room for faith. For this Kant started with the moral experience of the categorical imperative. From this he reached out to the "postulates of practical reason." Briefly his arguments run as follows :

"Two things fill the mind with ever new and increasing admiration and awe, the oftener and the more steadily we reflect on them : the starry heavens above and the moral law within."[9]

The fact that we experience a moral duty implies that we are free to fulfil that duty. I ought, therefore, I can. On the basis of pure reason it is not possible to prove the fact of free will. But on the basis of practical experience it is necessary to assume it. This is the first postulate of practical reason. Since, however, it is not possible within the limits of this mortal life to fulfil, all the demands of the moral law within, and moral perfection would require an endless duration of existence, the second postulate follows viz., the human soul is immortal. This idea comes very close to the Hindu idea of Saṃsāra. We thus see that both Hume and Kant touch Hindu Mysticism on some important point in the Hindu doctrine.

TURNING EAST

Turning East to Hinduism is like coming out of a confined room into the open. Unlike in the West, philosophy in the East is never pure speculation, but always some form of transcendental pragmatism. Its truths are to be tested operationally. They never tend to be cold exercises in abstractions. The Upaniṣads, for instance, are spoken of as *adhyātma—śāstra*—the science of Reality par excellence. Their central theme is self knowledge. The metaphysical question Vedānta asks is :

"What is that which being known everything is known ?[10]

Man's metaphysical quest presupposes man's essential unity with the core of Being. This unity is somehow, at some stage, for some reason, forgotten. Socrates looked for the abstract universals behind the sensible particulars. For Plato the soul of man had fallen from the world of Ideas and got entangled in a body after drinking the waters of Lethe or as Wordsworth put it :

"Our birth is but a sleep and a forgetting." That is, knowledge is "awakening" and "recollecting."

The attitude of the Hindu to man was one of self confidence. There is no logico-empirical or speculative streak involved. Inference, analogy, postulation have no place in his thinking. Throughout the Upaniṣads we notice that the utterances of the seers are couched in simple and direct language of discovery.

Where arguments are used it is only to clarify and make plausible for the benefit of the rational minds who lack intuitive knowledge. Besides (and this should be borne in mind) the various levels of reality are revealed gradually. Notice :

> "Then Gārgi Vācaknavi questioned him,
>
> 'Yājnavalkya' said she, 'Since all this world is woven, warp and woof, on water, on what, pray, is the water woven, warp and woof ?'
>
> 'On wind, O Gārgi.'
>
> 'On what then, pray, is the wind woven, warp and woof?'
>
> 'On the atmosphere-worlds, O Gārgi.'
>
> The questions and answers proceed ascendingly
>
> 'On what then, pray, are the worlds of Prajāpati woven, warp and woof ?'
>
> 'On the worlds of Brahma, O Gārgi.'
>
> 'On what then, pray, are the worlds of Brahma woven, warp and woof ?'
>
> Yājnavalkya said : 'Gārgi, do not question too much lest your head fall out. In truth, you are questioning too much about a divinity about which further questions cannot be asked. Gārgi do not over question.'[11]

Notice also how the various stages are gone through. The relatively external is taken and gradually eliminated. The final advice is not to push the questions too far because knowledge of Brahman is to be sought through instruction *and* immediate experience and *not* through inference. Notice again :

> "Teach me, Sir ! —with these words Nārada came to Sanatkumāra. To him he then said : "Come to me with what you know. Then I will tell you still further."[12]

Here again we see the progressive definition of Brahman. The Upaniṣads are sterling examples of the fact that Brahman is to be revealed progressively at various levels. Reality has various levels.

Admitting that there are various levels of Reality, the question arises : Can we apply a metaphysical method *per se* ? Dr. Pravas Jivan Chaudhury, in his article 'Vedānta As

Transcendental Phenomenology' suggests the methods of Husserl. He says :

"The method followed in his (Husserl's) transcendental phenomenology will not appear strange to a student of Vedānta, who finds in his disciplines the same transcendental analysis of experience, leading to the discovery of layers of subjectivity and their corresponding objective worlds constituted by the former's projective activity. This following of experiences back to their origin or home, stage by stage, ending in the all important and overwhelming result that the inquirer's self or his transcendental subjectivity is the metaphysical object he, in his ignorance, was searching for as an object apart from him, and, as such, never amounting to that true metaphysical object which being known everything is known."[13]

Vendānta enjoins that the aspirant first listen to the texts enshrining the reports of the great seers. Then try to understand them intellectually. Finally to use his own meditational search to realise these experiences for himself. In the initial stages, therefore, there is scope for discursive thinking, but this is only to build up momentum for the final assault. Various thinkers have used different methods to achieve this. But what all of them tried to do was to realise as immanent what appeared to be transcendent.

When the immanent appears as transcendent, it gives rise to illusion, errors, dreams, etc. The story of mysticism is enshrined in the great mystics' effort to realise as immanent what appeared to be transcendent. Each did it in his own way and in the process produced some of the greatest mystical literature in the world.

The study of this literature "can begin either at the bottom, with practice and morality; or at the top, with a consideration of metaphysical truths; or finally, in the middle at the focal point where mind and matter, action and thought, have their meeting place in human knowledge."[14]

Like Huxley we would prefer to start from the mid-point of doctrine, as in that case we are free to move both up and down. If, therefore, we are to achieve as immanent what appears to be transcendent, it will be our task to penetrate through objectivity or *avidyā* at the various levels of the self. This is what Dr. Chaudhury tries to do in his phenomenological method referred to above. We set a very brief summary of it below. We have chosen it as one of the ways to show how Eastern and Western methods can be fused together. All quotations are from Dr. Chaudhury's article : Vedānta as Transcendental Phenomenology.

The mind is endowed with the power of projection and retraction. When it projects it superimposes (*Adhyāsa*) on what is, what is not. When this illusion is dispelled there is retraction. This function of the mind is, however, indescribable (*Anirvāchya*). This "indescribability" derives from the fact that in ordinary experience no empirical analogy can be drawn. It would not make sense if we said "The snake perceived is only a rope" or "The man in the dream was nothing." The predicate term, it will be observed, does not qualify the subject term leading to a self contradiction in the judgement. So we see that illusory objectivity is no empirical fact to be described or explained in the usual way! It is to be recognised as an original function of the mind that freely projects objects before it, and adopts a mode of being such that it forgets, for the time being, their having been thus created and takes them for given objects." In other words what was immanent has appeared as transcendent. In order, to get over this illusion (*Avidyā*), which at the universal plane is known as *Māyā*, we have to (says Chaudhury) think in terms of phenomenological analysis of experience and so of levels of subjectivity and objectivity. He works out this in the following ways :

(a) S2 represents the second order self.
(b) S2 projects the first order objects O (illusion and dreams).
(c) S2 is sleeping in S1 (a lower self deluding mode adopted by S2).
(d) It is S1, which takes 01 for given objects.
(e) When S2, sleeping in S1, awakens, the breaking of illusion and dreams takes place.

In a profound sense, according to modern psychology, our dreams are wish-fulfilments. S2, in a manner of speaking, does not lapse completely but goes into a state of topor and holding itself in abeyance, takes on the pose of S1, in which pose it enjoys the experiences of S1, (both good and bad). In order to supplement its own waking experiences, which fall short of many desires, S2 creates dreams, which become wishfulfilments. Thus S2, through its play acting self's S1, enjoys it's unfulfilled desires.

Now lying dormant in S2, is S3, S2, in its turn is thus an assumed pose of a third order subjectivity, S3, which lies dormant in S2. It (S3) creates and enjoys the objects of the so-called waking reality. Says Dr. Chaudhury.

"This S3 has been realised by the mystics of all times and places as their reports show. The Vedic seers speak of a stage of self realisation when they are liberated though continuing bodily existence (*Jīvanmukta*). In this stage one feels the world to be a shadow-show, or a dream that is freely projected by one's higher—order self, just as we enjoy our day dreams. One lives his wordly life only for the sake of play acting, so to speak."

This third order self or subjectivity is the God of religions, "for it is the universal Creator and Correlator of images, who appears to the individual S2, to be a real object." In view of what is stated above Vedānta directs aspirants to listen to the reports of the Vedic seers, apply critical and speculative thinking to it. This latter is possible by analogy with everyday experience. And then to actually verify this, the knowledge gained, analogically, by realising it for oneself first hand.

The problem of "Realisation" is a persistent one in mysticism. It has been examined from various angles. We shall have much to say on it as we proceed. Before proceeding we digress a little to say a few words on Husserl. Almost on par with Śaṅkara, atleast in the spirit of his philosophy, the phenomenologists hold that the narrow framework of direct empirical knowledge should be transcended, to realise the "essential" core or basis of the finite. Viewed closely, this amounts to saying : Erase the world of practical awareness (*Vyāvahārika*) and go "behind" it to its essence viz. Brahman. For Husserl there were two kinds of experiences :

(a) The ordinary "experience" which he called individual intuition.

(b) Essential or what he termed *eidesic* intuition.

In the preview of the former would fall my present awareness. There are two pens and ten books on my desk. Within the preview of the latter fall not the particular but rather universal truths or essences (*eidos* is the Greek word). This Greek terminology is reminiscent of Plato and Aristotle. We are reminded of Plato's forms or Ideas. We are also reminded of Kant. Of course there is difference in their theories. Where, for instance, Kant insisted that it is the form of our intuition (as space and time) that makes the principles of arithmetic and geometry necessarily true, Husserl says that it is the content of our intuition that makes these principles true. *Eidos* or essence is the content. Like *Māyā-vādā*, in the initial stage, phenomenology differentiates between our world consciousness and transcendental consciousness. Whatever belongs to world consciousness is not free from uncertainty or perceptual illusioness. On the other hand, transcendent consciousness, which is the primitive basis, of our world consciousness is free from fantasies and is, therefore, purer and authentic. In striving to reach the essence, therefore, what Husserl would try to do would be to suspend the awareness of the world and grasp the reality of transcendental consciousness. But for the terminology, it will be noticed, how close this comes to genuine meditational methods. We shall revert to this discussion again and again particularly when we discuss the various disciplines prescribed by the Vedāntic seers and their great interpreters and by the unknown author of The Cloud. It is not our intention here to draw a comparison with *Māyā-vādā*. *Unlike the phenomenologists, the metaphysically enlightened Māyāvādin* does not make any effort to make a comeback in the world, as such a comeback, would defeat his purpose. By the experience of *Ātmānubhava* he has managed to prove the inauthenticity of the world.

Reverting to our discussion of the Transcendental phenomenology as applied to Vedānta, we see that to the realised soul this level (S3) gives a feeling of being an actor, in a world which is a stage. The joys and sorrows passing through his mind, pass, as they do in the mind of an actor portraying a particular role or character. The seers have a direct analytical-cum-meditational method of establishing S3. To those not initiated in this method, S3 may be presented as a "probable metaphysical postulate." They can employ "the hypothetico-deductive method of science to obtain explanations of phenomena."

Behind the third level of subjectivity, lies the fourth level, S4. "In this, too, we may follow the Vedic seers in their relentless self-analysis and arrive at what they have described as Brahman-without-differentiation, indescribable in empirical terms except by negation (*neti*)." In other words all objectivity disappears at the S4 level. At this level the self appears to be absolutely free and absolutely unconditioned. In the different schools of Indian Philosophy there appears to be a consensus of views on the fact that man is condemned to a weary and bound state in this empirical world. But perhaps more than this, there is consensus on the view that there are possibilities of an exit from this bound state. Such an exit, these thinkers believe, leads to *Mokṣa*. The enlightened seers have described this indescribable state as that of *Sat-cit-ānanda*, a sort of an incomparable state of being-intelligence-happiness. Ineffability is ineffability. Any attempt at description will naturally lead to contradictions. But more of this later. A state of complete and absolute freedom, absolute bliss and beatitude is established in S4.

The three-fold gradation of consciousness is well illustrated in the following verse from the Śvetāśvatara Upaniṣad :

"Sacred poetry (*Chandas*), the sacrifices, the ceremonies, the ordinances, the past, the future, and what the Vedas declare—This whole world the illusion-maker (*Māyin*) projects out of this (*Brahma*) And in it by illusion (*Māyā*) the *other*[15] is confined.

"Now, one should know that Nature (*Prakṛti*) is illusion (*Māyā*) And that the Mighty Lord (*Maheśvara)* is the illusion maker (*Māyin*). This whole world is pervaded, with beings that are parts of Him ."

The Lord of *Māyā* having created the world by his magical power, enters it and becomes bound by it. S2 takes the world as reality, S3 creates it and takes it as a make believe affair, S4 takes the creation act in the same manner.

"Brahman knows the empirical world of our common experience as a dream within a dream . . . . Therefore to know Brahman or S4, as a stage of subjectivity is to know that which, being known, everything is known."[16]

GOD

Traditional religion is on the decline, but the average man and woman continue to search for a deeper meaning behind existence. Science has demolished the old religious framework that gave man a definite place in the cosmos. Can science succeed in displacing religion by explaining the workings of nature? Can it provide the rich metaphysical and mystical foundation for existence that has traditionally been the prerogative of religion? Writers on topics relating to modern physics and cosmology find that there is a religious dimension to science. Problems of cosmology, such as the 'Big Bang' and the nature of matter, that had for centuries kept philosophers and theologians preoccupied, were now engaging the serious attention of scientists. Some scientists feel that some of the age-old problems of the universe might be on the verge of solution.

At the heart of all religions is the problem of Genesis. In recent years Cosmologists have made enormous efforts to understand the scientific version of creation — the socalled Big Bang from which all existing things sprang. When we contemplate the deep mystery surrounding the socalled Big Bang and wonder as to what must have triggered it, we are led to re-examine a long standing theological debate known as the cosmological argument.

In the scriptures of the Jews and Muslims there is no doubt about the principal actors (*Dramatis personae*). God is the *dramatis persona*. And there are persons (*personae*) acting in it. When we come down to Buddhism, *Karma* takes the place of *drama* and persons are merely the sum of conations, sensations and mental processes coming out of the universal flux. Inner coherence and permanence are absent. There is no personal God in the Hebrew or Muslim sense of the word. The transcendent element in man is bound by Karma giving a deceptive appearance of personality. But when we consider Hinduism we find that there is an unquenchable thirst for metaphysical ultimates. We shall observe, as we proceed, that great mystics like Śaṅkara, Rāmānuja and Madhva cause a metaphysical ferment while discussing these ultimates. If we take the first line of the Īśa Upaniṣad (one of the shortest and most important) we notice "By the Lord" to be the first words. It runs thus :

"By the Lord (*Īśa*) enveloped must this all be whatever moving thing there is in the moving world. With this renounced, thou mayest enjoy. Covet not the wealth of any one at all ."[17]

Thus there is the Lord and there is the world. The world should be enjoyed without clinging to it. Of the 'Lord' nothing is said for the time being. But Īśa 3 tells us that it is both the static and the moving, that it can be grasped in both its forms in a flash of intuition. It is without and within this universe :

"It is within this whole universe, and yet it is without it." (Īśa. 5). And finally in Ī śa- 6-7 cosmic consciousness is described :

"Now, he who on all beings looks as just (*eva*) in the self (*Ātman*) and on the self as in all beings — he does not shrink away from Him.

In whom all beings
have become just (*eva*) the self of the
discerner
Then what delusion (*moha*) what sorrow
(*śoka*) is there
of him who perceives the unity."
And the Īśa-8 says :
Āppropriately he distributed objects (*artha*) through the eternal years."

Reading Īśa 6-7-8 together we observe that this 'Lord' encompasses what is "radiant, without body, invulnerable, without muscle, pure, untouched by evil" that is, Ātman — Brahman, insofar as it is an eternal mode of being. Because he encompasses it, he is prior to it in the order of reality, just as he is prior to the world of space and time. He "has assigned to all objects duly their respective functions according to their nature, since endless times." He is what Aurobindo termed "Unknowable He."[18]

We shall discuss this point later, when we revert to Īśa, suffice it to say that since the 'Lord' encompasses, the two halves of existence together called Self or Brahman, they are, so to say, subject to the 'Lord.' Fluidity of terminology in Hinduism sometimes causes confusion. But Īśa exalts 'Lord' over and above Brahman — understood as the totality of eternal being and temporal becoming — a transcendentally immanent and immanently transcendent personal Absolute who encompasses both the world of appearance as well as the world of eternal unchanging essence — wisdom (*jñāna*) as well as action (*karma*).

Aristotle called it "unmoved mover." It is beyond both movement and rest. This was the God of Aristotle.

The cosmological argument reached its most developed form with Leibnitz in the 18th Century. Everything, it was argued, has a cause that precedes it : nothing can occur uncaused. We can trace the cause of cause and effect, back into the mists of time. But the cause, it was said, could not continue for ever. There must have been a first cause of everything and that cause we call God.

A related argument appealed not to causation as such, but to contingency. Everything must have an explanation for its existence outside itself. Nothing can provide an explanation for its own existence. Therefore, the explanation for the entire physical universe must be outside that physical universe and that explanation is God.

Long before science attacked these arguments philosophers had attacked them. What the philosophers objected to was the contradictory reasoning. The arguments first assume that everything must have a cause or explanation, but then go on to postulate God, who does not have a cause or explanation. If you can have an uncaused God, why not an uncaused universe?

In the bygone centuries theologians frequently appealed to evidence from design as an argument for the existence of God. Attention was directed to the complex structures that occur both in astronomy and biology, and they argued that these cannot be the result of blind chance. However, the fallacy of this argument is apparent when we realise that according to scientists, order and complex activity in many systems arise spontaneously. Even Darwinean evolution explains how biological organisms have achieved remarkable adaptation to the environment. Even in cosmology there is no real mystery about how the ordered universe we observe today had emerged from the chaos of the primeval fire.

But the existence of complex systems is only one sort of order. We can even call it the order of complexity. There exists another sort of order in the universe, which cannot be explained so easily. For a better term we will call it the 'order of simplicity.' The day to day running of the universe is one such example. Who doubts that each day the Sun will rise on schedule or that like poles of a magnet will repel? The rhythmic motion of planets bear testimony to the dependability of nature. To explain these felicitous regularities, physicists have coined elegant expressions like "God is a mathematician." After all, these regularities are the manifestation of the laws of nature. The question then arises : Did God create mathematics? Or does it exist outside of Him ? Why in fact are there laws at all? It is here that we come closest to the issue of meaning and purpose of the universe.

More and more scientists have been struck by what they regard as a string of improbable "accidents" and "coincidences" that are built into the laws of physics to enable the universe to produce the familiar systems, such as galaxies, stars, atoms and *Us.* These are what are termed the "constants of nature" and the slightest change in their numerical values would be catastrophic. A slight change in the relative strength of gravitational and electro-magnetic forces would turn stars like the Sun into blue giants or red dwarfs.

Conclusion : Nature got it just right. Is it possible, therefore, that these fundamental laws are the product of a designing mind — a mind with a capital M ?

One of the conclusions of all this would be to project God outside matter, space, time, into the abstract world or logic, mathematics and physical law. There would be no need of a creator in the traditional sense. At the same time even physics seems to demand some guiding influence, as it were, above nature, sustaining all of existence.

Our concepts of space, time and matter have undergone a drastic change. The absolute space and time of Newton have been swept away by the Theory of Relativity. Concrete matter perceived by our crude senses has been dissolved away on deeper inspection, into ghastly patterns of vibrating quantum energy. The result is that many of the word and abstract concepts thrown up by the new physics have struck deep chords with those of mystical persuasion. These results are far reaching and should not be ignored by both the new physics community and by the traditional religious communities.

With the old ways of looking at the world completely undermined by the onslaught of physical science, images of God up above, commanding a universe which works like a clock and which unfolds an area of absolute space and time according to his preordained plan makes little sense in a world of relativity and quantum cosmology. There is room for a meaning to existence but the language of the ultimate reality is not to be found in the familiar world of daily discourse.

We will refrain from drawing any hasty or preliminary conclusions at this stage. We can only remark that there appears to be little or no conflict between religion and science. That though science deals with phenomenal reality of things its final aim is to pass from phenomenal reality to ultimate reality.

The foregoing considerations are important if one is to understand the concept of God. When we say *concept* of God, we must remember that a concept merely succeeds in pointing to an experience. The concept cannot express the experience. It is like the finger pointing to the Moon, it is not the Moon. This is how the Zen masters would express it. Erich Fromm, calling himself a non-theistic mystic, in a radical interpretation of the old Testament writes :

"I believe that the concept of God was a historically conditioned expression of an inner experience . . . . 'God' is one of many different poetic expressions of the highest value in humanism, not a reality in itself.

"To which reality of human experience does the concept of God refer? Is the God of Abraham the same as the God of Moses, of Isaiah, of Maimonides, of Meister Eckhart, of Spinoza ? And if he is not the same, is there nevertheless some experiential substratum common to the concept as used by these various men, or might it be that while such a common ground exists in the case of some, it does not exist with regard to others?" [19]

To this aspect of God we will be reverting again and again in the course of this study. God and mysticism are inextricably connected. In the meantime we quote Erich Fromm again before proceeding. He says :

"When we know some fragments of reality we want to complete them in such a way that they 'make sense' in a systematic way. Yet by the very nature of the limitations of man we always have only 'fragmentary' knowledge, and never complete knowledge. What we tend to do then is to manufacture some additional pieces which we add to the fragments to make of them a whole, a system. Frequently the awareness of the qualitative difference between the 'fragments' and 'the additions' is missing because of the intensity of the wish for certainty.

"In the history of religious concepts we find the same process occurring. At the time when man had a fragmentary knowledge of the possibility of solving the problem of human existence by the full development of his human powers; when he sensed that he could find harmony by progressing to the full development of love and reason, rather than by the tragic attempt to regress to nature and to eliminate reason, he gave this new vision, this X, many names : Brahman, Tao, Nirvāṇa, God."[20] Writings such as above pose challenges. We have stated at the outset of this chapter that this generation has a desperate need to fill the vacuum left by the decline of the old beliefs. Its agnosticism (if we may call it that) is tinged with a certain wistfulness — it would like to believe, yet cannot. This shows that the need to believe is one of the root causes of our present discontents. But it is doubtful whether the old beliefs can fill the bill. Atleast organised and institutionalised religion cannot fill the bill. In fact, man in his desperation is driven to make an idol of the state and to accord to men the reverence due to God. Can mysticism fill the bill ?

These are not easy questions to answer. In some form or the other they have existed from time immemorial and great thinkers have endeavoured to answer them. Consciously or unconsciously we are all seeking, seeking something. Says Sri Aurobindo :

"All spiritual seeking moves towards an object of knowledge to which men ordinarily do not turn the eye of the mind, to someone or something Eternal, Infinite, Absolute, that is not the temporal things or forces of which we are sensible although he or it may be in them or behind them or their sources or creator. It aims at a state of knowledge by which we can touch, enter or know by identity this Eternal, Infinite and Absolute, a consciousness other than our ordinary consciousness of ideas and forms and things, a knowledge that is not what we call knowledge but something self existent, everlasting, infinite."[21]

This is nothing but a mystical quest, a journey of the soul, by an inner ascent, to immediate knowledge of God and communion with Him. From Plotinus to Sri Aurobindo, we find all of them agreeing on one point : Reticence, silence. All have agreed that it is necessary to refrain from uttering the unutterable. The sages of the Upaniṣads and the masters of Zen, all tell us the same thing. "God," says the author of The Cloud of Unknowing, "may well be loved, but not thought."[22]

Let us revert to the cosmological argument before passing into Vedānta. Let us for a moment consider Kant — the critical mediator between dogmatism and scepticism. It is not necessary for us to discuss all the aspects of the problem, but only so much as will serve as a background to our study of mysticism. Irrespective of the fact whether Kant succeeded or not in reaching the objective he set for his new critical philosophy, his achievements were monumental. Perhaps his mistakes were more important than most men's successes. It is, therefore, impossible to philosophise without taking his views into account.

Kant summerised the traditional argument in one sentence :

"If anything exists, therefore, an absolutely necessary being exists."[23]

By an absolutely necessary being Kant assumed the traditional meaning — a union of being and perfection (*ens realissimum*) since Kant assumed that a necessary being had to be a perfect being, he went right on to press the contention that we certainly cannot move from an imperfect existent world to a being complete in the absolutistic sense of perfection. We quote :

"The transcendental idea of a necessary and all sufficient being is overwhelmingly great, so high above everything empirical, the latter being always conditioned, that it leaves us at a loss, partly because we can never find in experience material sufficient to satisfy such a concept, and partly because it is always in the sphere of the conditioned that we carry out our search, seeking there ever vainly for the unconditioned . . . ."[24]

What Kant wants to convey is that there is no way of gaining insight into the unconditioned if we seek clues in the realm of the conditioned. Kant views the idea of the unconditioned, necessary and all sufficient being as "so high above everything empirical." For Kant the gap between the conditioned and the unconditioned cannot be bridged. Kant argued that the proof of God could not be demonstrated or shown that it is capable of absolute certainty.

Perhaps Kant could have followed the teleological approach as he himself had said that it best suited the ordinary human reason. (Design/goal, etc.). Obviously he did not do it as it would lead him to an "architect" not a "creator." Thus both cosmological and teleological arguments did not appeal to him. For Kant, knowledge and certainty were synonymous. In these circumstances reason faces a "veritable abyss." Even the teleological yields only a conditioned architect. Are we, therefore, led into a blind alley ?

The human search for God or the nature of being — cannot even get off the ground unless one presupposes that the searcher and the object of his search are in some sense one. The knower and the object to be known cannot afford to be ontological strangers. If we put this in theological terms it will be tantamount to saying that, if a man discovering himself does not discover God, then God can only be reached on the basis of conjecture and probability. The cosmological argument by itself may not take us to the classical God of the ontological argument. But can we for that reason disregard it? It atleast forces us to understand that the orderly world as we observe it is not understood in its completeness until we see it as the involvement of a creator-ground, whose unity is expressed in this world. If this way of arguing has mystical overtones, it is because mysticism is inevitable if we are to get-out-of the impasse. Without being rhetorical or emotional it can be stated that the Majesty of God is by definition such that no reasoning based on human experience in the world can ever penetrate the abyss between God and man-world.

The question, therefore, arises as to whether there exists a way from God to man-world, which will meet the ideal of knowledge. God by definition being perfect and man imperfect there appears to be no way by which a perfect being can manifest itself *in its perfection.* In a way, this closes the flow both ways. Śaṅkara as we shall see later, worked out a way out of this by his two tier reality. Brahman and Īśvara.[25] No matter how much we say that God is not this, not that, for such statements to take on any cognitive content, God at some point must, in some sense, be continuous with what is given in finite experience, otherwise we run the risk of making God totally irrelevant. Statements like neti neti lead us into the sphere of probabilities.

Perhaps a mystically based absolute certainty of Being could save us from the scepticism of mere probabilities. Even here, we must admit, the moment we start expressing or describing, words fail us. Ineffability takes over.

We have seen that Kant was dominated by the ideal of truth and of Being without a flaw. A cosmic architect was not acceptable to him. At the same time his claim of "ordinary human reason" to use his term, which led to cognition in general was not unacceptable to him. If, therefore, had Kant been able to entertain seriously the possibility that cognition in general, and in religion and morality specifically, did not require demonstrative certainty or unconditioned submission, he might have correlated moral, aesthetic and religious data with the cosmological teleological considerations.

It is not for us to suggest any alternative arguments for a certain kind of God. All that we would do is not to argue from a fixed point. We have before us three traditions, viz., Hindu, Christian and Jewish. Any fixed position would militate against their being discussed dispassionately. Insofar as "God" is concerned the psychological, theological (now scientific) cold war has been going on and will probably never stop. The basic concern of man should be to view the qualitative variety and range of human experience in the world in a sensitive fashion. That is, to appraise and appreciate them for what they are in themselves. Such experiences will yield unique and complex features. Thereafter to examine and see how far they can be related to each other. Religious and mystical experiences which form the subject matter of our study, for example, have been sensitively described in more than one mode and mood : The Dark night of the Soul, Nothingness, Satori, Mukti, Union, I-Thou, Oceanic feeling. Alfred North Whitehead's words are relevant here.

We quote :

"Religion is the vision of something which stands beyond, behind, and within, the passing flux of immediate things; something which is real, and yet waiting to be realised; something is a remote possibility, and yet the greatest of present facts; something that gives meaning to all that passes, and yet eludes apprehension; something whose possession is the final good, and yet is beyond all reach; something which is the ultimate ideal, and the hopeless quest."[26]

He adds that the vision claims nothing but worship, then writes :

"The power of God is the worship, He inspires. That religion is strong which in its ritual and its modes of thought evokes an apprehension of the commanding vision. The worship of God is not a rule of safety — it is an adventure of the spirit, a flight after the unattainable. The death of religion comes with the repression of the high hope of adventure."[27]

This is no rhetoric. It makes us feel that there is an order of reality other than that of the familiar world.

HINDU MYSTICISM

The metaphysics of the West does not exist in the East. Hinduism encompasses all disciplines — religion, philosophy, science, etc. Air tight compartments are unknown and as we read the Upaniṣads and the Hinḍu scriptures in general, we find one discipline treading on the heels of another. So vast is the subject that it is not possible for us to touch on every aspect. We shall, therefore, confine ourselves to the major traditions (systems) of Vedānta Advaita, Viśiṣṭādvaita and Dvaitā and their famous advocates, Śaṅkara, Rāmānuja and Madhva. We shall also touch upon Buddhism, making reference to the intermediate systems as and when they touch the above systems and our study in some significant way.

In Hinduism the Vedāntic approach to God has played a very important role in shaping the views of the thinkers who advocated the various systems. But if we were to search for the key concept of Vedānta, it would be the concept of Brahman and Brahman's transcendental nature. We read in the Chāndogya:

"Then his father said to him : 'Śvetaketu, my dear, since now you are conceited, think yourself learned, and are proud, did you also ask for that teaching whereby what has not been heard of becomes heard of, what has not been thought of becomes thought of, what has not been understood becomes understood?"[28]

Brahman is not open to empirical enquiry. But this very reason makes enquiry necessary. Even Śaṅkara declares that Vedānta's principal goal is to know and interpret Brahman. But more than this is to acquire its transcendental status. Intertwined with its transcendence is also its immanence. It is not that these two are considered to be poles apart, but in the history of Vedānta they have endangered the transcendental perfection of Brahman. The diverse ways the Vedāntins took were the result of trying to define the immanently transcendent Brahman.

Hindu, Buddhist and even Jain religions agreed that their chief aim was to free themselves from the chain of bondage imposed by the karmic process. The transcendence of Brahman had, therefore, to be guarded. But if Brahman had to be attained there had to be immanence. One without the other, soteriologically speaking would be meaningless. At some stage, moreover, Brahman had to become self consciousness, to become God. If Brahman is transcendent then it should transcend something. There has to be a relation with *something* for reference. The only question would be to understand this relationship. This is not an easy question to answer, because what the answer to the question is, is what philosophy and the scriptures are all about. Take a short quotation from the Gītā :

"And whatever states of being there may be, be they harmonious (sāttvikāḥ), passionate (rājasāḥ), slothful (tāmasāḥ) — know thou that they are all from Me alone. I am not in them, they are in Me."[29]

"While He contains and comprehends all, they do not contain and comprehend Him. This is the distinction between God and His creatures."[30] Here, in other words, we have the Supreme Being, which without being exhausted by other beings includes them.

In fact immanence — transcendence are not seen as two contradictory states. Notice :

"Verily, this whole world is Brahma."[31]

"This Soul of Mine within the heart is greater than the earth .... This Soul of Mine within the heart is smaller than a grain of rice . . . "[32]

The transcendent, immanent question has been admirably described by Dr. S.G. Mudgal : Talking about Śaṅkara in his two tier system he writes :

"But the two tiers are not different, though they are not identical. The lower subsists in the higher; the higher transcends the lower. The lower is, because of the higher; and yet the lower is not, in spite of the higher. The higher is lower, only when spatiotemporally conditioned. The lower is the higher *sub specie aeternitatis.*"[33]

From what we have said so far it would be clear that the problem round which the Vedāntins would build their system is the transcendence-immanence of the Supreme Self, Brahman.

Śaṅkara, for instance, would say that Brahman is unknowable in the cognitive or empiric sense and knowable in the intuitive sense. To Rāmānuja all knowledge was necessarily relational. Karmic bondages result in Ignorance : Relationship of loving Devotion—Desired Knowledge of Brahman. There is the knower-known relationship. (This problem comes up sharply in the 'Cloud of Unknowing.')

Madhva's Dualism "while admitting two mutually irreducible principles as constituting Reality as a whole, regards only one of them viz., God, as independent and the other as dependent."[34]

For the mystic and those interested in the study of mysticism these systems and the Vedic and Upaniṣadic scriptures are veritable gold mines of mystical knowledge. No wonder Plato called philosophy "a dear delight." We shall now proceed to deal with each one of the advocates of the Vedāntic system trying to see what lessons they have for our mystical knowledge and how they are related to the other mystical traditions of the world particularly Christian and Jewish traditions.

ŚAṄKARA

Having discussed God, we are now in a position to proceed to the three great Vedāntists — Śaṅkara, Rāmānuja and Madhva. Vedānta's sole aim was soteriological. This meant that man's effort and energy should be directed somehow towards transcending the consequences of his own actions. Though Buddhism differed in some respects, its foundation was also soteriological. Arnold Toynbee writes :

"Hinduism regards man's universe as being an illusion; the Buddha, anticipating some of the schools of modern Western psychologists by about twenty-four centuries, held that the soul is an illusion too. He saw in the human psyche only a fleeting series of discontinuous psychological states, which are held together only by desire, and which can be dissipated if and when desire is extinguished. In Buddha's view, the extinction of desire is the proper goal of human endeavour, because the achievement of this brings with it the extinction of suffering, and for Buddha life and suffering were synonymous. Not death, *but rebirth,* is the arch ordeal for a human being. The Buddha took it for granted that the effect of desire, precipitated in the form of Karma (the cumulative spiritual effects of action taken in a succession of lives upto the present), is to keep a series of rebirths going *ad infinitum,* unless and until, in one of the lives in this chain, the sufferer, by successfully performing the strenuous spiritual exercises that the Buddha has prescribed, manages to bring the series to an end by attaining the state of extinguishedness (Nirvāṇa) in which all passion is spent and rebirth ceases ."[35]

We have quoted extensively above as we feel that in some respects the mysticism of Buddha and Śaṅkara's mysticism are similar. Perhaps their dissimilarity lies in the fact that the former resorts more to illustrations and stories which drive the point home more effectively.

If Buddhism made Nirvāṇa its goal in shaking off Karma, Vedānta made *Mukti* or *Mokṣa* the chief motivating factor in its enquiry. But this enquiry was not purely intellectual. Stress was laid more on the dynamism of the underlying doctrine, rather than on its epistic or ontic structure. The message continuously dinned into the ears of the pupil is :

"Whoever thus knows 'I am Brahman'!" becomes the All; even the gods have no power to prevent his becoming thus, for he becomes their self (*ātman*).[36] Or take the Muṇḍaka : "As flowing rivers get themselves disappeared in the ocean losing their special names and distinct forms, so the wise man free from all his identifications with names and forms goes unto the highest of the high —the Supreme Divinity."[37]

Like all great Vedāntists, Śaṅkara resorted repeatedly to the Upaniṣads to reinforce his ideas and points of view. Besides, he used lilting tuneful songs (hymns) to express his experience. Like Aquinas, he accepts the full authority of his country's scriptures as a divine revelation. But having done that he sets out to find proofs in experience, and reason for all scriptural teachings. Unlike Aquinas, he feels that the power of reason has been exaggerated and that for every argument we can have an equal and opposite argument, resulting in scepticism. What is needed, therefore, is not logic, but intuition —a faculty that is capable of grasping the essential and the eternal, discarding the non-essential and temporal.

"A mere intellectual understanding of reality is not enough. The end of all knowledge is spiritual realisation."[38]

Though all schools of thought do not consider truth as self revealing, for Śaṅkara, it was self revealing. Truth was its own criterion. These criterions have differed with the differing metaphysical views. The various views do not concern us here. Suffice to know that value of a criterion lies in its instrumentality. Śaṅkara adopted the mystical criterion. To him, as to any great mystic, such a criterion comes naturally. Mysticism and intuition go hand in hand. Hence their eminent suitability for Śaṅkara. In this context we quote R.D. Ranade :

"If we were to enquire about the psycho-metaphysical nature of Anubhava, we find that it is an immediate, first hand intuitive apprehension of Reality. It satisfies all the requirements of a good criterion. It alone gives truth and does not require any other criterion for its validation. It is self evident. When there is direct approach to Reality there is no necessity of an intermediate criterion and it can be dispensed with forthwith. The direct experience becomes its own criterion. Reality though ineffable is experienceable. Therefore, Anubhava is the only appropriate criterion of it. There is no otherness at this stage. Here the faculty of intuition leads us on to the beatific vision. Anubhava thus blinks at intuition on the one hand and beatification on the other."[39]

Śaṅkara's criterion was the mystical criterion. The mystic in him was paramount. If he could not express in terms in which Rāmānuja and Madhva expressed their mysticism, it was because of the nature of the system he advocated. Despite this, sometimes, in his poetry the barrier is broken and Śaṅkara the mystic emerges like the Sun emerging from out of the clouds. Śaṅkara composed innumerable hymns, some of them highly philosophical. He has covered all deities. He advocated worship of God's forms. By reciting names, for instance, one is able to get rid of his obsession with name and form world. If Śaṅkara advocated worship, it did not, as some tend to think, detract from his Advaita position. In fact it reinforced it.

Prayer and worship, as we shall see later, constitute a very important and integral part of mysticism. Mysticism is a "process" going from the grosser to the subtler. Between name and form, the former is more subtle. The name Lord Ramachandra is more potent than the person Rama. It is for this reason that the tantric proceeds from outer worship (*bāhya-pūjā*) inward by chanting hymns (*stava*) muttering of mantra (*japa*) and meditation (*dhyāna*) to Reality (*Advaitabhāva*). Śaṅkara, or Rāmānuja or Madhva, none can bypass with impunity the basic disciplines leading to the final mystical experience. And for this purpose all have to make use of name and form. The classic example of sinner Ajamiḷa, on his death bed, calling his son Nārāyaṇa, and earning, though, unintentionally, Vaikuṇṭha is an illustration in point.

Coming back to Śaṅkara we find that pure Advaita is not possible. Dr. S.G. Mudgal has aptly described Śaṅkara's philosophy as :

"He is not Absolutist for hisBrahman is not the Absolute as understood in Western philosophy. He is not a Monist, as his Brahman is not one (*aneka*) yet not two (*Advaita*). It is not one, though not two, yet not none."[40]

His is a two tier system. For him lower truth is not synonymous with falsehood. It is a truth, conditioned by other truths. The phenomenal world becomes an illusion only when it is viewed in the light of the experience of Reality. What the Advaitin denies is not the phenomenal world or its reality. What he denies is its ultimacy. When, therefore, Śaṅkara is asked what is the cause of bondage and suffering, he does not reply, as a Christian would, that it is original sin. He would say it is original ignorance. (*Avidyā*) *Māyā* and ignorance were the two potent weapons in the spiritual armoury of Śaṅkara. In answer to those who flouted morality on the ground that evil, being *Māyā*, was part of the unreal world, could, with impunity be trifled with, he replied that good and evil are real within the world of space and time and are, therefore, binding for those who live in the world. On the other hand a true *Mukta* is a law unto himself, free from desire and action.

Confusions arise because words like, *Māyā*, ignorance, are misunderstood or more often than not, misinterpreted. Stale and worn out clichés are employed (by Hegel for instance) to demolish concepts whose meaning and significance and philosophical implication have not been understood. This misunderstanding can be imputed to thinkers from both East ad West. We will not go into the wild and unfounded accusation made by a philosopher like Hegel. It will not serve our purpose. In fact it will deflect us from our course. However, we will touch upon it at the end of this section. Moreover, a discussion on time and history with reference to Śaṅkara's mysticism will help us to assess the position in its correct perspective. As the views of Buddhism on Time and History are identical, we propose to deal with them together. Later, we will revert to the subject when dealing with Christianity and Judaism. The way God reveals Himself in history is in fact the great theme of the Bible itself. We cannot, therefore, divorce History from Religion or the Bible. The way in which a system or culture interprets time and history depends upon its presuppositions and philosophical concepts. The history of Indian Philosophy clearly shows that views on time and history were always implicit in the Indian Philosophical traditions. When time and history form the basic of thought, mysticism comes in. Atleast this is true of India, because the question of transcending both these arises. Let us see how.

For the moment let us forget that there is any rivalry (if any) between Buddhism and Advaita. What are the central concepts of Advaita? They are :

1. *Brahman*
2. *Ātman*
3. Ignorance (*Avidyā*)
4. *Māyā*
5. *Karman*
6. *Mokṣa*
7. Knowledge

We comment very briefly on each of the above. Brahman is the unchanging reality, eternal, unborn, uncreated, immutable. The

Ātman, which is the inmost self of man is also eternal, unborn, uncreated and immutable. It is not to be confused with the empirical ego. (The ego is subject to constant change.) *But* Brahman and Ātman are identical. In other words they are two different labels for one and the same Ultimate Reality. Brahman is beyond names and forms, neither He nor She but It —not to be thought of as God. When we think that the Ultimate Realty is the empirical ego and that the knowledge of the world coming through our senses and reason, is the knowledge of the Ultimate reality, we are the victims of Ignorance (*Avidyā*). Though this is beginningless (*anādi*), it can be ended. Identity of Brahman and Ātman brings an end to Ignorance. The power of Brahman by which it manifests itself in the phenomenal world is *Māyā*. Being co-existent with Brahman, it is beginningless and endless. But this should not be taken to mean that there are two ultimate realities, because *Māyā*, apart from Brahman, has no existence. There is a serious misunderstanding when —

Phenomenal world Māyā

Māyā Illusion and Unreality.

Such an equation leads us to believe that the phenomenal world is "illusion and unreal." Such a view does not present the correct Advaita view of *Māyā* because Advaita does not deny the phenomenal world or its reality. As we said above what it denies is its ultimacy. Reality for the Advaitin is that which exists without depending for its existence on any thing other than itself. The position is described as "neither real nor unreal nor both." This could be interpreted to mean that the phenomenal world is neither ultimately real nor wholly unreal, illusory and non-existent. Like the snake-rope illustration —there can be no pure illusion —every illusion is grounded in reality. We will not go into the mechanics of illusion. It is a word lending itself to several interpretations. Sigmund Freud wrote a book on it : "The Future of an Illusion."[41]

How does the concept of Karma come in? Karma is a bondage created by our thoughts, actions, deeds. It can be got over with by the realisation of the identity of Ātman and Brahman. *Mokṣa* (or *Kaivalya*) is freedom from Karma and bondage, which in turn is freedom from ignorance. *Mokṣa* is not something to be looked forward to after death. It is to be attained in this world

(*Jīvanmukti*). And finally we have knowledge of two kinds : Lower (*Vyāvahāra*) and higher (*Paramārtha*). The former knowledge is sublatable. The latter, unsublatable. Name and form are the warp and woof of the former. The latter is absolute.

Buddhism : The chief concepts of Buddhism are :

1. Existence
2. Suffering (*Duḥkha*)
3. Ignorance
4, Karma
5. Nirvāṇa
6. Knowledge

A little later in this Chapter we will be disçussing in some detail these concepts of Buddhism. Here we will run through them briefly.

There being no eternal and unchanging entities either within or outside man, existence is pure flux. Existence for Buddha was impermanence. The very concept of impermanence brought in its trail suffering : moral, psychological, physical. Close on the heels of suffering followed ignorance. In fact it was the other way round. Suffering was the result of ignorance. Ignorance was not only the absence of knowledge of reality but also wrong views held in regard to it. Karma was also generated by ignorance. Insight into reality i.e. freedom from ignorance, led to Nirvāṇa.

Knowledge was of two kinds : the lower or mundane, the higher or supramundane. (*Samvṛti-satya, paramārtha-satya*). The former was born of the senses and intellect : The elements of relativity, opposition of identity and difference governed it. It had limited validity. The latter knowledge was non-conceptual, non-relative and intuitive. Both in the case of Advaita and Buddhism, in the final mystical state a profound transformation is brought about.

Though it cannot be said that these concepts are on all fours, it is clear that there is a striking similarity between them. Both hold that impermanence, giving rise to plurality, distinctions, division, conflict, lead to pain and suffering. Man feels the fleeting nature of phenomenal existence hanging over him like the sword of Damocles, in the form of Death. Man naturally worries whether life has any meaning. In fact man has always been in search for an answer to this question. Going from one thing to another, often aimlessly, he does get a respite, but for a short time only. He realises that he cannot escape suffering. Advaita and Buddhism will tell him that the methods he is using to overcome suffering and the fear of impending death are themselves an integral part of the phenomenal existence. They are time bound. Naturally such methods are doomed to failure. Man cannot overcome time bound things with the help of methods that are themselves time bound. Phenomenal existence, by virtue of its being phenomenal is in the grasp of time (*Kāla*). In short both the malady and the method of curing it are time bound. They are, therefore, doomed to failure. If suffering and death are to be overcome, what is required is the use of the knowledge of the eternal and the timeless. Brahman is the timeless and the eternal ground of all existence. The only way to liberate man from the time bound condition is to have knowledge of Brahman. It is only through knowledge which transcends everything that is time bound that man rises above suffering and death.

So far so good. Both Advaita and Buddhism advocate that we should "know" ourself. But how? This is the million dollar question answered by Advaita and Buddhism in slightly differing ways. Both advise transcendence and rising above time. The Advaitin says that Brahman and Ātman are identical. By knowing the Ātman, Brahman is known. Even if similar considerations hold for Buddhism, yet here the knowledge is not of *Brahman* or *Ātman* but of the fundamental emptiness (*Śūnyatā*) which is the underlying structure of existence. For the Buddhist such knowledge constitutes Nirvāṇa. Nirvāṇa in simple words would mean a release from pain and suffering which is part and parcel of the phenomenal existence. So in short, Advaita says that one knows Brahman by knowing Ātman. For the Buddhist the liberating knowledge is of emptiness (*Śūnyatā*) for the rest this knowledge defies logic, it is beyond language, beyond names and forms, can be described in negative terms, it is non-conceptual and intuitive, non-relative, absolute and timeless.

The mystic knows that the *Brahman* and the world of phenomenon are not two numerically different ontological realms. If the phenomenal world is penetrated by the removal of the veil of names and forms we "see" Brahman. Conversely by drawing a veil of names and forms and concealing Brahman, gives us the phenomenal world. Similarly in Buddhism the phenomenal world (*Saṃsāra*) and Nirvāṇa (*Śūnyatā*) are one and the same reality viewed from the lower and higher stand point.[42] Language is not sufficient to meet the demands of expressing such experience adequately. Hence words like 'veil' etc., have to be employed.

One conclusion we can draw from the above discussion is that both in Advaita and Buddhism time belongs to the phenomenal world. Phenomenal world has no independent reality. It follows, therefore, that time too has no independent reality.

If we convert the remarks above into Advaitic terminology we can say that the phenomenal world and time are the children of *Māyā*. They require our senses, concepts and imagination for their working. If a parallel could be drawn for this with the Western philosophical tradition, we could compare the Advaitistic and Buddhist time with Kant's *a priori* form of our sensible intuition. Time cannot, therefore, be said to have any ontological status.

If the above conclusions are admitted (insofar as Advaita and Buddhism are concerned) then, history, being by its very nature time bound cannot have any ontological status. By History we mean all history, that is, human, celestial, geological, biological. Knowledge of Ultimate Reality cannot be sought in history.[43] A study of history will only reveal that man has been in bondage and continues in the same state today. It is not surprising, therefore, that a secondary place is allotted to history in India. We will not go into the charge levelled against Indian tradition that it lacks historical consciousness. The Indian's historical consciousness is not to be viewed in isolation but within the framework of its philosophical and religious traditions. A gross misunderstanding of these traditions has led to such wild charges. In fact Śaṅkara's teaches that the phenomenal world is neither illusory nor non-existent. It is a practical reality but not Ultimate Reality. What is to be borne in mind is that just as the unreality of the imaginary stand point (*prāti-bhāsika*) is to be assessed from the empirical stand point (*Vyāvahārika*), the neither real nor unreal state of the empirical stand point is to be assessed from the ultimate stand point (*paramārthika*). The Buddhist position is not very different. Hīnayāna with its dharmas[44] and Mahāyāna even in its most radical form, (*the Mādhyamika*) does not claim that the empirical world is unreal and illusory. (Unreal it is, illusory it is not). We leave the detailed discussion of this for later. The point we wish to make is that the charge that Indian tradition regards the world of phenomenon as unreal and illusory is without foundation and sometimes, even malicious.

Liberating knowledge (*Pāramārtha satya*) is *different*, but not opposed to practical knowledge. The mystic, therefore, can attain this liberating knowledge by transcending the time bound existence. A mere study of the empirical world will lead him nowhere. History as such can have no place in the mystic's make-up, in the same way as Time can have no place.

But history occupies a very important place in the Christian/Jewish traditions. Historicism is an attitude, a paradoxical one, in which history is given the status of an ultimate reality. In the Christian and Jewish civilisations God intrudes into human affairs. The drama of the crucifixion of Jesus is a part of history. Will Durant in his monumental Story of Civilization III, Caesar and Christ, begins by saying "Did Christ exist?"[45] Whatever be the answer to this question, for the Christian, history is the unfolding and realising of God's will and purpose. It is not surprising, therefore, that the status of Ultimate Reality is granted to history. This remark holds good for both the theistic and atheistic historian. History being a theatre of God, is Ultimate Reality for the theist. For the other, it is ultimate, *ex hypothesi*, because there is no other reality. We shall revert to this in a later chapter when dealing with Christian and Jewish mysticism. Christ was so much a part of history that it prompted Will Durant to write :

"On the annual journeys that all good Palestinian Jews made to Jerusalem for the Passover Festival, Jesus must have learned something of the Essenes, and their half monistic, almost Buddhistic life."[46]

Will Durant adds a footnote :

"Aśoka had sent his Buddhist missionaries as far West as Egypt and Cyrene very likely, therefore, to the Near East."

Time, temporality, *Māyā*, these are the perennial problems of philosophy. No less, time is the perpetual problem of physics. An enquiry into time, leads to an enquiry into Reality. Says. T.M.P. Mahadevan :

"From the standpoint of the Absolute —if Absolute it may be called—there cannot be time. In the plenary experience, Brahmānubhava, time cannot be, even as in perfection, imperfection, cannot be. But to the inquiring intellect time must present a perpetual puzzle. Like *Māyā*, time is indeterminable". (*anirvacanīya*).[47]

Marcea Eliade has aptly put it :

"For after having understood the dialectic of *Māyā*, the Indian tries to deliver himself from its illusions whilst these Europeans seem to be content with the discovery, and to put up with a nihilistic and pessimistic vision of the world . . . . Now, for an Indian, there is no sense in the discovery of the cosmic illusion if it is not followed by the quest of the absolute Being; the notion of *Māyā* is meaningless without the notion of Brahman. In occidental language, we might say that there is no point in becoming aware that one is conditioned unless one turns towards the unconditioned and seeks deliverance. *Māyā* is a cosmic play and, after all, illusory, but when one has understood it to be so, when one has torn away the veil of *Māyā*, one finds oneself before the Absolute Being, before Ultimate Reality."

He adds finally :

"It is the consciousness, of your own historicity that makes you anxious, and no wonder; for one has to die to History before one can discover and live true Being."[48]

BHAKTI : RĀMĀNUJA AND MADHVA

It was Swami Vivekānanda who advocated the blending of knowledge and devotion. He was wont to say that an ideal sage would be one with the brain of Śaṅkara's and the heart of Rāmānuja. In some of his impassioned poetry Śaṅkara forgetting his obdurate monism, describes his mystical experience in terms that would do great credit to the followers of Bhakti.

What then is Bhakti? Bhakti and its kindred word *bhagavad* comes from the common Sanskrit root *bhaj*. It means to deal out, apportion, divide, share, etc. But like the English word 'share' it carries both the meaning of 'to give a part of' and 'to have a part of.' The word is rich in meaning and carries within itself the various implications of love. It means possession, enjoyment, honour, loyalty, devotion and so on. It can also mean enjoy, possess, embrace, worship, adore, revere, esteem.

Bhakti is the central theme of the Bhagavadgītā, The Epics, the *Upaniṣads* and other scriptures. Sanskrit literature has made use of the word in all its nuances and shades of meaning. The meaning, therefore, ranges from the Erotic to the devotional to the mystical, having innumerable intermediate meanings. For Rāmānuja Bhakti was paramount. P.A. Shrinivasachari has summed up the position and meaning of Bhakti admirably. (Caught in the causal cycle of *avidyā-karman*, the *mumukṣu* yearns to return to the Absolute where his home is.) He writes :

"Karma Yoga is the path of his disinterested duty illumined by the knowledge of the distinction between the eternal *ātman* and the empirical ego of *Prakṛti* and the gradual renunciation of egoism or the conceit of *aluṁ-kāra* and *mamakāra* or the feeling of 'I' and 'Mine.' *Jñāna Yoga* is the process of self-realisation in which the self retires from the circumference to the centre, and regains its own state. But it is the orison of quiet, which may lapse into the pitfalls of quietism, and is not the supreme end of life, as it is a godless state of aloneness without the glow of love. *Upāsanā* or *Bhakti* is the unitive way in which the *mumukṣu* sheds his egoism and egocentric outlook, attunes himself to the will of God as Puruṣottama, and yearns for eternal communion with Him."[49]

The meaning of the word 'Bhakti' discussed above brings out one significant feature. Bhakti is not only the love of man for God, but also the love of God for man. The latter part of the meaning is noteworthy. In an age when science and anti-religious philosophy are blamed for the decline of religion, it is forgotten that religion declined not because it was refuted, but because it became irrelevant. What actually happened is that creed has taken the place of worship and love (*Bhakti*) has become a habit. Today religion speaks with the voice of authority, not of compassion. It is for this reason that its message becomes meaningless.

And why is this ? Because we forget that religion is an answer to man's ultimate questions. The problem, therefore, is not to answer the question, but to rediscover the question to which religion is an answer. In such circumstances, Bhakti assumes an important role. It is not merely the love of man for God, but also the love of God for man. God is in search of man. Philosophically speaking man is trapped between the fundamentalist on the one hand and the logical positivist on the other. The former says that all ultimate questions have been answered and the latter says, that the ultimate questions are meaningless. Bhakti assumes relevance because it does not have the conceit of the former and the unconcern of the latter.

When we qualify the word 'Bhakti' by adjectives like *Puj* (reverential bow) it assumes a reverential character. But what is important to remember is that *Bhakti* has a personal connotation. It implies a personal relationship and communion with God. Of course, this itself does not prove that with the advent of Bhakti birth is given to the deep doctrine of the mysticism of love. Bhakti can only be a way. Words are ambiguous. If the word "faith" is used as a synonym for 'Bhakti' it would make 'Bhakti' into "Belief," which could be better translated by the word "Śraddhā" which in its turn would mean "an intellectual belief." The full meaning of Bhakti is "loving self Surrender." It is the foundation on which Rāmānuja builds his Viśiṣṭādvaita.

When Bhakti is assigned this meaning it follows that all techniques prescribed for self-realisation become subordinate, priority being given to Divine initiative. In spite of this initiative assigned to God, the implication of reciprocity remains. Man needs God as much as God needs man. The equation would run roughly as follows :

Bhakti self surrender of the devotee
God's surrender to the devotee
(He is known as Bhakta Parādhīna)
Mukti

The word Bhakti has been used in its purest form in the Gītā. No reference is made to sex symbolism —a feature so common in Sanskrit literature and in descriptions of mystical experience given by Western and Eastern mystics. It is a truism to say that the Gītā is the "gospel of bhakti." Let us take a few illustrations:

"In whatever way men worship Me, in the same way do I fulfil their desires (It is) My path, O son of Pārtha (that) men tread in all ways."[50]

If we analyse these lines we observe that the subject of *bhajāmy* is Sṛikṛishṇa and the object "his devotees." Sṛikṛishṇa loves his devotees to suit the path chosen by them. The implication is that God comes half way to meet man. There is reciprocity. Another example :

"I am the same in all beings, to Me there is none hateful, none dear. But those who worship Me with devotion, they are in Me and I also am in them."[51]

Here "*ye bhajanti tu māṁ bhaktyā*" will have to be translated as those who with love worship me. Occasionally the relationship of love between God — Devotee is a little toned down because of the use of adjectives, like *bhaktimān* (12.17) but even here love between God and man is emphasised by the addition of (*me priyaḥ*). (12.17).

When we come to the *Upaniṣads* the position is altered. While in the Bhagavadgītā, Bhakti is paramount, in the Upaniṣads, with its innumerable trends, both doctrinal and religious, the dominant trend is *Brahman - Ātman*.

Upaniṣads like Īśā, Kaṭha, Śvetāśvatara, Muṇḍaka clearly show a theistic current. It is not necessary at this stage to give illustrations from them. Suffice it to say that despite being called Brahman or Puruṣa, in passages where comparison is made with rivers flowing into the ocean, or salt dissolving in water, the undercurrent of conception of God cannot be completely ruled out.

We can conclude by saying that compassion and graciousness are the chief characteristics of the God of Bhakti. On the one hand man surrenders, on the other God gives himself as a gift. Bhakti and Grace go hand in hand. The divergence between the Monist and Theist assumes seriousness on the question of Grace. The Theist tends to visualise the highest form of transcendence (immanently) in Grace. The Monist dismisses such views as projections of an anthropomorphic mind. In fact the very quotation from the Gītā (4.11) cited to illustrate the love — surrender relationship with God is cited by Śaṅkara to illustrate that the Rain-giver (Parjanya) showed no discrimination and partiality in showering rain on earth. The growth of the resultant crops depend on the seeds sown and their inherent potentialities. To put it in the words of Bṛihadāraṇyaka Upaniṣad one becomes good through good work and evil through evil work.

The theory of Grace would be tantamount to saying that God was prepared to break the causal chain in which Karma binds man. The Gītā admitted that man gets what he deserves. So on the one hand we have cold, impersonal, speculative Monism : on the other we have concrete, personal Bhakti, with little or no stress on the abstract. The realisation of complete identity of the soul with Brahman brings liberation for the former. For the latter the personal God is concrete with attributes : Kṛṣṇa is a friend of Arjuna. Liberation, therefore, means meeting with God through Bhakti, which includes both love and Grace.

So here we have the two tier system of Śaṅkara and the lively pulsating Bhakti of Rāmānuja. Like the proverbial East and West of Kipling the twain cannot meet. Writing on Śaṅkara Dr. Mudgal says :

"The lower tier has a warmth of its own. And yet this very world is unreal. God is unreal, men and their morals are unreal, the world is unreal, all this is ultimately a make-believe. Of whom? Why? These questions should not be raised, as they cannot ever be answered. And when answered we find ourselves 'coming in from the same door from which we went out . . . . in the upper those questions are never raised and in the lower tier they cannot be answered."[52]

Grace is the very heart of Rāmānuja' s system. Without it, it falls. In the Cloud of Unknowing, the anonymous author writes :

"God may be reached and held close by means of love, but by means of thought never."[53] The constant refrain of The Cloud is God cannot be known by 'thought.' He can be known in darkness. He can be known by unknowing. He can be known by love. He can be known by his Grace, but by thought, never. All these words are reminiscent of Bhakti, of Rāmānuja. Love and Grace are the chief factors in Rāmānuja's system. So are they in The Cloud. On some rare occasions Śaṅkara comes close to admitting Grace. Commenting on Gītā 2.39 he says : "You have to severe the bond of Karma only by attaining that knowledge which is caused by the Grace of the Lord." (*Īśvara-Prāsāda*). Such instances in Śaṅkara are very rare and he explains that what is meant is that there should be devout meditation. Śaṅkara has been so consistent throughout his commentaries that one cannot but accept his subsequent explanation.

The position differs radically when we come to Rāmānuja. As we said above, Grace occupies a very important place in his system — so important that he gives it an ultimately real status. We may sum up what Rāmānuja says by quoting B.G. 8.14.

"I am easily attainable, O Partha, by that ever steadfast Yogi, who constantly remembers me daily and thinks of none else" (*sulabhaḥ* Easily attainable).

A general view of Rāmānuja's commentaries both on Brahma-Sūtras and Bhagavadgītā shows that there is Divine Grace *outside* the working of Karma. Grace within the operative power of Karma would not have the same status as the Grace that comes from God, *gratis.* In fact it would not be in keeping with the great stature of God, if the Grace were obtained within the limits of Karma. It would not be commensurate with so great a gift. Just as the ultimate means to release must be the gracious Lord Himself, so also the Ultimate End is the attaining of His Being. And where the attaining of such a Great End is concerned, it cannot be said that it is achieved merely on the basis of *just deserts principle.* As we shall see later while discussing The Cloud, no matter how intense the devotion or exalted the worship, man can only attain that end with the extra something he receives from God by way of a gift, something that is not his just deserts, something that is not attracted by his Karma, something that comes to man as a bonus. Why does God so go out of the way for his devotee ? For the answer to this question we have to revert to Bhagavadgītā 8.14. Commenting on it Rāmānuja writes : "Unable to put up with his separation (from Myself) I Myself want him. The meaning is that I Myself give him that progress in his worship, which is required for attaining Me." Rāmānuja then quotes (*Muṇḍ*. III. 2.3) "The self is not attained through discourses nor through memorising scriptural texts nor through much learning. It is gained only by him who wishes to attain it with his whole heart. To such a one the self reveals its true nature." Rāmānuja also says (*See* Bhagavadgītā X.10-11) "I give them Buddhi-Yoga by which they come unto Me."

It cannot be denied that this theology of Lord's Supreme Grace puts Rāmānuja in a dilemma. The question arising out of this (that is, deserts principle discussed above) was why did God not save everyone ? Besides this view puts the related issue of soul's freedom of action in jeopardy. Rāmānuja gives great weight to the aspirant's human action and devotion, but attributes the attaining of the Goal to Divine Grace only.

The door is to be opened from inside. No magical formula or *mantra* or secret method of meditation can work miracles and carry the devotee to his goal by the momentum of his own efforts, without Divine Grace. It is not we who decide when audience will be granted. The initiative is always with God. All we can do is to show our loving devotion, our Bhakti, we can knock, and keep on knocking until our prayers are heard and the door is unlocked.

The question then arises : Is the devotee to give up all hope of attaining the Goal except through unmerited Grace? Has he merely to cast himself (*Prapatti*) in utter and total surrender on the Grace of God? Has he to take shelter (*Śaraṇāgatī*) in the Grace of God only?

Gītā answers (18.66) : "Relinquishing all Dharmas take refuge in me alone. I will liberate thee from all sins, grieve not."

Total surrender is the last stage of spiritual life. This verse is the climax of the Bhagavadgītā. Rāmānuja commenting on it says : "All Dharmas" are *Karma Yoga, Jñāna Yoga* and *Bhakti Yoga*, which were the means of achieving the Goal. God is to be loved for Himself alone as He is in Himself, not for what the worshippers can get out of Him and not as He is after passing through the refractive medium of a human personality. Bhagavata story of *Gopi Vastraharaṇa* is significant. Unreserved and *unabashed nakedness* of self and its total surrender, resulting in complete denudation of the 'I' and the 'MINE' and full awareness of being 'His.' Without Him 'I' am 'NONE.' With Him 'I' am 'HIS.' I belong to Him.

What is to be renounced is not action, as such, but attachment to it, because attachment to it would generate an improper state of mind. Such attachment would lead to arrogance, pride and the belief that the devotion was meant to benefit oneself. An arrogant attitude would give the devotee the impression that he was the agent. But God is both the agent and the Goal. Arrogance would shift the agency from God to the devotee. It is for this reason that both Rāmānuja and The Cloud emphasise that the thinking about God has to be continuous without any sort of intrusion from outside. So long as the devotee is in an embodied state he *cannot* give up work. But he can give up attachment to it.

Generally speaking for Rāmānuja life is determined by the laws of Karma. Good works are rewarded by the Lord. The Lord is pleased by the services done to Him. But scattered all over Rāmānuja's writings are intimations of soul's desire for immortality through God's Grace. At such moments his whole philosophy is grounded in Grace to the exclusion of everything else.

Madhva alone makes his theistic attitude towards Grace clear at the very outset. For him the enquiry into Brahman is made possible because of the Grace of the Lord. Sharma writes "According to Madhva, this knowledge of God is not a mere intellectual realisation of the Deity. It is more a feeling of deep attraction and attachment arising from the knowledge of *Bimba-Prātibimbabhāva* between God and Soul, and sustained by a sense of spontaneous attraction and affection flowing from it. Hence, in Bhakti, there is the element of knowledge and attachment combined. In the last analysis, then, it is not pure knowledge that puts an end to the bondage of souls, but the Grace of God in gracious acceptance of the soul's surrender."[54]

Madhva is categorical in his statements. For Madhva the soul's release is the gift of the Independent Lord, in the same way as he is the cause of the soul being obscured and in a state of ignorance. The essential being of the Lord is completely outside and beyond the reach of the soul irrespective of the intense devotion of the devotee. His Grace is like a ray of light that reveals him.

But Madhva's system cannot be restricted to such a simple view. Let us, therefore, examine his conception of Grace in relation to that of Rāmānuja and incidentally, (the views held by some Christian Mystics).

MADHVA — DVAITĀ

INTRODUCTION

With the discussion of Advaita, Viśiṣṭādvaita, Dvaitā and Buddhist mysticism, we can by no means exhaust the variety of Hindu mysticism. But we would not be far wrong in saying that a short discussion of the three great forms of Vedānta together with Buddhist mysticism gives a fair idea of the main types. Insofar as the three forms of Vedānta are concerned, the other systems left out from the classical forms represent variations or intermediate positions between these points of view.

We now turn to Madhva. He rejects Śaṅkara's non-dualism (Advaita), Rāmānuja's qualified non-dualism (Viśiṣṭa-advaita) and advocates a thorough going duality between the world and Brahman. But it would be a mistake to understand the word "dualism," in the usual sense of the word. B.N.K. Sharma has taken considerable pains to show that the Sanskrit terms "Dvaitā" and the English term "Dualism" have associations which preclude their being applied to Madhva's philosophy. Sharma sums up the ontology of Madhva by the following quotation : "There are *two orders* of reality — the Independent and the dependent."[55]

As a world view dualism means the belief that 'real' is of two kinds. Such a definition would fit the Western conception of dualism, where two equally independent ultimate principles or reals exist. It would not fit the Dvaitā of Madhva. For him reality consists of three eternal absolutely real and irreducibly distinct entities, namely, Brahman, selves and matter, the latter two being completely dependent on the first. Madhva thus regards Śaṅkara's Saguṇa (qualified) Brahman as Ultimate Reality. Like Spinoza's God, Madhva's Brahman is both essence and existence. He is *causa sui*, caused by itself and *res completa*, complete in itself, determined by itself and capable of being explained by itself. God or Brahman is a "Svatantra — Tattva."

Thus the reaction against Śaṅkara's doctrines expressed by Rāmānuja, was carried to its logical conclusion by Madhva, who to all intents and purposes abandoned the monistic system altogether. It is not necessary for us to enter into the complete philosophical system of Madhva. We propose to deal with those portions that pertain to his mysticism.

Ignorance plays a very important role in Śaṅkara's philosophy. It is not possible, as we have already seen, to explain his mysticism without discussing ignorance. The condition that causes souls to be bound down to the beginningless round of rebirths is ignorance. Madhva too holds this view. But the "ignorance" in Śaṅkara and the "ignorance" in Madhva are different. To Śaṅkara, ignorance was a unitary phenomenon. The structure of Śaṅkara's mysticism was based on this conception. Madhva, however, did not conceive ignorance in this way. To him *each* individual's ignorance has its own characteristics. There is thus a difference between the "release" enjoyed by one person from that enjoyed by another person. Madhva is thus unique in holding that some "selves" would continue to transmigrate whereas some others would suffer eternal punishment in hell.[56]

It is not necessary for us to enter into the details of this problem. Suffice it to say that for Madhva there were not only various levels of release but also various levels of non-release. For Rāmānuja the way of destroying ignorance was through *Prapatti*. Through Bhakti and total surrender man makes himself worthy of Divine Grace. This eliminates ignorance, egoism and Karma. However, such surrender does not result in complete effacement of the self or its uniqueness. Man preserves his individuality and consciousness while enjoying eternal communion with God. Madhva held similar views. Thus like Rāmānuja, he recognises total devotion and self surrender to God as the only means of salvation.

Though devotion and worship form an integral and central part of the path to salvation, Madhva also prescribed meditation. But the meditation prescribed by him differed from that of Advaita or Buddhism in that the latter required the emptying of the mind of images and objects of all thoughts. In this manner a pure state of consciousness was achieved, which led to realisation. On the other hand Madhva's meditation had as its object the "Lord." This meditation or *dhyāna* involved continuous thinking *on* God and of God, setting aside all other things. But to Madhva this was not just thinking. It had to be backed by full conviction acquired as a result of rational thinking and scriptural studies. In order to dispel all doubts and false ideas, such knowledge about the nature of God, generates devotion (*Bhakti*) for the Lord, which in turn gives rise to a continual flow of love. The flow of this love would be such that it would remove and remain unimpaired despite thousands of obstacles. The list of the things a meditator had to follow was a very long one. Among other things it included reflection on the five differences : (a) between God and Soul, (b) soul and soul, (c) soul and the matter, (d) God and the matter, (e) one object of the world and another.

For Madhva, Brahman is the source of everything. He does not admit, as some other theists do, that there is an independent potency in the universe (e.g. in Prakṛti, Puruṣas, etc.). His conception of God in an absolute sense, leads him to give God complete metaphysical independence, and complete metaphysical dependence upon Him, to all else. The entire finite reality both sentient and non-sentient, is permeated with God's immanent power. Says Sharma :

"It also shows in what respect he differs from other Theists like Patañjali, who limit the controlling power of God to a serious extent. Prakṛti, according to Patañjali, has the 'intrinsic potency of change, and development. It is not derived from the *Will of God* ' (Italics mine). All that Īśvara does is to help Prakṛti to manifest her latent powers."[57]

In fact he goes to the extreme of saying that the potencies present in things are subject to Will and control of God.

BUDDHIST MYSTICISM

During the course of this book we have occasionally referred to Buddhist mysticism, but had left the development of the theme for later. We accordingly take it up now. Since, however, we are concerned with the mystical element in Buddhism, we do not propose to deal with the doctrines in detail, except insofar as they pertain to mysticism, though there is bound to be unavoidable overlapping.

Buddhist mysticism simply means Nirvāṇa, it being the only mystical element, all other elements being rationalistic and sceptical. What is *Nirvāṇa* ? Generally speaking *Nirvāṇa* is not a state of annihilation but the attainment of the unchangeable reality which can positively be described as the eternal peace (*Nirvāṇam Śāntam*). What this peace really is, no words can define; all definitions can only offer a vague suggestion. Buddha employs negative terms for the description, such as freedom from misery and death, freedom from sensuality, from the ego, from delusion, from ignorance. This state of freedom is attainable by the "noble kind of wisdom," what the Vedānta calls transcendent knowledge. The 'wisdom' referred to is not the wisdom of the intellect, which presumes a knower and the known or an object of knowledge. It is rather a state (*Śūnyatā*) in which there is no subject-object relationship, but in which both the mind and intellect are transcended. (Hindu psychology separates these two). Expressed in the words of Christ : "Ye shall know the truth and the truth shall make you free." *Nirvāṇa* is the state of actual realisation of the oneness of life and that the many are one. *Para-Nirvāṇa* is the withdrawal from activity entirely and dissolving into *Para-Brahm,* or non-Being, to return no more in incarnation — *Saṃsāra* entirely escaped. *Nirvāṇa* is attained in the flesh, and is not an 'annihilation' as has been said by some, but a state of, to use the words of Dr. Bucke, cosmic consciousness — a glimpse of the *sat-cit-ānanda* (Existence, knowledge — bliss). Absolute — a desireless being. The soul (as understood by the Buddhist is a bundle of desires, habits, etc.) may pass out of the body after Nirvāṇa, and may dwell on certain planes of Being, helping the race to escape its bondage — such are the masters and Adepts the Elder Brethren of the Race, who forgo the Bliss Absolute for aeons in order to render service to the race. Beyond all this is the entrance into *Para Nirvāṇa* — dissolution into Para-Brahm — a sinking into Eternal Peace and Rest Absolute. The following comments of Dr. D.T. Suzuki on *Nirvāṇa* are illuminating. He says :

"All the Buddhist teachings unfold themselves around the conception of Buddhahood . . . . The Buddha is endowed with transcendental knowledge (*Prajñā*) and a great compassionate heart (*Karuṇā*). With the former he realises that this world of particulars has no reality, is devoid of an ego-substance (*anātman*) and that in this sense it resembles *Māyā* or a visionary flower in the air. As thus it is above the category of being and non-being, it is declared to be pure (*Viśuddha*) and absolute (*Vivikta*) and free from conditions (*Animitta*) . . . . *Nirvāṇa* is not the ultimate abode of Buddhahood, nor is it enlightenment. Love and compassion is what essentially constitutes the self-nature of the All-knowing One (*Sarvajña*)."[58]

Buddhism is wholly the product of Buddha's enlightenment experience, and, therefore, mysticism is the very essence of it. So far as purely mystical element is concerned, there is no important difference between *Hīnayana* and *Mahāyāna*, because the only properly mystical element in Buddhism is *Nirvāṇa*, and *Nirvāṇa* must be conceived as having the same nature in both. The differences lie in the emotional atmosphere in which the experience of *Nirvāṇa* is embedded, interpretive beliefs and moral ideas. We need not go into a detailed discussion on them here, being concerned as we are exclusively with mysticism. But then it would not be proper to ignore the issue altogether. Stated briefly, *Mahāyāna* distinguishes itself from *Hīnayāna* by terming itself Mahā (great/superior) and Hīnayāna as little/inferior. The former comprises a wealth of methods (*Upāya*) for the realisation of *Nirvāṇa*. Its methods range right from the dialectic of Nāgārjuna to the Sukhavati or Pure Land Doctrine of Liberation of Amitābha, the Buddha of Boundless light. In Japanese it is known as Jodo. Incidentally, this doctrine developed around the vow of the Buddha Amitābha and uses for its single operative means, the invocation of his name. The name itself means "Infinite Light" and the Buddha thus denoted is the one who presides over the Western quarter where his own "Buddha-land" is symbolically situated. It is interesting to note that Westerners who are drawn to Buddhism are inclined to avoid this form because of its insistence on *Grace*. It has importance for us inasmuch as it insists on Grace, an issue of some dispute in Buddhism and a very important issue wherever mysticism is discussed. It is quite likely that the Westerners drawn to mysticism tend to avoid, this form because it reminds them of Christianity which they have left behind to embrace Buddhism. They are, therefore, drawn to *Jiriki* (own power) methods.

Hīnayāna, which is also termed small vehicle or *shoja* in Zen takes the aspirant from one state of mind (delusion) to another (enlightenment). It is designed to accommodate only one's self. This is not according to the highest teachings of Buddhism. Buddha's enlightenment meant that existence is an inseparable whole, each one of us embraces the cosmos in its totality. It follows, therefore, that we cannot attain genuine peace of mind merely by seeking our own salvation while remaining indifferent to the welfare of others. A short parable illustrates Hīnayāna. A mother who lost six children had one daughter remaining who too died and left the mother disconsolate. The Buddha came to see her and consoled her by saying that many hundreds of children we have buried, you and I, several kindred, in the times gone by. He posed her a question : Which among them is the one for whom you mourn ? If we are to accept Buddha's fundamental teaching that all things are without a self (*an-attā*) then an ontological problem arises. In what sense can the woman with all the children have lived through the thousands of lives? The Hīnayānist attempts to answer this question by stating "*Yat sat tat kṣanikam*" — Literally means "that which is real is momentary," "all things are as brief as winks." They cease the moment they spring. Even then they are like a chain of cause and effect, which is beginningless and eternal. These transitory dharmas are what appear to be Gods, men, ocean, trees. In other words, every phenomenal being should be looked upon as a flux of particles, that are themselves short lived and fleeting. After all throughout the transition from birth to death and the endless rebirths the so-called individual is no more than this causal sequence, always different from what was a moment ago and what it will be a moment later. Simile of the flame of the lamp is sometimes given to illustrate this point. During the three parts of the night the flame is the same flame and yet not the same flame. In other words what appears to us as pseudo-individuals are just the aggregates of small and brief realities. In the final analysis there is no thinker but thought, only feelings but no one to feel. This is how world illusion is formed. Soul and the individual are ruled out. When we realise and cease to think that these phenomenal effects constitute reality, *Nirvāṇa* is attained. The Hīnayānist treats *Nirvāṇa* as negative. If he treats it as positive he breaches his conclusion, *yet sat tat kṣanikam.*" And finally we may state that Hīnayāna is also known as Theravāda or the way of the Elders. It is so called because the Hīnayānist claims to represent the original Buddhism as taught by Gautama himself.

Reverting to Mahāyāna we note that the Mahāyānist lays more stress on the life of Buddha instead of on his teachings. He contends that Buddha did not want to slip off into Nirvāṇa all by himself, but to help others to attain it also. As against the negativism of Hīnayāna, Mahāyāna approached the non-dualism of Vedānta : In fact, after enlightenment, Buddha spent some forty-five years teaching people how they could achieve enlightenment. John Whitter's poem "The Meaning" has lines that express Mahāyana succinctly :

"He findeth not who seeks his own
The soul is lost that saved alone."

Historically coinciding with the revival of Hinduism were the decline of early Buddhism and the rise of *Mahāyāna*. Elements of *Mahāyāna* had been present in Buddhist thought and practices, almost from the beginning, but they co-existed with the original Buddhism or *Hīnayāna*, until this time, when they achieved a definite form. The tendency of Mahāyāna was to popularise the original teachings of the Buddha, giving a mystical and devotional turn to his doctrine. Thus it preached that higher than Arhathood (or personal sanctity, which was the ideal of *Hīnayāna*) was Buddhahood, the state of prime perfection which Buddha reached and a state which is within the grasp of all. While *Hīnayāna* laid stress on asceticism and monastic seclusion, *Mahāyāna* visualised the attainment of perfection in the midst of the tumult of this life. And what is more important, unlike *Hīnayāna*, it urged dependence on worship of Buddha as an incarnation of God. It was this view that created in Buddhism a place for Grace, which was otherwise absent in the unaided spiritual effort of the Hīnayānist. Besides Bodhisattva was the exalted conception for the Mahāyānist. The Bodhisattva was required to take a vow in the beginning of his spiritual life, undertaking to postpone his own salvation until all have achieved that cherished goal. This was in marked contrast to the exclusive personal salvation which was the desideratum of the Hīnayānist.

For Mahāyāna, Grace is a fact. A boundless power dwells in everyone, drawing each in its good time to the goal. Examples are not lacking in the Pali Canon (Udāna 7 : 1—1) wherein the key to the understanding of what "Grace" means in a Buddhist setting are found. The passage (from a Hīnayāna text) also throws considerable light on Nirvāṇa. We quote :

"There is, O Monks, an unborn, an unbecome, an unmade, an uncompounded : if, O Monks, there were not here this unborn, unbecome, unmade, uncompounded, there would not here be an escape from the born, the become, the made, the compounded. But because there is an unborn, an unbecome, an unmade, an uncompounded, therefore, there is an escape from the born, the become, the made, the compounded."

This famous passage can be used for a preliminary study of both Nirvāṇa and Grace; the two most important aspects in any major mystical tradition.

This oft quoted passage can no doubt be taken to represent Buddha's thought. It can be likened to the thoughts of Heraclitus.

All things flow and there is nothing permanent, with no underlying "Substance" of things. Everything is in a state of flux. Many interpretations of Buddha's philosophy give the impression that this concept of "flux" constitutes the whole of Buddha's thoughts. This is not so. Nirvāṇa does *not* form part of the flux. Making allowance for some divergent views in some branches of Mahāyāna, it may be stated that Nirvāṇa stands in contrast to Saṃsāra. The fleeting world of temporal events constitute Saṃsāra. Looked at from the human angle it is the endless round of reincarnate lives; as everything in Saṃsāra — world is compounded of parts, which dissolve, whatever arises, is produced by some cause. But Nirvāṇa is neither produced nor caused. Causes and effects lie in the flow of time. Nor can we give the attribute of permanency to "Nirvāṇa" because that would again bring it within the purview of time. After all permanency means "enduring through time." Nirvāṇa is what Eckhart called "the Eternal Now." It is the "unborn reality." And because of this unborn reality there is escape from Saṃsāra.

It is thus clear that Nirvāṇa is not a subjective state of mind or being where the aspirant 'arrives.' It transcends the individual mind. It may be likened to the Buddhist version of the Eternal. If we say that Nirvāṇa is not produced, then it may be asked, what do the various exercises like breathing, concentration etc. do? Do they not produce Nirvāṇa? The answer is a categorical "NO." There is but one Nirvāṇa and the various exercises and disciplines help us to participate in Nirvāṇa. We will not enter into the question whether such an exposition of Nirvāṇa does or does not make Buddha a metaphysician — a position he always tried to deny.

If we take another small passage from the questions of King Milinda, belonging to a later period, where the speaker is not Buddha but the Monk Nāgasena, we find that despite the lapse of time and change of the cultural setting, the passage concurs with the passage quoted above.

"Revered Nāgasena, is Nirvāṇa uncompounded?" "Yes, Sire, Nirvāṇa is uncompounded, it is made by nothing at all. Sire, one cannot say of Nirvāṇa that it arises or that it does not arise or that it is to be produced or that it is past or future or present, or that it is cognizable by the eye, ear, nose, tongue or body."

"If, revered Nāgasena, Nirvāṇa neither arises, nor does not arise and so on, as you say, well then revered Nāgasena you indicate Nirvāṇa as a thing that is not Nirvāṇa is not."

"Sire, Nirvāṇa is."[59]

The passage speaks for itself. For a moment let us revert to the quotation from Udāna. There is no doubt that the language is the language of transcendence. A Christian mystic or a Sufi could have used the very words while referring to God and the world. The passage holds out hope. But what it does not do is to define the link. There is apparently no indication to show the bridge over which changefulness must traverse to reach the Eternal. This bridge in fact represents the function of Grace. It is at this juncture, before proceeding further in our discussion of the various aspects of Nirvāṇa and the problems connected with it, we ask the question : "Is there any room for Grace in Buddhism?" It is generally presumed that a mystical tradition that does not include the idea of a personal God, is most unlikely to develop the concept of "Grace," which afterall is to be received by the aspirant as an unsolicited gift independently of any effort on his part : Grace is a translation of a divine Function. Generally speaking, it has to be admitted that "Grace" is a word that corresponds to the whole dimension of spiritual experience. Would it be possible, therefore, that it should be absent from one of the great religions of the world? Of course this does not answer the question we asked above.

Let us look at it this way. Apparently there is an incommensurable gap fixed between enlightenment and the seeker after enlightenment. By definition the seeker is ignorant. On the face of it, it does not make sense. Imagine the seeker and enlightenment to be the two ends of a pole. The way things are explained it would appear that enlightenment (God for that matter) in relation to man's endeavour is situated at the passive end of the pole, i.e., Enlightenment becomes the object of man, the subject. In other words man becomes an active agent in an operation in which Enlightenment plays a passive role. But things cannot be read this way. By definition Enlightenment falls outside the scope of "becoming." From these observations it would appear that on its own showing the pursuit of enlightenment becomes paradoxical inasmuch as this results in the encompassing of the greater by the less, of the imperishable by the ephemeral, of absolute knowledge by relative ignorance. As we just said man becomes the subject and Enlightenment the object. History of religion will testify that this is equally true of theistic forms of religion. Is it possible, therefore, we ask, to unilaterally, perceive the Divine Truth, even across one of its aspects, leave alone its essence ? Reduced to Buddhistic terms no human effort, however great and however stretched, can possibly match to the suchness of enlightenment. And yet Buddhism is just this : Nothing less than this is offered. As human beings we are all on the axis of Buddhahood. Why should we not, therefore, reach enlightenment, when as the saying goes, it is within the scope of every being even "down to the last blade of grass," via of course, prior attainment of a human birth. We again quote Dr. Suzuki :

"There is a gem known as Maṇi which is perfectly transparent and colourless in itself, and just because of this characteristic it reflects in it varieties of colours (*vicitra rūpa*). In the same way the Buddha is conceived by beings; in the same way his teaching is interpreted by them; that is, each one recognises the Buddha and his teaching according to his disposition (*āśaya*), understanding (*citta*), prejudice (*anuśaya*), propensity (*adhimukti*) and circumstances (*gati*). Again, the Buddha treats his fellow-beings as an expert physician treats his patients suffering from various forms of illness. The ultimate aim is to cure them, but as ailments differ medicines and treatment cannot be the same."[60]

As a result, if there is to be any wooing of enlightenment, it (i.e. enlightenment) remains the real subject of the quest as well as the ostensible object. Some mystics have insisted that in enlightenment the subject-object distinction is wiped out. This has always remained an enigma in mystical tradition. However, intuition allows one to know that despite initiative and effort the aspirant remains the passive term in the equation.

If we turn our attention to Mahāyāna Buddhism we see that it speaks of the three bodies (*Kāyas*) of Buddhahood. Some have called this the three mansions of enlightenment :

(a) Essence or Suchness (*Dhama Kāya*)

(b) Bliss (*Sambhoga Kāya*)

(c) Avataric projection into the world (*Nirmāṇa Kāya*).

It is the third Kāya which relates to the question of grace in its appearance among beings.

And finally a short story to clinch the point. Before his enlightenment the Buddha-to-be proceeded to Bodhgayā to take his place on the seat standing ready for him at the foot of a spreading pipal tree. When he was about to sit, Māra the tempter challenges him. "I am the prince of the world," he says, at that moment the Bodhisattva stretched forth his right hand and touched the earth calling on her to witness that the throne (seat) was his by right and earth testified that it was so.

In the classical form of this image Buddha is always shown sitting upon a lotus, right hand pointing towards the earth, touching it, while the left hand turned upward to support the begging bowl — a sign of a bhikku state. It symbolises the acceptance of heavenly grace. This classical pose sums up the entire gamut of man's spiritual exigencies.

The general tenor of the above discussion shows that there is place for Grace in Buddhism. If 'Grace' is accorded its proper interpretation and meaning, then one can hardly find a major religious tradition where it does not exist. Even for those who think that Zen is pure "self power" without any "other power" tend to lose sight of the fact that a very important part is played by the Guru or Roshi, who not being the disciple must necessarily be the "other power" in relation to the latter. A story is told about Patriarch Bodhidharma (of Zen). The Patriarch came to the sea shore wishing to cross to the other side (ocean Saṃsāra). Not finding a boat he espied a piece of reed with the help of which he crossed the waters and landed safely on the other shore. Being a sage he knew that "own power" and "other power" represented "free will" and "Grace," which in essence are the same. His own use of the reed (Bamboo) as a vehicle rests on this very awareness. But this is not all. The question also arises as to who put the reed there. Obviously the "other power." Parables and stories, works of art and paintings have all been used to convey the idea of the presence of "Grace."

With the above as a backdrop we proceed to discuss Nirvāṇa and make a brief comparison with Vedānta and other traditions.

Buddhistic mysticism is concerned with the fact of suffering and the possibility of escape from it. If anything distinguishes

Buddhist mysticism from the mysticism of other religious traditions, it is the fact that it combines a practical rule of personal conduct with a consistent transcendentalism. If we narrow down to Hindu mysticism, we find that there are, no doubt, points of differences between them, but in the last analysis Buddhist mysticism is a new interpretation rather than a repudiation of Hindu mysticism. Buddhist mysticism does not see something different, but sees differently the same thing. In spite of Buddhist dissent from certain methods of religious practices and pedagogy, common at that time, there are rooted in Buddhism a number of ancient Hindu beliefs expressed in terms like *Karma, Nirvāṇa, Dharma* (the law), *Saṃsāra* (the endless round of existence), *Māyā*, and others. Not only did the Buddha take some of these Hindu doctrines, but he sought to give them a more direct relevance and dynamism.

Buddha was a pragmatist *par excellence*. He did not waste any time and effort in speculation and sterile metaphysical discourse. His concern was solely with deliverance. Like the ocean which has only one taste, that is of salt, so also his doctrine has one flavour, that of deliverance. Deliverance or salvation or Nirvāṇa meant only one thing : Breaking through the chain of births and rebirths. Rendered in modern idiom it could be stated that his teaching was not speculative but therapeutic. According to him we can help one another and also be helped by a Guru, but ultimately everyone has to save himself by the momentum of his own efforts.

Existence involved suffering. The cause of suffering is desire and attachment to existence. The way to escape from suffering and existence is to be rid of these desires. The goal the Buddha set before his disciples was the achievement of Nirvāṇa or the cessation of suffering. Nirvāṇa, therefore, became the pivot and the spiritual destiny of Buddhism. For Buddhism the question was not "what is Nirvāṇa" but "How is Nirvāṇa attained."

Buddha realised the futility of posing impractical questions. He was aware that even if the hearer or disciple understood the implication of metaphysical questions, such questions would be impractical and lead the hearers or disciples into a metaphysical morass. What is Nirvāṇa ? and like questions cannot be answered by ontological analysis. The mind is inadequate for the task. (Cf.

Kant, Critique of Pure Reason). The Buddha, therefore, bypassed all this and taught :

(a) The Four-fold Noble Truths.
(b) The Twelve-fold Chain of Causation.
(c) The Eight-fold Path of Righteous Living.
(d) The Doctrine of Non-ego (Anātman).
(e) Attainment of Nirvāṇa.

The Buddha knew that in the higher reaches only a Buddha could understand another Buddha. No amount of sun staring could make an eagle out of a crow, nor could the Buddha turn a jackal into a lion. Every aspirant has, what we term in modern psychology, a threshold, beyond which he cannot go — no matter how much ontological analysis and metaphysical arguments were employed.

Between our intellectual knowledge and the forthcoming experience lies a vast area of symbols and concepts. Buddha was well aware that for thousands of years men had gained experience in meditation, profound thought and applied action. They essayed to describe all this in words, through metaphysics, philosophy, psychology and religion, but failed to put it in words. How much more difficult it would be, therefore, to convey the highest experience to the generality of hearers and disciples? It was for this reason that the Buddha thought it proper to remain silent or as Radhakrishnan says "suspend judgement."

But strangely enough while discussing such matters we tend to begin, where we should end, at the top. It has no name, but human beings have never tired of supplying a name. The Christians call it 'Godness' (Gottheit), the Hindus call it 'That' and the Buddhist refer to it as "the unborn, unoriginated, unconditioned." Buddha, therefore, took the world as he found it and tried to formulate methods and disciplines by which mankind could be freed from the chains of suffering and ignorance, the two important ingredients in the way of achieving Nirvāṇa. Besides, Nirvāṇa was to be achieved in this present life. It is not an after-death experience. As the Gītā says :

"Transitory existence is overcome even here by them whose mind rests on equality. Brahman is flawless and the same in all, therefore, they are established in Brahman."[61]

Nirvāṇa, here and now, (*Samdiṭha Kam Nibbanam*) is the clarion call of Buddhism. It has much in common with Jīvanmukti of Hindu Mysticism.

Buddha's was a philosophy of flux. (We use the word "philosophy" for want of a better word). But unlike other philosophers who professed a similar philosophy, Buddha's was a philosophy that showed a way out of the flux. In the escape from this flux lay the way to Nirvāṇa. In fact his philosophy has often mistakenly been compared with that of Bergson. On a superficial examination there does appear to be a similarity. But then the similarity is to some extent, deceptive.

According to Bergson the Ultimate Reality is a constant flux, a creative evolution. While the Buddha also believed that the universe of experience is a constant flux, he did not admit that this constant flux was the Ultimate Reality. It is not necessary for us to analyse in detail the philosophical views of Bergson. Suffice it to say that to him time and duration are real. To Buddha the universe of flux is neither real nor unreal, *it is*, and *it is not*. Put in simple words Bergson would like nothing better than to whirl within the bonds of *Māyā*. Both Buddha and Bergson see the flux, but the latter does not want it to be viewed as *sub specie aeternitatis* (from the aspect of eternity) but *sub specie* duration is. Buddha rises above the flux, time, space and causation. Shelley in lines reminiscent of Plato writes :

"The One remains, the many change and pass;

Heaven's Light for ever shines, Earth's shadows fly;

Life, like a dome of many — coloured glass,

Stains the white radiance of Eternity."[62]

Even Plato points out the weakness in assuming flux and change to be the Ultimate. In the event of such as assumption knowledge would be impossible. Plato even shows his impatience with the later Heracleiteans when he puts the following words in the mouth of Theodorus :

"For, in accordance with their text books, they are always in motion; but as for dwelling upon an argument or a question, and quietly asking and answering in turn, they can no more do so than they can fly."[63]

Like Plato, Buddha sought to find the state beyond flux (*Bhava —Nirodha—Nibbanam*). This withdrawal from the state of flux was for the Buddha the attainment of Nirvāṇa.

Even if we admit for a moment that Bergson pointed out that the Ultimate Reality could not be discovered by the intellect alone, he has egregiously failed to find a way with the help of which one may transcend the intellect and reach the very source of knowledge itself.

TURĪYA AND NIRVĀṆA

No two mystical experiences can be said to be on all fours. Being individual they are *sui generis.* But if at all a comparison is to be made Buddhist Nirvāṇa would come closest to the *Turīya* or transcendental consciousness of the Upaniṣads. It comes closest to the description of *Turīya* as neither subjective nor objective experience, nor an intermediate experience, nor is it a negative condition which is neither consciousness nor unconsciousness. It can only be clarified that *Turīya* (fourth) is not a state, like the others, but is present in all the states and is the whole of reality.

The Nirvāṇa of Buddha like the *Turīya* is beyond conception, beyond knower, time, space, causation, unthinkable, inconceivable and yet attainable. It is for this reason Buddha refused to define it, as a definition would bring it within time, space and causation.

We may not know Nirvāṇa but we know its effects on life. It is what Christ called : "By their fruits Ye Shall Know Them."[64] St. Paul enumerated these fruits as "Love, Joy, Peace, Long Suffering, Gentleness, Goodness, Faith."[65] Aśoka carved on stone "compassion, liberality, truth, purity, gentleness, peace, joyousness, saintliness, self-control." If one could imagine consciousness without the contents of consciousness, one could come close to Nirvāṇa.

Buddha did not deny a permanent reality, but he did consistently deny the possibility of positing it so long as we dwelt within the limitation of sense experience. Buddha was afraid that the element within man, which is commonly known as the self, but which in fact is the ego, dependent on the flux for its existence and character, would be mistaken for the true unchangeable self, S.N. Dasgupta has admirably summed up this point : "It is indeed very difficult to describe satisfactorily the ultimate mystical stage of Buddhistic Nirvāṇa. For in one sense it is absolutely contentless. It is the state of deliverance from all sorrow and from all happiness . . . . Whether we read the teachings of the Upaniṣads or of the Yoga of Patañjali, the ultimate state representing the goal of all the spiritual quest and spiritual strivings of the sages is set forth as absolutely contentless and non-conceptual . . . . It is a state of absolute dissolution of all world process. Though a blissful state, there is no distinction here between the bliss and the enjoyer of the bliss . . . . To call it blissful is not to understand bliss in an ordinary way. For this mystical bliss is incomprehensible by the intellect."[66]

We could put things in another perspective. Is Nirvāṇa attained ? In Buddhism the unconditionality of Nirvāṇa is present in the superstructure from the beginning. And if it is already there, there can be no seeker of Nirvāṇa and no process of liberation. Gauḍapāda's description of these notions make illuminating reading :

There being "na nirodhaḥ" and "na utpattiḥ" that is, there being no dissolution and origination, bondage etc., do not exist.[67]

"There is no dissolution, no origination, none in bondage, none striving or aspiring for salvation, and none liberated. This is the highest truth.[68]

But all this does not mean that a path is not prescribed. The structure of the Buddha's teaching was based on his personal enlightenment—Six years of hard thinking and meditation. It is for this reason that he emphasised (nāna) *Jñāna* (knowing) and (passa) *Pasya* (seeing). In the Buddha's teaching of the Eight-fold noble path, *Sammadassana* (right seeing) comes first and *Sammasan Kappa* (right knowing), comes next. By seeing, he meant seeing things in their right state of suchness (tathatā) or what we call is-ness. In other words, the whole structure of Nirvāṇa has for its foundation the "seeing."

Like all great teachers, the Buddha set forth recondite truths in the form of parables. In the parable for the "crossing over" he explains how a raft is to be constructed out of twigs, dry leaves and so on.

The bank hither is fraught with danger. The bank yonder is secure and safe. What has the disciple to do after crossing over safely and landing on the other side ? Has he securely to pack the raft and carry it further on his head or shoulders? No, says the Buddha. The raft was for getting across not for retaining. It had served its purpose. He says :

"You monks, by understanding the parable of the raft must discard even right states of mind, and all the more, wrong states of mind."[69]

Before we end, we may remark that Buddhism, like Advaita, has one of the greatest mystical traditions in the world. We shall examine in our last chapter as to how close the concepts of Advaita and Buddhist mysticism come to modern physics.[70] We shall see how contemporary physics finds a remarkable echo in the Eastern and not Western metaphysical system. The reason for this is the monistic view of Reality, not monotheistic view. The religious scientist has discarded what may be termed 'objectifying monotheism' in favour of "subjectifying monism." This is exactly what the Buddha taught : objectifying leads to the perception of differences and perception of difference leads to suffering. To quote Aśvaghoṣa :

"As soon as the mind perceives differences, it awakens desires, grasping and suffering and then the mind notes that some relate to himself and some to not-self. If the mind could remain undisturbed by differences and discrimination, the concept of an ego (the root of moral evil) would die away."[71]

It is for this reason that the Buddha refused to discuss Brahman, laying sole stress on Nirvāṇa, which is a subjective form of the mystical enlightenment. It is also for this reason that we do not come across (unlike Hinduism) any theories of cosmos or permanent self, or Brahman or any ontological propositions concerning the universe or man. Sometimes Buddhist mysticism sounds like depth psychology. This is because in this mysticism all problems and solutions are to be found in the subject. To the Buddha the real is what you experience. What you think does not matter.

Finally, however much and however hard we try to describe Nirvāṇa, we have to admit defeat because we are trying to describe the indescribable. All that we can say is that in this unique experience there is an immediate apprehension of Being in which there is no sense of union with the Divine conceived in terms of personality or super-personality or even an identity as conceived in the Hindu Ātman-Brahman concept. This knowledge is referred to as "Eye of knowledge" (*Jnānacakṣus*). While early Buddhism was analytical and tried to free Being from the imposition of subjectivity, Mahāyāna, continuing to be analytical, rejected both subjectivism and objectivism by laying stress on Being as such, which was finally experienced in enlightenment. The Buddha's directions for meditation and concentration were perhaps of the simplest kind : 'In what is seen there should be what is seen. Similarly there should be just the heard, the smelt, tasted, sensed and thought. Each act should be just that completely, to the exclusion of everything else. More simple and direct words could not have been used to explain meditation and concentration.

Thus Nirvāṇa is not to be looked upon as a psychological insight or a highly charged ecstasy, because it leads to complete transformation and revaluation of the personality. It revolutionises the entire framework. Subject–object duality is completely lost resulting in a fresh dimension. This lasts so long as the experience lasts. However, the aspirant finds his place in the flux of life identifying himself with and loving everything that exists.

In the Buddha and the great Avatāras the experience is present continuously. The everyday activities and bodily wants being attended to mechanically.

CONCLUSIONS

It will be observed from the foregoing discussion that a thorough study of Nirvāṇa would result in the study of the history of Buddhism. After all the history of Buddhism is nothing else but the history of Nirvāṇa. And what lessons do we draw from all this discussion ? We find that Nirvāṇa is a kind of critical and reflective awakening, which has nothing to do with what we experience empirically. It is neither existence nor non-existence, each taken separately. Nor is it both at once or neither at once. It transcends linguistics. Can we equate it with extinction ? If we did we would take away the very mainspring of moral endeavour. Can we then identify it with eternal persistence as an individual? This would lead to selfishness.

Instead of giving positive answers, the Buddha answered negatively by saying that Nirvāṇa would put an end to the ills of life, which was tantamount to an escape from a world covered with flames of desire — attachment, aversion and delusion. However, if there was one thing that gave Nirvāṇa a positive character it was its uncompounded element — the state of attaining bliss, a state of peace that passes all understanding resulting in deliverance or emancipation (*Vimokha*), which is supposed to correspond to absolute cessation of consciousness. (*Sanna Vedayita — Nirodha*).

Dr. Suzuki has put it thus :

"Buddhism is the story of relationship between the two groups of beings; the one is called Buddha who is the enlightened, the Tathāgata, the Arhat and the other is generally designated as Sarvasattva, literally 'all beings,' who are ignorant, greedy for worldly things, and, therefore, in perpetual torment. In spite of their hankering for worldly enjoyments, they are conscious of their condition and not at all satisfied with it; when they reflect they find themselves quite forlorn inwardly, they long for real happiness, for ultimate reality, and blissful enblightenemnt."[72]

According to Buddhism the desire for enlightenment is latent in every one of us. Potentially we are all Buddhas. But we experience Buddha in accordance with the level at which we are at a particular point in time. Suzuki adds : "The Buddha leaves his transcendental abode. He is seen among sentient beings, each one of whom recognises him according to his own light."[73]

It is not the scope of this book to explain the various stages through which an aspirant passes to reach the absolute cessation of consciousness. Suffice it to say that the four sublime contemplations viz. :

1. Maitri (benevolence towards others)
2. Karuṇā (compassion towards the distressed)
3. Mudita (joy at others' happiness)
4. Upekṣā (indifference towards others' faults) are imperative for the aspirant to be able to roam in Brahman. (*Brahmā — Vihāra* — bhāvanā)

These will no doubt have to be reinforced by —

(1) constant Remembrance (anusmṛiti) (constant remembrance of the immediate present).

(2) breathing exercises and such other formulas (which were presumably added in later ages).

All these prescriptions were intended to take the aspirant from the gross to the subtle, from the physical to the psychical and from feeling to intuitional aspects of life. Elaborate instructions exist on the subject. In this connection the following quotation throws considerable light, though it is strictly for the Hīnayānist. *Mutatis mutandis* it can be applied to Mahāyānist :

"The teachings of the Buddha offer a great variety of methods of mental training and subjects of meditation, suited to the various individual needs, temperaments and capacities. Yet all these methods ultimately converge in the 'Way of Mindfulness' called by the Master himself 'the Only Way' (or : 'the Sole Way' — ekāyano maggo). The Way of Mindfulness may, therefore, rightly be called 'the heart of Buddhist meditation' or even 'the heart of the entire doctrine' (*dhamma-hadaya*). This great Heart is in fact the centre of all the blood streams pulsating through the entire body of the doctrine (*dhamma-kāya*)."[74]

We need not go into the details of this procedure. It is enough to state that the chief purpose of *satipaṭṭāna* is to aid in final liberation from suffering which is the highest goal of Buddha's teaching — Nibbana. This doctrine appears twice in the Buddhist scriptures. Once as the 10th Discourse of the 'Middle Collection of Discourses' (*Majjhima Nikāya*) and as the 22nd Discourse of the 'Long Collection' (*Dīgha Nikāya*) where it is called the Mahā – Satipaṭṭhāna Sutta. It is here that the Four Noble Truths are treated in detail. What are the Four Foundations of Mindfulness?

'What are these four? Herein a monk may dwell practising body-contemplation on the body . . . . practising feeling-contemplation on feelings . . . . practising mind-contemplation on mind . . . . practising mind — object contemplation on mind objects, ardent, clearly comprehending and mindful, having overcome covetousness, and grief concerning the world."[75]

The quotation above is merely a sample of what satipaṭṭhāna has for the aspirant and how it guides him "to the methodical development of Insight (*Vipassanā*) which may well lead him, in this very life to a stage ('Stream-entry' or *Sotāpatti*) where final deliverance is irrevocably assured."[76] Such a deliverance comes at the latest after seven existences. Such a procedure would not suit the follower of the Mahāyānic Bodhisattva Ideal, whose aim is to bring salvation first to those others who are walking about in ignorance. To such a one his salvation is not enough until he has helped others to achieve theirs. To such a follower the nihilistic contemplation of Nirvāṇa practised by Hīnayānists would, therefore, not be suitable.

For the Mahāyānist the *Daśabhūmi* (ten stages of Bodhisattvahood) as given in the Avatāmśaka Sūtra would be most suited. Lucien Stryk in his book, 'World of the Buddha' gives an admirable paraphrase of these ten stages as set-forth by Dr. Suzuki in his 'Outlines of Mahāyāna Buddhism.' We give below a short resumé from this paraphrase. (This is given by Asanga in his Mahāyāna Sūtrālankāra) :

THE TEN STAGES OF BODHISATTVAHOOD

1. *Pramuditā (JOY)* : In this first stage the aspirant realises that self salvation is not enough. It is only when others are made aware of suffering, that the greatest joy possible to them, (sacrifice for others), can be accomplished. Once this initial, but important, stage is reached, the enlightened man can move about and spread his teaching.without any difficulty.

2. *Vimulā (PURITY)* : This stage is the direct result of joy. The aspirant is selfless, free from anger, greed or malice. He develops a sense of mission.

3. *Prabhākarī (BRIGHTNESS)* : Next the awakened man acquires the intellectual condition that makes him capable of fathoming the depths of things and to realise that all is impermanent, impure and subject to sorrow. He also realises that the real nature of things is neither created nor subject to death. All partake in the selfsame Essence which is beyond space and time.

4. *Arciṣmatī (BURNING)* : The enlightened man develops a purifying crucible of his newly acquired insight, in which all elements of evil and illusion are consumed.

5. *Sudurjayā (INVINCIBILITY)* : Equipped with these virtues, the enlightened man frees himself from evil passions and develops an intense love for humanity. To him absolute and relative knowledge are one.

6. *Abhimukhī (REVEALING ONESELF)* : Reflecting on the essence of all Dharmas, which are of a piece, he perceives the

truth and feels compassion towards those who are still straying in Saṃsāra.

7. *Dūraṅgamā* (*GOING FAR AWAY*) : Though resident in the highest sphere of spirituality, he still remains in Saṃsāra for the benefit of mankind.

8. *Acalā* (*IMMOVABILITY*) : When the Bodhisattva attains the highest knowledge, that is, when he acquires the knowledge that everything in the world partakes of suchness (*Tathatā*) he reaches this state. This knowledge is both unconscious and intuitive and is not amenable to the rules of logic. Suchness can be said to be the positive expression of voidness (*Śūnyatā*). "Possessing such knowledge, the awakened man enters a stage where all is immediately brilliant and his actions are spontaneous, innocent, even playful. He wills and it is done, he is nature itself."[77]

9. *Sādhumatī* (*GOOD INTELLIGENCE*) : This stage is reached when the enlightened man's works begin to benefit sentient beings.

10. *Dharmameghā* (*CLOUDS OF DHARMA*) : In this last stage, the enlightened one reaches the acme of all activities. He is Love and Sympathy personified whatever he does, no matter how insignificant, benefits mankind.[78]

For Mahāyāna, the idealisation of the Buddha, positive view of Nirvāṇa and Salvational mission of the Bodhisattvas, are imperative. Throughout Buddhist teachings, if there is one word that occurs most, it is Nirvāṇa. Saya Radhakrishnan :

"He is a dialectician, arguing with his opponents to lead them to liberation. He presents to his followers the experience through which he himself has passed and exhorts them to verify for themselves his views and conclusions. The doctrine is not based on hearsay, it means 'Come and see'."[79]

REFERENCES

1. The Eye of Shiva, William Morrow and Co. Inc., New York, 1981, p. 13.
   divi sūryasahasrasya bhaved yugapad utthitā
   yadi bhāḥ sadṛśī sā syād bhāsas tasya mahātmanaḥ
   (*Bhagavad Gītā*, XI.12).
2. Ibid, p. 14.

3. Psychotheraphy East and West, Jonathan Cape, London, 1971, pp. 8-9.
4. Mysticism, A Study in the Nature and Development of Man's Spiritual Consciousness, Methuen and Co. Ltd., U.K., Reprinted, 1967, p. xiv.
5. Hindu Mysticism, Motilal Banarsidass, Delhi, 1983, p. ix.
6. Discourses on Method, Penguin, 1960, p. 48.
7. A Treatise of Human Nature, Ed. by Selby-Giggs, Clarendon Press, 1955, pp. 252-3.
8. History of Western Philosophy, Unwin Paperbacks, London, 1987, p. 637.
9. Critique of Practical Reason, Trs, Thomas Kingshil, Abbott, Longmans, 1967, p. 260.
10. Muṇḍ. 1.1.3.
11. The Thirteen Principal Upaniṣads, Tr. R.E. Hume, Oxford University Press, London, 1934, Brih. 3:6.
12. Chānd. 7 : 1.
13. Philosophy and Phenomenological Research, Qr. Vol. 20, No. 2, Buffalo, New York.
14. Aldous Huxley, The Perennial Philosophy, Chatto & Windus, London, 1946, p. 7.
15. *Note* : 'Other' = individual soul.
    Śvetāśvatara, IV.9.10, Trs. R.E. Hume, The Thirteen Principal Upaniṣads, Oxford University Press, London, 1934.
16. Dr. Chaudhury, Vedānta of Transcendental Phenomenology.
17. *Īśa,* 1. Trs. R.E. Hume, The Thirteen Principal Upaniṣads, Oxford University Press, London, 1934.
18. Ten Classical Upaniṣads, Vol. 1, Ed. P.B. Gajendragadkar, Bharatiya Vidya Bhavan, 1981, p. 121.
19. You shall be as Gods, Fawcett Premier, New York, 1986, p. 18.
20. Ibid, pp. 19-20.
21. The Synthesis of Yoga, Aurobindo Ashram, Pondicherry, 1986, p. 273.
22. Chapter VI/I, Delta Book, Tr. Ira Progoff, 1978.
23. The Critique of Pure Reason, Ed. Norman K. Smith, London, MacMillan, 1930, Auo 5, B633.
24. Ibid, A621, B645.
25. *Note* : "The spatio-temporal world, with a God and men, with sinners and saints, life and death, good and bad, with all the variety, plurality, differences and richness between them,

constitute the lower tier. From a rarefied breathtaking, uninhabited differenceless, colourless, attributeless, barren, indescribable, ineffable absolute, the upper tier." (S.G. Mudgal, Advaita of Śaṅkara, Motilal Banarsidass, Delhi, 1975, pp. 15-16).

26. Science and the Modern World, A Mentor Book, New York, 14th Printing, p. 171.
27. Ibid, p. 172.
28. 6:1:3. Hume.
29. The Bhagavad Gītā, 7 : 12, Tr. Radhakrishnan, George Allen and Unwin Ltd., London 1967.
30. Ibid, p. 217.
31. Chānd. 3.14.1.
32. Chānd. 3.14.2.
33. Advaita of Śaṅkara, Motilal Banarsidass, Delhi, 1975, p. 16.

    Note : *Subspecie aeternitatis* the consideration of things in relation to the perfection of God — Spinoza.
34. B.N.K. Sharma, History of Dvaitā School of Vedānta and its Literature, Motilal Banarsidass, New Delhi, 1981, p. 2.
35. Man's Concern with Death, P. Robin Dennison Publishers, Arnold Toynbee and others.
36. Brih. 1.4.10.
37. III. 2.8—Swami Chinmayānanda.

    Note : For Śaṅkara the Muṇḍaka was very important. In his commentary on the B.S. he quotes it as many as 129 times. (Deussen, Vol. 2, Sixty Upaniṣads, p. 569).
38. Radhakrishnan, Brahma Sūtra, George Allen and Unwin Ltd., 1960, p. 30.
39. Vedānta, The Culmination of Indian Thought, Bharatiya Vidya Bhavan, Bombay, 1970, p. 41.
40. Op. cit. Advaita of Śaṇkara, p. 2.
41. Doubleday & Co. Inc., London, 1964.
42. Na Samsārasya Nirvāṇāt Kincidasti Viśeṣaṇam

    Na Nirvāṇasya Samsārāt Kincidasti Viśeṣaṇam

    Yah Kleśah Sa Bodhih, Yah Samsārah, Tat Nirvāṇam.
43. The absolute has no history, though there is history in the Asbolute —Bradley F.H.
44. *Note* : Hīnayāna maintains that the world of phenomenon is constituted of certain number of dharnas, basic elements of existence.
45. Simon and Schuster, p. 553.

46. Ibid, p. 559.
47. Time and Timeless, Upaniṣad Vihar, Madras, 1953, p. 53. "Time if properly approached, can be our friend inducting us into Eternity," ibid, p. 54.
48. Myths, Dreams and Mysteries, Collins, The Fontana Library, 1977, pp. 240-241.
49. The Philosophy of Viśiṣṭādvaita, The Adyar Library and Research Centre, 1978, p. 354.
50. ye yathā māṁ prapadyante
tāṁs tathai' va bhajāmy aham
mama vartmā' nuvartante
manuṣyāḥ pārtha sarvaśaḥ

(B.G. 4.II)

51. samo' haṃ sarvabhūteṣu
na me dveṣyo' sti na priyaḥ
ye bhajanti tu māṁ bhaktyā
mayi te teṣu ca'py aham

(B.G. 9.29)

52. Advaita of Śaṅkara, p. 16.
53. Tr. Ira Progoff, VI : 3.
54. B.N.K. Sharma, Philosophy of Sri Madhvācārya, Motilal Banarsidass, Delhi, 1986, p. 417.
55. *Svataṁtramasvataṅtram cha prameyam dvividham matam*

(*Tattvaviveka*)

Madhva's Teachings in his own Words, Bharatiya Vidya Bhavan, Bombay, 1979, p. 31.
56. *Note* : This view goes against the very genius of Hinduism. The superficial view held by some that Madhva may have been influenced by Christianity or more correctly Christian missionaries, does not appear to be correct. Sharma writes : "There are several passages which lie scattered in the Ṛgveda, out of which one could piece together a rosy picture of the joys of heaven and gruesome pictures of the horrors of hell. Madhva has naturally drawn on these in setting forth his idea of *Mokṣa* and of *Tamas* (Hell)." — History of Dvaitā School of Vedānta and Its Literature. p. 12.
57. Madhva's Teachings, p. 125.
58. The Lankāvatāra Sūtra, Routledge and Kegan Paul, London, Reprinted, 1978, p. xii.

59. The Teachings of the Compassionate Buddha, Ed. E.A. Burtt, New American Library, Mentor Books, New York, 1955, p. 115.
60. Op. cit., p. xiii-xiv.
61. Ihai 'va tair jitaḥ sargo
    yeṣāṁ sāmye sthitaṁ manaḥ
    nirdoṣaṁ hi samaṁ brahma
    tasmād brahmaṇi te sthitāḥ

    (B.G.5.19)
62. P.B. Shelley, Adonais, LII, Complete Works, Oxford, London, p. 443.
63. The Dialogues of Plato, Vol. 2, Trs. B. Jowett, Random House, New York, p. 182.
64. Matthew, 7 : 20.
65. Galatians, 5 : 22.
66. Hindu Mysticism, Motilal Banarsidass, 1983, pp. 89-90.
67. na nirodhaḥna uḥtpattia na baddhḥna cha sādhaka
    na mumukṣuh na vai muktah ityeṣa paramārthatā

    (Ṃandukya Karika, II. 32)
68. anirodham anutpannam anuchedam aśāśvatam
    anekārtham anānārtham etat tatvasya lakṣaṇam

    (Nagarjuna).
69. World of the Buddha, Ed. Lucien Stryk, Doubleday Anchor Book, New York, 1968, p. 202.
70. See Appendix Two.
71. Quoted by W.T. Stace, Religion and the Modern Mind, New York, 1960, pp. 263-264.
72. Lankāvatāra, p. xx.
73. Lankāvatāra, p. xx.
74. Satipaṭṭhāna, Nyanaponika Thera, 'The Heart of Buddhist Meditation,' Rider and Co., London, 1969. p. 7.
75. Ibid, p. 139.
76. Ibid, p. 13.
77. World of the Buddha, Ed. Lucien Stryk, A Doubleday Anchor Book, pp. li-liv.
78. Ibid.
79. Indian Philosophy, Volume I, p. 359.

CHAPTER II

The Mysticism of the Īśa, Kaṭha, Muṇḍaka and Kena Upaniṣads

A BRIEF BACKGROUND

All scriptures, irrespective of the tradition to which they belong, have in lesser or greater measure, mystical overtones. In scriptures like the Bible, both the Old and New Testament, and Koran, the mystical element is considerably lower than that in the Hindu scriptures. (We refer particularly to the Upaniṣads and the Bhagavad Gītā). In the Upaniṣads and the Bhagavat Gītā, mysticism, religion and philosophy freely mingle together. They flow, so to say, from one to the other. But through them all runs the central theme of mysticism. The basic thought and theme of the Upaniṣads may be summed up in the prayer :

From the unreal lead me to the real.
From darkness lead me to light,
From death lead me to immortality.[1]

Says Sri Aurobindo :

"The idea of transcendental unity, Oneness, and stability behind all the flux and variety of phenomenal life is the basal idea of the Upaniṣads; this is the pivot of all Indian metaphysics, the sum and goal of our spiritual experience."[2] When we look around, however, we see nothing but change, instability. All seem to be forever shifting and rearranging itself. Sri Aurobindo continues :

"Yet if one thing is certain, it is that the sum of all this change and motion is absolutely stable, fixed and unvarying, that all this heterogeneous multitude of animate and inanimate things are fundamentally homogeneous and one."[3] The overall impression left by the Upaniṣads is that they are the cumulative mystical experience of the ancient sages of India. The wonder and poetry that characterised the hymns of the Vedas, are there in the Upaniṣads. Only, in the Upaniṣads, they are deepened, widened and elaborated in the calm of meditation. This was due to the shift of emphasis of spiritual longing from the wonder of the universe outside to the self within. In Christianity, Judaism and Islam the pursuit of Mysticism came as a parenthesis. For the seers of the Upaniṣads everything was imbued in mysticism. This is because the Hindu mind has been traditionally exercised over the problem of the nature of Reality. In short, the springs of the Upaniṣads reach down deeper than theory. Hindu mysticism is never pure speculation. It is invariably some form of transcendental pragmatism requiring its truths, like the truths of modern physics, to be actually tested. To Śaṅkara, for example, the main purpose of all Vedānta texts is Brahman "tat tu samaṅvayāt."

"Brahman is the meaning of all scriptural passages. Their differences are only apparent and are capable of reconciliation. The many passages have one purpose."[4]

We have already pointed out in the foregoing chapter that mysticism is not just plain intuition — intuition in the sense in which Bergson interpreted it, where time or duration entered. For the Upaniṣadic seers, mysticism is not only intuition of what is extra-empirical but also of what is timeless or eternal, of something which ordinary experience is impotent to reveal. While studying the Upaniṣads, therefore, there is no need to doubt the mystical validity when the seer tells us of a remarkable experience. That he has *had* an experience of a peculiarly personal and ineffable character may be admitted. What is open to question is the interpretation of the experience.

The catholicity of the Upaniṣads and Hindu scriptures is so all-encompassing that saints and seers have interpreted the mystical experience in keeping with their own light. It is this interpretation that has not only enriched the Hindu scriptures and Hinduism, but it has also been the cause of considerable controversy. We are not concerned with the controversies. What concerns us is that irrespective of these interpretations, Brahman remains central to the Upaniṣads. These Upaniṣads vividly illustrate that the knowledge of Ātman is an evolutionary process.

It has perforce to be acquired at various levels of consciousness. "Hindu thought," writes Dr. Radhakrishnan, "believes in the evolution of our knowledge of God. We have to vary continually our notions of God until we pass beyond all notions into the heart of the reality itself, which our ideas endeavour to report. Hinduism does not distinguish ideas of God as true and false, adopting one particular idea as the standard for the whole human race. It accepts the obvious fact that mankind seeks its goal of God at various levels and in various directions, and feels sympathy with every stage of the search. The same God expresses itself at one stage as power, at another as personality, at a third as all comprehensive spirit, just as the same forces which put forth the green leaves also cause the crimson flowers to grow. We do not say that the crimson flowers are all the truth and the green leaves are all false."[5]

In the study of the Upaniṣads our guiding lines should be from the Kaṭha:

"This self cannot be known through much study nor through the intellect, nor through much hearing. It can be known through the self alone that the aspirant prays to, this self of that seeker reveals its true nature."

We come across this verse in the Muṇḍaka (III.2.3) also. "ayam" and "eṣaḥ" would be interpreted by the Advaitin as 'which Ātman' and 'This aspirant' whereas the Dvaitin would interpret as 'Whom' and 'God.' Thus according to the Advaitin the translation would read 'which Ātman this aspirant longs to gain' and according to the Dvaitin it would mean 'The aspirant whom the God chooses.' On a superficial reading there appears to be a contradiction between these two stand points. But such is not the case. To Śaṅkara, the Godhead is an 'ascent.' To Rāmānuja and Madhva it is a descent of God into man. Descent is another word for 'Grace.' The end result is the same. After all there is no difference whether the river reaches the ocean or the ocean receives the river. The ocean is, the river is not, at this crucial stage. Whatever position the Advaitin, Viśiṣṭādvaitin, or Dvaitin takes, all ensure that the basis is always the Upaniṣads and they equally INSIST that the Ultimate is protected from any possible imputation of imperfection. Moreover, each perspective grounds its conviction about the perfection of God's nature on what are claimed to be revelations of religious and mystical experiences. While confining ourselves to the four Upaniṣads referred to above, we will also take a bird's eye view of the theories propounded in the Upaniṣads. This is not with a view to iron out the differences and paradoxes that obtain in the Upaniṣads. They will perhaps never be ironed out. But such a bird's eye view will serve as a background for the study of the four Upaniṣads. Even if the concept of Brahman runs through the Upaniṣads, there are features which differ one from the other when viewed from the points of view of the three main schools of thought.

If there are negative ways of describing Brahman, there are also affirmative ways of describing. Advaitists, for instance, will simply dismiss such descriptions as symbolic, not to be taken literally. Existence, consciousness, Bliss[7] condenses, as it were, all that can be asserted about the nature of Brahman. Perhaps it is more adequate to define Brahman, as Existence-consciousness-Bliss than to define it as the cause of the world. Existence-consciousness-Bliss leads us closer to Brahman than originator — sustainer — destroyer. The latter characterises Brahman as the cause of the world. This view not only serves no purpose, but takes away pure non-duality. For the Advaitists Brahman is knowledge *per se*. Rāmānuja holds that belief in God rests on revelation. Madhva represents an intermediate position.

To return to our discussion we find that both the negative and affirmative positions vie with one another in the Upaniṣads. In a general way it could be said that their positions are evenly balanced. In an arbitrary way we could assert that the negative position predominates. Positive statements (see Tait. Up.) like satyam jñānam anantam are not uncommon. Here again these should be taken as value concepts. It would be incorrect to classify them as existential categories. The statement above could be analysed as follows :

satyam : being i.e. unchanging, that which can neither cancel nor alter.

jñānam : consciousness. This value stands for transcendence of the subject-object relation. The real is not a knower as distinct from the object known and the process of knowing. It is what we have referred to before, knowledge *per se*.

anaṅtam : Endless. Here Endless will have to be taken to include 'Timeless.'

All these words are symbolic. Even here some words are more adequate than others. W.T. Stace has something to say on this :

"The relation between the symbol and symbolizandum is not that of resemblance, but that of greater or less nearness to the full self-realisation of God. Certainly 'near' and 'far' are mataphors, but it is easy to interpret them. In the scale of being, one level is nearer to God's self-realisation than a second, if between it and that full self-realisation there intervene fewer levels of being than between the second and that full self-realisation."

Stace goes on to observe :

"Thus it is truer to say that God is a mind or a person than that He is a force. For the word 'force' refers primarily to such existences as gravitation, cohesion and the like, which belong to the lowest order of beings, those furthest away from the divine self-realisation."[8] Another thing carefully to be borne in mind while interpreting the mysticism of the Upaniṣads is that words like Existence, Consciousness, Bliss and so on *do not* mean that Brahman has *Being and Consciousness and Bliss.* They are merely three different symbols for one and the same symbolizandum. If we consider the major texts of the Upaniṣads : That Thou Art, I am Brahman and so on as a consolidated whole, we find them to be more adequate. If we take them separately as 'I,' 'Brahman,' 'That,' 'Thou,' they are meaningless, 'That' cannot be 'Thou,' and 'I' cannot be 'Brahman.' Only when we take them symbolically or in their secondary meaning (*Lakṣana*) does it yield some meaning. But the Upaniṣads, as we shell soon see, are not concerned about the meaning as such. What such words are ultimately meant to do is to evoke an experience. Only when we talk about words or symbols evoking an experience, do we come close to understanding what the Upaniṣads have to convey.

The refrain of the Upaniṣads is self-realisation. It is the final goal of man. (*Paramapuruṣārtha*). The Westerners call it 'spiritual freedom.' We call it *Mokṣa.* All sorts of words are used while discussing it — as if it is something to be acquired or attained. Briefly, it is simply the regaining of what is the eternal nature of the soul. This idea is perhaps *The Idea* in the Hindu scriptures. Śaṅkara used two words when talking about it :

Nitya (eternal) and *a-Sadhya* (not what is accomplished). So *Mokṣa* is the very nature of Brahman.

We often find such thoughts in the poetry of great poets, who in ecstatic moments visualise the experiences of the sages and saints. In such poetry the order of time and the order of eternity meet at a point. But this meeting does not last. Whereas the experience of the sage and saint is timeless. There is no parting of company. *Mokṣa*, therefore, can be experienced here and now. As the *Kaṭha* says : "When all the desires that dwell in the heart are destroyed, then the mortal becomes immortal and he attains Brahman even here."[9]

The Jīvanmukta's body continues to function as long as the unspent portion of his Karma, which is responsible for his present body, still remains (termed *Prārabdha*). He will attain liberation from the body (termed *Videhamukti*), when *prārabdha* will have spent its force. This is the view generally held. In fact it is the logical corollary to the theory of Karma. But Śaṅkara has something different to say. He says that the *Mukta* has no *prārabdha* attached to him. He writes in Aparokṣānubhūti :

"Once knowledge of reality (*Tattva Jñāna*) has arisen there can be no results of *prārabdhakarman*, just as after waking there is no dream."[10]

Śaṅkara would explain this by saying that the body is unreal. In any event what is stated about *prārabdha* has wide implications for mysticism and mystics and for the conception of salvation, as understood not only in Hindu but also in the Christian traditions.

Mysticism in general and Hinduism in particular have been accused of solitariness, that it does not have any conception of universal history. There is no doubt that this accusation is baseless. We will be going beyond the scope of this book if we enter into a detailed discussion on this point. Only one illustration should suffice for our purpose.

Hinduism (and its mystical tradition as seen in the Upaniṣads) takes a cosmic view of things. Well known passages both from the Bhagavad Gītā and Upaniṣads are often repeated without realising their import. Passages like :

"Whenever, O descendant of Bharata, there is decline of *Dharma*, and rise of *Adharma*, then I body myself forth."[11]

The word 'Avatāra' relates to the descent of the God principle on Earth. The Hindu conception is that such 'Avatāras,' descend from time to time in order to accelerate the advance towards eternal perfection. This acceleration does not relate to *Hindus only*, but to *the whole of mankind*. Stating this in mystical terms we would say that each *descent* of the Avatāra helps in the *ascent* of *mankind* to God. The Avatāra by his grace serves the whole of mankind. Looked at from this stand point it can hardly be said that Hinduism has no cosmic conception of history. In fact such a cosmic conception is inherent in Hinduism.

Dedication of the intellect to the exploration of Reality and a disinterested love of truth, does not lead to an *a priori* concept of Pure Being or to an intuition of it. After all Reality is not something behind the phenomenon or experience or behind the relational outlook of things. It is for this very reason that words like 'veil,' 'lid' lend themselves to diverse interpretations (hiraṇmayena pātreṇa). Golden vessel which is like a lid that hides from view.[12]

To say that 'veil' is *Māyā* and its removal discloses Brahman or Reality, is to offer a facile explanation of a very difficult problem. We cannot pretend to understand the mystic or hope even to understand him in a fragmentary manner unless we are equipped with properly tuned up sensibilities. But this should not deter us from at least examining the record of mysticism with the aid of our reason, however frail it may be. Sri Aurobindo's words in this regard are significant :

"The reader (of the Upaniṣads) or rather the hearer, was supposed to proceed from light to light confirming his intuitions and verifying by his experience, not submitting the ideas to the judgement of the logical reason."[13]

The aspirant always proceeds from light to light. If this were not possible there would be no hope and we would be at the end of the tether. The nuclear physicist who, despite the wall of the unknowable facing him, continues to explore into the reality of matter. The very act of observation alters the observed ultimate unit of behaviour, the particle loses its identity in time. Similarly thought can only uncover the complexity of the relational processes. It can never uncover the Absolute which must include thought itself, and to which these processes are relative. We must not forget that records like the Upaniṣads span centuries in a dimension which is altogether different from the dimension we are in on this earth. With man's adventure into outer space, it will always remain a big question mark as to whether man cannot similarly embark on a similar journey into inner space — the *terra in cognito* of mysticism. Of course, it is no journey to anywhere. For It is Now, Here. In this moment, where one is, one finds oneself, which was not lost, yet sought after.

"A stark companionless Reality
Answered at last to his soul's passionate search :
Passionless, wordless, absorbed in its fathomless hush,
Keeping the mystery none would ever pierce,
It brooded inscrutable and intangible
Facing him with its dumb tremendous calm.
It had no kinship with the universe :
There was no act, no movement in its Vast."[14]

The Upaniṣads by themselves are sufficient to serve as an adequate basis for discussing Hindu mysticism. Even the great Vedāntists, Śaṅkara, Rāmānuja and Madhva, have derived their systems, by and large, from the Upaniṣads. Originally, the words 'Upaniṣads' and 'Vedānta' were synonymous. It was only in the course of history that the Vedānta Sūtras too fell within the purview of the term Vedānta. it can be said that the Upaniṣads occupy a central position, the Vedānta Sūtras being subsidiary to them. As for the Bhagavad Gītā, being a *Smṛiti,* the position it occupies, despite its high philosophical and mystical value, is derivative. For all intents and purposes, therefore, the Upaniṣads, even a few selected ones, are sufficient to serve as an adequate basis for the discussion of Hindu mysticism.

Moreover, a brief recapitulation will demonstrate that both Śaṅkara and Rāmānuja resort to the Upaniṣads to show that their doctrines agree with the Upaniṣads. Not that they do not refer to other works, they do. But even here, while Śaṅkara depends wholly on the Upaniṣads and so to say, makes them a powerful instrument to prove that there was a single philosophical impulse in the Upaniṣads, Rāmānuja, however, takes recourse to other scriptures too like Purāṇas, Pāncharātras, etc. in addition to Upaniṣads. So by and large, the Upaniṣads which are equated with Vedānta can also be equated with Hindu mysticism. Some other books would also come within the scope of the definition of Vedānta, as defined by Sadānanda.[15]

The Śāriraka works would refer literally to the body aphorisms by Bādarāyaṇa which rightly determines the nature of the 'embodied self.' 'Other works' would include the commentaries on the Upaniṣads and the Gītā etc. But one fact stands out, bright and clear, staring us in the face, that all scriptures, Hindu, Christian, Jewish, have mysticism, in lesser or greater measure : that when the volume of evidence increases quantitatively we shall have to revise our opinions and come in line with the findings of mysticism. With these words we will now proceed to examine the mysticism of Īśa, Kena, Kaṭha and Muṇḍaka. In this examination we shall try to use the cumulative experience of the mystics of the East and West.

The very first verse (Invocation) in the Īśa presents us with a mystical statement of great import. It also presents us with a paradox which is apparently insoluble. Looking at the various commentaries on the Upaniṣads it appears that the Īśa is perhaps the most commented upon Upaniṣad. All schools of Vedānta have commented on it. Even in those interpretations which are purely Advaitic there is an under current of difference. However, we will not attempt to answer the question as to whose exposition comes nearer the Upaniṣadic spirit. The Upaniṣads not being the work of one author and Sanskrit language being what it is (susceptible to varying interpretations, and manipulations) it would be presumptious to hold that the interpretations of one Ācārya comes more close than that of another. Thibaut and Radhakrishnan feel that Śaṅkara's system is the best devised. When we come down to Īśa we find that for Śaṅkara (basing his views on Verses 1 and 3-8) the Īśa teaches the Supreme Self. Madhva has his own interpretations. According to Madhva, the proper place for the Lord's residence is the creation. Creation cannot function without such residence. *Jagati* means Lakṣmī, the presiding deity of Prakṛti, which depends on the Lord for her activity.

We thus have views which are apparently opposed to one another. In the course of this chapter we shall discuss some of them and try to find out whether there *is* real opposition or not. both Śaṅkara and Madhva, interpret the first verse of the Īśa mystically, but the difference in the interpretations seems to be in their temperament.

All this whatsoever moves on the Earth — should be covered by the Lord. Protect (yourself) through that detachment. Do not covet anybody's wealth. (*Īśa*.1).

For Madhva, it is action, for Śaṅkara it is cessation of action, that is necessary for the realisation of the self. Both paths lead to realisation : Śaṅkara's is more difficult than that of Rāmānuja or Madhva. Unity in multiplicity is the consistent doctrine of the Gītā.[16]

"Others, too, sacrificing by the *Yajña* of knowledge (i.e., seeing the Self in all) worship Me, the All Formed, as one, as distinct, as manifold. All Formed is He who has assumed all the manifold forms in the universe." As one, as identifying with All-Formed-the Advaitic view.

ĪŚA UPANIṢAD

Keeping the above comments in view let us examine the Śāntipātha.

"That is whole, this is whole, from the whole the whole becomes manifest. From the whole when the whole is negated, what remains is again the whole."[17]

Practically all Upaniṣads have such *Śāntipāthas*, obviously to induce the right attitude for the spiritual quest. Apparently this is the reason why such an invocation has been placed at the head of the Īśa. (Also at the end). But so closely does this invocation merge with the very first verse that one wonders whether it is not an integral part of the Upaniṣad. Its interpretation is definitely difficult. Many commentators, for this reason, just slur over it or omit it altogether. Prof. Nikam explains as follows :

"The invocatory verse of the Īśa points to a contradiction in the notion of the infinite. The verse says that the infinite arises out of the infinite; that if the infinite is deducted from the infinite, the infinite alone remains. And the Īśa Upaniṣad exhibits this contradiction in practical life as enjoyment through renunciation."[18]

But is it enough to say that this verse illustrates "this contradiction in practical life as enjoyment through renunciation?" The seer has brought in mathematics (knowingly or unknowingly) to present his point of view. One guess could be that the verse was drafted by a mathematician — philosopher. This is not uncommon. The borderline between mathematics and philosophy is so thin that mathematical-thought more often than not leads to philosophical and mystical thought. Therefore, to say that the Śāntimantra was placed there merely to generate the right attitude for spiritual quest, even if true, would only be partly true. The lines are more than *Śāntimantra* — they carry a philosophical mathematico-mystico message. We quote from Bhāskarācārya, a great mathematician :

"Bhāskarācārya, one of the greatest mathematicians of India stated in his book, Bījagaṇita' Zero multiplied by any number is Zero. Zero divided by any number is Zero. But any number divided by Zero is termed Khahara (infinity). If any number or infinite is added to or taken away from Khahara, it remains unaltered.' It is like the infinite Brahman without a second, which remains unaltered both by creation and absorption. Bhāskarācārya has explained the mathematical idea of Advaita. He states that any number divided by Zero is called Khahara, a value which neither increases by addition or decreases in value by subtraction. It has already been shown that infinity minus infinity continues to be infinity. It can also be shown that infinity plus infinity or any finite quantity is also infinity.[19] Anything which neither increases nor decreases, numerically, may be either 'Śūnya' or Nirguṇa Brahman of Vedānta, which is ultimately inexpressible."

Īśa thus starts on a very high mystical note, so much so that a French Commentator, Patrick Lebail was prompted to say[20] :

The profundity of the verse is so deep that it condenses in itself complete Upaniṣadic thought. Even a general and superficial study of the Upaniṣads shows that the demonstrative pronouns 'that' and 'this' carry a profound connotation in the Upaniṣads. 'This' is the phenomenal world outside. It is the sum of its sights, sounds, etc. as they impinge themselves on our senses.

'This' in other words stands for the impact the external world makes on us. But this impact does not stop here., We continually try to relate it to something that is 'inside.' The very inexpressibility of this action makes us use words like 'inside,' 'internal.' At this juncture we could enter into a comparison with the scientific attitude. But we will leave that for later. Suffice it to state that Brahman is the ALL of the spiritual and non-spiritual (as manifested by Māyā). Science deals with the latter. For it the ALL constituted the physical aspects of the universe. The scientific aspect may be termed as looking at the universe from one level. The picture is only complete when we take a holistic view and look from 'within.' It is not enough to answer as to what the world looks like when we view it from the outside. The question is what does it look like when we view it from within. The mysticism of the Upaniṣads lies in the synthesis of these two. True knowledge is the whole knowledge of that which comes from 'without' and 'within.' The Muṇḍaka says[21] :

It is the support of all kinds of knowledge since it is source of them all. It is only when things are viewed relatively that 'inside' and 'outside' exist. From the total point of view they do not exist. When a relative point is adopted, the view is partial and we take a point of reference for our view (like the body, etc.). But this relative viewpoint is also important because it helps as a stepping stone. The 'idaṁ' (This) thus implies the unity back of the many. And this unity, which, is not perceptible, is the 'adaḥ' (that). The former is the changeable aspect : This latter, unchangeable aspect. The former is near (this), the latter is far (that). A somewhat similar situation arises in 'Tat Tvam Asi,' in which we have 'That' signifying consciousness characterised by remoteness and 'Thou' signifying consciousness characterised by immediacy, both referring to the same consciousness viz., Brahman.

What this verse, interpreted mystically, says is that, behind the phenomenal universe, is Brahman who is the fullness of Pure Being. This fullness is nothing but absolute existence, absolute awareness and absolute bliss. It is a state in which the past, present and future merge.[22]

I know, O Arjun, the beings of the whole past and the present and the future, but Me none knoweth. Therefore :

pūrṇasya pūrṇamādāya pūrṇamevāvaśiṣyate

The fullness of the universe has come from the Fullness of Brahman, leaving a Remainder which is also Fullness. Patrick Lebail writes :

"*Brahmaṇ* ne diffère ni de la totalité des êtres, ni de celle des possibles. Il est donc plénitude, *pûrnam* ('plein' 'parfait') Rein n'est hors de lui, tout est en lui. Il est à la fois l'essence et l'existence."[23]

'Nothing is outside of it, all is in it. It is at the same time the essence and existence.'

Only when the Invocation is viewed in the light of the remarks above does it yield some meaning. Arbitrarily to declare that it contains a contradiction is tantamount to brushing it aside without giving it a hearing.

We now proceed to the first and second verses of the Īśa :

Īśāvāsyam idaṁ sarvaṁ
yat kiṁ ca jagatyāṁ jagat,
tena tyaktena bhuñjīthā, (1)
mā gṛdhaḥ kasyasvid dhanam.
Kurvanneveha karmāṇi
jijīviṣecchataṁ samāḥ,
evaṁ tvayi nānyatheto, sti
na karma lipyate nare. (2)

The traditional interpretation of these verses would be that all that moves in the universe, including the universe, is pervaded by the Lord. Detach yourself. Lust not after wealth, yours or anybody else's. After all whose is wealth ? Doing verily works in this world, one should wish to live, a hundred years. Thus it is in thee and not otherwise than this; Action cleaves not to a man!

(According to Aurobindo [kurvanneveha] the stress of the word evaṁ gives the force, "doing works indeed, and not refrain from them."[24]

References to Lord, God, Panduranga, pervading the universe, are found in the writings (particularly, the spontaneous poetry) of great mystics. Those following Bhakti are more prone to such out-bursts. For instance :

Tukā mhaṇe devā sarvanthaee jālā
bharūni uralā Panduranga.[25]

or

Tukā mhaṇe mazā sakhā Panduranga
vyāpiyele jaga tene eke.[26]

Tukaram says God pervades the universe. Though pervading, remains aloof, that Panduranga.

Tukaram says : "My companion is Panduranga.
He alone pervades the entire universe."

If, as we have seen, paradox prevails in the Invocation, paradox also prevails in the first verse, especially when it is read with the second verse. There is in the Īśa, what Aurobindo termed "the uncompromising reconciliation of uncompromising extremes."[27] In classical and serious mysticism such paradoxes are more the rule than the exception. As far as Īśa was concerned there were historical as well as spiritual reasons for this. Īśa was one of those Upaniṣads that was close to the Vedic roots, and had yet emerged far enough to counter antipragmatic Vedānta. Despite the fact that the Īśa belonged to the early Vedic group, it carried more effectively than most Upaniṣads the germs of Monism. Thus it oscillates between human life and activity on the one hand and the Monistic standpoint on the other.

At times, the way of action is regarded as the lowest truth. Obviously a Vedic heritage. Acts constituting external practices, etc. Disinterested action is, however, exalted. Austerity (*tapas*) is higher still. There is also the Tantric way, which involves a sort of reversal of values and release of inhibitions. Above all the path of knowledge is the result of integrated contemplation. Ultimately it is transformed into spiritual realisation. It is not surprising, therefore, that different paths are suitable for different aspirants. There are psychological and spiritual reasons for this. Psychologically, the inclination and mental make up of one aspirant differ from those of the other. It is inclination and mental make up that prompt the aspirant to choose a particular path. Spiritually, the aspirant chooses a particular path because he is at a particular level of spiritual development. We may even call this reason eschatological.

The non-liberated man is subject to enslavement by his actions. His actions follow him indefinitely. Every action, after all, in a lesser or greater degree, is tainted and polluted. In Hinduism, therefore, for better or for worse, karman as a consequence of action and Saṃsāra as a recurring transmigration of living, have to be accepted as inescapable religious dogma. In other words, these have to be accepted as postulates not open to discussion. While such a theory appears, especially to many a Westerner, pessimistic, in the last resort it is not. Whether East or West, retributive accountability is an inescapable psychological fact. (As you sow, so you reap, etc.). But the Westerner tends to forget that there is a corollary. Action can, to a certain ex'ent, direct man's destiny. Man is not, as is incorrectly assumed, hopelessly caught in the cycle of birth and rebirth. Actions which determine later stages can create fruits which ripen in exact proportion to what the original action was like. In other words human initiative has its proper place in Hinduism. It is not totally impotent. This is so because ethics too has its proper place in Hinduism. Man is urged to perform meritorious action.

But a stage is reached when the prime importance of renunciation is stressed. This consists in ceasing to act at all, thereby exhausting all the reserves of karman.

Looking back at the two verses we have quoted above, we have full corroboration in what we have just said. Synthesis of opposites, knowledge and work. On the one hand we have the wellknown tat tvam asi of Chāndogya. For this everything is to be given up except the bare necessities. Someone else's wealth is not to be longed for. Even what's one's own is to be kept to the barest minimum. On the other we have the path of activity. The Vedas, when viewed as a whole, also teach two paths, the path of renunciation and the path of activity.

But the purpose of all mysticism is *to know*. That by knowing which everything else is known. If we take the first line of Mantra 18 in Īśa, it reads :

agne naya supathā rāye asmān

"O Agni! Lead us on to wealth by a good path."

Here again the word 'wealth' (rāye = wealth) is significant. This line is translated by Aurobindo as :

"O God Agni! Lead us by the good path to the felicity."[28]

Words like 'wealth,' 'Treasure' often lend themselves to multifarious interpretations. As we shall see in Christian Mysticism, Christ used it in more senses than one. The treasure 'here' and the treasure in 'Heaven.' When, therefore, the poet in the present verse wants to be led by supathā (good path) to wealth, it obviously means that what is sought is spiritual wealth. Aurobindo's 'felicity' will also have to be taken in this manner. With all its oscillation between knowledge and action, the Īśa is mainly 'knowledge oriented.' Let us for a moment go back to verse 17 :

> vāyur anilam amṛtam athedaṁ bhasmāntaṁ śarīram,
>
> Oṁ krato smara kṛtaṁ smara krato smara kṛtaṁ smara. (17)
>
> "(May) this life merge in the immortal Breath!
>
> And (may) this body end in ashes! Oṁ! Mind, remember remember thy deeds. Mind, remember remember thy deeds."

The aspirant has come to the end of his journey. The journey of life. As also the journey of his spiritual efforts. He has, therefore, to remember whatever *karma* he has done till now. But spiritually he has to remember (Christian mystics would use the word 'recollect') what he has meditated upon. The repetition signifies earnestness. What is prayed for is 'Entrance'. A close look at this verse will show that there are undertones of *Bhakti*. But then Pure Advaita is a rare phenomenon. In the aspirant's ascent he is bound to touch *bhakti*. What the Īśa shows is that on the upward path, the transition, more often than not, is from Action to Knowledge. It is never the other way round. In this connection Aurobindo's comment is illuminating. Referring to krato in verse 17 above he writes :

"The Vedic term "*kratu*" means sometimes the action itself, sometimes the effective power behind action represented in mental consciousness by the will. Agni is this power. He is divine force which manifests first in matter as heat and light and material energy and then, taking different forms in the other principles of man's consciousness, leads him by a progressive manifestation upwards to the Truth and the Bliss."[29]

Aurobindo's translation is :

> "Oṁ! O Will, remember, that which was done, remember!
>
> O, Will, remember, that which was done remember."[30]

Knowledge and Action cannot go together. In the realm of mysticism Karma may precede knowledge. Never knowledge precede Karma. It is recognised that Karma prepares man for true knowledge. No such position is possible for Karma to succeed knowledge. Notice in Kaṭha[31] :

Dūramete viparīte viṣūcī
avidyā yā ca vidyā iti jñātā
vidyā-bhīpsinam Naciketasaṁ manye
na tvā kāmābahavo' lolupanta

"That which is known as knowledge and that which is known as ignorance are widely contradictory and they follow divergent courses. I consider Naciketā to be an aspirant for knowledge (because) the enjoyable things, multifarious though they be, did not tempt you."

KAṬHA UPANIṢAD

The idea underlying all the major Upaniṣads as we have seen in our discussion so far, is unity, oneness and stability. These are the stratum of the flux and variety which the phenomenal world is. The central problem of the Kaṭha is this unity and stability. But unlike some other Upaniṣads, not an unimportant place is given to sacrifice. Ritual as we shall see while discussing the mysticism of the Muṇḍaka, plays an important role in the spiritual life of the mystic. Prof. S.N. Dasgupta's words in this connection are significant. He writes :

"The most important characteristic which distinguishes the science of Brahman from the science of sacrifices consists in the fact that the former springs entirely from inner spiritual longings, while the latter is based almost wholly on mundane desires."[32]

The story of the Kaṭha is simple and straightforward. The son of Vājaśrava (vājaśravasa vāja = food, śrava = fame) Gautama gave in sacrifice all that he possessed. He has a son Naciketās.

Seeing the decrepit condition of the cows offered in sacrifice, he asks his father : "Father, to whom will you offer me?"[33] On being pressed for an answer, the father says : "To Death I offer you."[34] And so to Death goes Naciketās. He has to wait for three days before meeting Death. At last when Death does come he is touched by Naciketās' zeal in waiting for him. So Death offers him warm hospitality and as a bonus also offers him three boons.

The story is not new. It, however, serves to expound a unique mystical tradition. The teacher is Death. Teachers have played a great role in the Hindu mystical tradition. He forms an indispensable part of the tradition. In fact, in no other tradition does he play the role nor occupy the status that he does in the Hindu tradition. Swami Vivekananda said :

"First have something to give. He alone teaches who has something to give, for teaching is not talking, teaching is not imparting doctrines, it is communicating. Spirituality can be communicated just as really as I can give you a flower. This is true in the most literal sense. The idea is very old in India and finds illustration in the West in the theory, in the belief, of apostolic succession."[35]

So when the teacher was Death and the seeker Naciketās, the former a teacher *par excellence*, the latter the very embodiment of inner discipline and one-pointed love of truth, the resultant philosophy could not but be of a very high order. Unlike the other Gurus imparting spiritual knowledge, here we observe the knowledge of Brahman being imbibed through the ever-present mystery of death. If not for any other reason, for this reason alone, the Kaṭha can be placed in a class by itself. Swami Ranganathananda says :

"It (Kaṭha) blends in itself the charm of poetry, the strength of philosophy, and the depth of mysticism; it contains a more unified exposition of the spiritual insights of Vedānta than is found in any other single Upaniṣad."[36]

In the first boon, Naciketās wants his father, Gautama, to be freed from anxiety, be calm of mind[37] (śānta - saṁ kalpaḥ). The boon is granted instantly. Through the second boon Naciketās wants to know about the Fire that is the means for the attainment of Heaven (saḥ tvam agnim svargyam).[38] This, too, is granted. The theme of sacrifice is elaborated here. As a special favour for the aptitude Naciketās displayed in grasping the idea of the sacrifice, Death named the Fire after Naciketās. This Fire sacrifice shall be named after thee (tava eva nāmnā bhavitā yam agniḥ).[39] With the third boon commences the mystical portion. Naciketās asks :

"This doubt that arises, consequent on the death of a man — some saying 'It exists,' and others saying, 'It does not exist'—I would know this, under your instruction. Of all the boons this one is the third boon."[40]

This question sets the scene for action. Death employs all the delectable means at his command to dissuade Nachiketas from pressing for an answer. But in vain. Nachiketas, who is the symbol of an ideal aspirant, ready in all respects to receive the highest mystical knowledge, is not prepared to let go an instructor like Death (Vaktā ca asya tvādṛk anyaḥ na labḥyaḥ).[41] The rock-like stand taken by Nachiketas impresses Death, who proceeds to grant the third boon.

We enter rightaway into the mystical portion. The first six verses display a juxtaposition between Ignorance and knowledge. Man is faced by a choice between the preferable and the pleasurable (śreyas and preyas). In the world of spirituality, many are called but few are chosen. Only when the aspirant goes through a rigorous test successfully, without wavering in his determination (even in thought) does he become eligible for mystical instruction. In Naciketās we see the ideal seeker after Truth. Naciketās rejects all the temptations without the least hesitation "The path of wealth in which many a man comes to grief" (Na etām sṛṅkām vittamayīm avāptaḥ yasyām majjanti bahava ḥmanuṣyāḥ).[42]

Thus we have here a perfect combination of an ideal seeker after Truth and an ideal Guru to impart mystical instruction to him. Only a teacher like Death could have at one stroke placed the goal of ignorance preyas and the goal of knowledge śreyas before the seeker.

Maitri (7.9) or Bṛhadāraṇyaka (IV(iv) II) or Muṇḍaka (I.2.8-10), repeat the same concept that the Kaṭha does. For instance—

"Living in the midst of ignorance and considering themselves intelligent and enlightened, the senseless people go round and round, following crooked courses, just like the blind led by the blind."[43]

Compare with—

"Miserable are those worlds enveloped by (that) blinding darkness (Ignorance). To them, after death go those people who are ignorant and unwise."[44]

Here we notice the words 'ignorant' and 'unwise' occurring together. It is not simply 'ignorance' that will take one there, but the lack of knowledge, that is, one will have to be ignorant *and* unwise. Īśa expresses this concept as under :

"Those worlds of devils are covered by blinding darkness. Those people that kill the Self go to them after giving up this body."[45]

Therefore, it is necessary to have knowledge of Brahman. This knowledge cannot be attained by mere speculation (tarka) concerning it. It is to be won through instruction.

"Of that (Self) which is not available for the mere hearing to many (and) which many do not understand even while hearing, the expounder is wonderful and the receiver is wonderful, wonderful is he who knows under the instruction of an adept."[46]

This knowledge is to be communicated by a profound perceptor (kuśalānuśiṣṭaḥ).[47] 'Communication' is all that the perceptor can do : Revelation is the act of Grace. The oft-repeated verse, which also occurs in Muṇḍaka, says :

"This Self cannot be known through much study, nor through the intellect, nor through much hearing. It can be known through the Self alone, that the aspirant prays to; this Self of that seeker reveals Its true nature."[48]

In the ultimate analysis, revelation is an act of Grace. (ātmā vivṛṇute tanūm svām).[49]

But the ground for the reception of Grace has to be prepared. And this can only be done by co-operation between the aspirant and his Guru. The Upaniṣads have consistently emphasised the paramount importance of a Guru. In matters spiritual the Guru himself must be fully qualified :

"The Self is not certainly adequately known when spoken of by an inferior person; for It is thought of variously. When taught by one who has become identified with It, there is no further cogitation with regard to It. For It is beyond argumentation, being subtler even than the atomic quantity."[50]

This is one of those Upaniṣadic verses that sum up Vedānta in a magnificent way. If analysed we notice :

"not adequately known" (suvijñeyaḥ)
"when spoken by an inferior person"
(avare ṇa nare ṇa prokta ḥ)
"subtler" (aṇīyān)
"than the atomic quantity"[51] (aṇupramāṇāt)

Here we notice that for final realisation a Guru is a *must*. But the implication is that one can start on the journey without a Guru, though in that case *adequate* knowledge cannot be acquired. In other words, commencing the journey without a Guru would be tantamount to receiving instruction from an inferior person. The knowledge to be acquired being subtler of the subtlest, only a person who has already acquired it can impart it. Śaṅkara, whom we have already quoted, says, while commenting on Muṇḍaka (I.2.12) :

"One though versed in the scriptures should not search independently after knowledge of Brahman."[52]

The Guru is necessary, not because he would impart instruction like any other teacher but because, besides being a realised soul himself, he would shower Grace on the disciple. Grace is one of the most important factors in the disciple's attainment of knowledge. Even though, Śaṅkara does not explicitly attach much importance to Grace in his Advaita, his insistence that the disciple seek a suitable Guru, is a tacit admission that in the ultimate analysis, knowledge of Brahman is only obtained through the Guru and, therefore, through Grace.

Of course in the end the disciple has to go it alone. The Guru, the scriptures, can take him to a certain stage, from where he has to proceed on his own. Only Grace can take him from here.

In the words of Śaṅkara :

"Commentaries on philosophies constitute a thick jungle in which a roaming mind may easily get lost, in its own delusion. Therefore, true seekers of *Brahman* should, through right efforts, come to experience the Real Nature of the Self."[53]

Scriptures have been termed by Śaṅkara as a great forest of words. For him who has been stung by the serpent of ignorance merely repeating the mantras is of no avail. It is like repeating the name of the medicine without taking it.

Whether it is the Hindu or Christian or Jewish tradition, the advice is similar. Scriptures are merely the scaffolding, meant to act as an aid or a means. The Path, which is like the proverbial razor's edge, is to be trodden alone, without scaffolding of any kind. A time comes when the aspirant who so far had the guidance of his Guru, is left completely alone. All that can take him to the final goal is the momentum of his spiritual strength and intensity of purpose.

Max Mueller commenting on the Kaṭha says : "The Upaniṣad was rendered into English by Ram Mohan Roy and has since been frequently quoted by English, French and German writers as one of the most perfect specimens of the mystic philosophy and poetry of the ancient Hindus."[54] Mysticism and Alchemy are both to be found in the Upaniṣad. Naciketās represents the spirit which constantly echoes and re-echoes the words of the Upaniṣads, "From the unreal lead me to the Real." He is an Alchemist trying to transmute faith into knowledge. The price for realisation is very high. He has to offer himself. Naciketās' father fails in this. He has withheld himself. It is this that provokes his precocious son who asks :

"He said to his father, 'Father to whom will you offer me' ."[55]

Naciketās is the most valuable possession of the king. He is his very self.

The mysticism of the Upaniṣad emerges the moment we comprehend the inner meaning of such passages. Let us take : "This doubt that arises, consequent on the death of a man—some saying 'It exists,' and others saying, 'It does not exist'—I would know this, under your instruction."[56] Let us set aside the traditional interpretation of this passage for a moment. Naciketās was aware that "Man decays and dies like corn, and emerges again like corn."[57] Therefore, one way of looking at it would be that he did not want to know about survival after death. What he actually wanted to know was, what happens to the individual soul after the attainment of liberation (*Mukti*). Can the liberated soul be said to exist in this state ? Yājñavalkya explains the mystery surrounding the final state to his wife Maitreyī. His wife is confused. "Just here you have thrown me into confusion, Sir—by saying that after attaining (oneness) the Self has no more consciousness." Yājñavalkya said, "Certainly, I am not saying anything confusing, my dear, this is quite sufficient for knowledge, O Maitreyī."[58]

"Because when there is duality, as it were, then one smells something, one sees something, one hears something, one speaks something, one thinks something, one knows something. (But) When to the knower of Brahman everything has become the Self, then what should one smell and through what, what should one see and through what, ...Through what should one know that owing to which all this is known, through what, O Maitreyī, should one know the knower?"[59]

The problem in Kaṭha is similar to that in Bṛhad Āraṇyaka. It would, therefore, be more correct to say that the burden of the third boon is! What is the state of those who have attained liberation?

Buddha, dealt with this problem in almost a similar way as did Yājñavalkya.

"Monks, there are these five sense-organs, of different sphere and different domain, which do not separately enjoy the sphere and domain of one another. They are the sense-organs of the eye, ear, nose, tongue and body. Of these five sense-organs, of different sphere and different domain, the mind is the repository. Mindfulness is the repository of mind. Freedom is the repository of mindfulness. Nirvāṇa is the repository of freedom. But if you ask what is the repository of Nirvāṇa, the question goes too far and is beyond the compass of an answer. The Brahma-faring is lived for immergence in Nirvāṇa, for going beyond to Nirvāṇa, for consummation in Nirvāṇa."[60]

The Self resides in us "Subtler than the Subtle and Greater than the Great,"[61] "bodiless in the midst of bodies."[62] The Upaniṣad assigns to it a place, which it calls 'heart',[63] the secret refuge, the cavern, where the meditator perceives it in the course of his meditation. No doubt this 'heart' is not the physical organ nor is it the *Anāhata chakra*[64] envisaged in Tantrism, although this last sees it precisely in the centre. Nor is it the small 'lotus' (of eight petals). Talking of Kaṭha, S.N. Dasgupta writes : "We are here face to face with the real Mysticism of the Upaniṣads. The highest essence of man, the Self, the Brahman, is difficult of perception, it is hidden, as in a deep cavern, in that deathless being who exists from the beginning of all time and beyond all time."[65]

The Kaṭha sums up the various aspects of mysticism in a manner that no other Upaniṣad has been able to do. It has combined the opposites in a very deft and telling manner—the subtlest of the subtle and the greater than the great—It cannot be known by much learning or scholarship and yet it is seen through a pointed and fine intellect.[66] The seers in framing their experience in this manner were demonstrating the fact that it was impossible to conceive Brahman in empirical terms, that the Brahman cannot be brought within the ambit of a definition. The opposing predicates so applied to Brahman, while on the face of it contradict one another, in fact cancel one another. To put it into the words of Bṛhad Āraṇyaka[67] : The Brahman is "Truth of truth," "Reality of reality." These words can be interpreted by saying that even if the universe is reality,[68] the real in it is Brahman alone. Sometimes a term confirms, or better still, removes doubt. (For instance, when the unconditioned Brahman is described as Satchidānanda, existence, knowledge, bliss, pure and absolute). Existence, knowledge and bliss are not attributes of reality, they are its very stuff. Pure existence is the same as pure knowledge and pure bliss. The word Existence emphasises the fact that Brahman is not non-existence, the phenomenal universe. Brahman does not exist as an empirical object, but as absolute existence, without which the material objects would not be perceived to exist. It is something like saying that the mirage exists because of the desert. Therefore, the term existence as applied to Brahman, is to be understood as the negation of both the empirical reality and its correlative unreality.

When the Kaṭha, as also many other Upaniṣads apply irreconcilable attributes to the unconditioned Brahman, it does so with the purpose of showing that empirical predicates cannot be applied to it and that it is totally different from anything we know. It is only when we view the opposing words in this light do they assume meaning. When, in other words, the opposing attributes are cancelled, what remains is an independent pure consciousness free from all attributes.

The Kaṭha, at such moments, appears to be the cry of a mystic, for whom the empirical must be rejected *in toto*.

In the classical simile of the chariot, the Kaṭha examines discrimination. The simile is not new and has been used in some form or another by other traditions. In early Jewish mysticism, for instance there exists a branch of mysticism known as Throne (Hebrew : *Kisse*) mysticism, which is the object of the ecstatic vision. It is more often called Chariot (Hebrew *Merkabah*). Merkabah mystics sought the visionary experience of divine splendour of the throne of God, which was usually referred to as a chariot, probably under the influence of the great vision of prophet Ezekiel.

In the Kaṭha, the Ātman (Self) is the Lord of the Chariot, the body is the chariot, intellect the driver, the mind is the reins, and the horses are the senses.[69] Both Buddhism and Judaism have similar descriptions of chariot imagery.

" 'Straight' is the name that Road is called,
And 'Free from Fear' the Quarter wither thou art bound,
The Chariot is the 'Silent Runner' named
With Wheels of Righteous Effort fitted well,
Conscience the Leaning-board the Drapery,
Is Heedfulness, the Driver is the Norm (Dharma),
I say, and Right Views, they that run before,
And be it woman, be it man for whom
Such chariot doth wait, by that same car
Into Nībbāṇa's (Emancipation's) presence shall they come."[70]

The burden of the whole Upaniṣad is that self-realisation should not be postponed. Efforts should be made to attain it while one is on this earth. All that is necessary is to polish the intellect and make it spotless like a mirror in which the self will be distinctly reflected. There is in fact no other place where the Self appears so distinctly reflected as on this earth. *Brahmaloka* is the only other place where it so appears. But then *Brahmaloka* is difficult to obtain. The Upaniṣad says : "When all the knots of the heart are destroyed, even while a man is alive, then a mortal becomes immortal. This much alone is the instruction (of the Upaniṣad)."[71]

"Anyone else, too, who becomes a knower thus (like Naciketās) of the indwelling Self, attains Brahman."[72] All that he has to do is to become free from virtue and vice, and also desire and ignorance.

MUṆḌAKA UPANIṢAD

The central teaching of Muṇḍaka is pure mysticism. This Upaniṣad like The Cloud, is a hand-book meant for all those aspirants who strive for Self-Realisation. Muṇḍaka is divided into three sections, each section being further divided into two sub-sections. The first deals with the preparatory stages leading to the knowledge of Brahman. The second, deals with the doctrines of Brahman, and the third, the way to Brahman. These divisions are not airtight compartments, as there is spilling of one section into another. The upshot of the Upaniṣad is that superficial study of scriptures, neither the observances of religious rites, nor good works, nor all these put together, can lead to Brahman. Self-Realisation can only be achieved through the practice of renunciation and discrimination. The central idea is :

> "Which is that thing, which having been known, all this becomes known ?"[73]

We have already examined this from the phenomenological view point (Chapter II). These lines express the gist of the whole of Vedānta. The goal of all mysticism is to lead man back to the primordial state. Vedānta says that this can be brought about by removing superimposition (adhyāropa). Man sees that, after all the snake was not a snake but a rope, mistaken by him for a snake in the darkness of his ignorance. The whole problem thus revolves around the removal of Ignorance.

Chāndogya has a similar verse :

"To him the father said, 'O Śvetaketu, O good looking one, now that you are conceited, proud of being a learned man and immodest like this, did you ask about that instruction?' "[74]

Though passages like these occur in other Upaniṣads, they do not occur very often. With words like these a height is reached where it is not easy to remain for long. It is something like going up the Everest, tarrying for a while and then descending. It was not easy for the aspirant to grasp the significance of such words. Such words also afforded a golden opportunity for the exposition of higher knowledge. So it is not surprising that the Muṇḍaka attempts to define the indefinable.

Dividing knowledge into two parts the Upaniṣad refers to the knowledge of the Vedas, rituals, grammar, astrology, etc., as lower knowledge. "Then there is the higher (knowledge) by which is realised that Immutable."[75] The implication and importance of this verse and the following verse is very great for the understanding of mysticism. Once and for all it has been stated, and stated categorically, what is mysticism and what it is not. The lower knowledge does not constitute mysticism. The higher knowledge does. But for the aspirant the lower knowledge is a stepping stone to the higher. Lower knowledge has for its content, Ignorance, Higher knowledge, Brahman. In fact higher knowledge, involves freeing oneself from everything however good or exalted it may be. The Cloud (Privy Counselling) says : "Reject all thoughts be they good or be they evil."[76]

"(By the higher knowledge) the wise realise everywhere that which cannot be perceived and grasped; which is without source, features, eyes and ears; which has neither hands nor feet; which is eternal, multiformed, all pervasive, extremely subtle and undiminishing; and which is the source of all."[77]

Here we notice the Seer's attempt to express in finite terms that which is infinite. An endeavour is made to define the indefinable. It is reminiscent of the description in the Bhagavad Gītā.[78]

"If the splendour of a thousand Suns were to rise up simultaneously in the Sky, that would be like the splendour of that Mighty Being."

To define the "ineffable" is an impossibility. Nobody can truly attain to any such knowledge other than by a strictly personal effort. The aspirant has to verify the nature of such knowledge for himself. When we attempt to define, as the Upaniṣad has done, we limit what we are defining. That with which we are concerned is, in itself truly and absolutely unlimited and cannot be confined to any formula. When therefore, we say that It is invisible, ungraspable, Eternal and so on, we are only giving a partial definition. Thus for example, when Aristotle envisages metaphysics as a knowledge of being *qua* being, he identifies it with ontology, that is to say, he takes the part for the whole. That is why in all true metaphysical conception, it is necessary to go beyond being. In all true metaphysical conception, it is necessary, therefore, to take into account the inexpressible. We employ terms like 'metaphysical conceptions 'or' higher knowledge' for lack of adequate terms. They stand for that which we comprehend by intuition. Even in intuition, we have to differentiate between Pure Intellectual intuition and sensible intuition. The former, that is intellectual intuition, can be said to be the attaining of intuitive and immediate supra rational knowledge. It is often termed as 'see' ing or 'Perceive' ing. This intuition lies beyond reason, whereas the other can know only the world of changing and becoming, that is to say, nature and the inferior part of nature. Higher knowledge can, in a way, be associated with pure intellectual intuition, that is, with the eternal and immutable principle, whereas lower knowledge can be associated with sensible intuition, with the world of changing and becoming. In order to comprehend the universal principle directly, the transcendent intellect must be of the universal order.

It does not follow, therefore, that lower knowledge (theoretical or discriminative knowledge) is irrelevant and useless. It is necessary by way of preparation for higher knowledge. Lower knowledge, moreover, is the only knowledge that is communicable, unlike, higher knowledge, which is not communicable. A non-mystic cannot understand a mystic. But one mystic can understand another even if no words pass between them, as they can communicate without words.

So in the process of self-realisation, the aspirant has first to go through lower knowledge, then higher knowledge. Both of which finally take him to the Absolute state. Rituals etc. are, therefore, as a preparatory step, very essential. These means, indeed, must be within man's reach, since it is in the human state that the Being exists. Subsequently this same Being will assume the higher stages. Thus it is in these formal means appropriate to this world as presently manifested that the Being finds a suitable fulcrum for raising itself beyond this world. Words, symbols, signs, rites, rituals or any other preparatory methods have no other function. They are supports and nothing else. How is it possible, it can be asked, that merely contingent means can produce an effect that immeasurably surpasses them and is at the same time of a totally different order? The answer would be that these means, in fact, are only fortuitous. The results they help to attain are by no means consequential. What they do is to place the Being in the position conducive to attainment. That is all. No understanding of the mysticism of the Upaniṣads is possible, if one fails to grasp this. The rituals *etc.* are simple *means* not *cause.* The word *cause* gives rise to the idea of effect. There is no such thing here. Realisation is not the *production* of something that does not yet exist; but the knowing of that which is, in an abiding and immutable manner, beyond all temporal succession. All states of being, considered under this primary aspect, abide in perfect simultaneousness in the eternal *NOW*.

One of the ways a scientist or psychologist would look at Canto I, Section II, relating to rituals etc. of Muṇḍaka, would be to view it as a psychological means to prepare the aspirant psychologically, through religious rituals, for the final act of Realisation. Such means can be compared to a horse that helps a traveller to reach his destination earlier than he would have reached had he footed out the distance. But that does not mean that he could not have completed the journey on foot, only it would then take him more time and involve more trouble. If the traveller were asked to exercise his option, he would choose to go on horse-back. The case with rituals is not any different.

GURU

Between the performance of actions and the attainment of realisation, there is one important step — Guru. It is this aspect that the Muṇḍaka considers next. In Hindu mysticism Guru has occupied a place of great importance. Even great saints like Rāmakṛṣṇa, Kabir and others had to take their directions and inspiration from the Guru. Kabir placed the Guru above God. The Muṇḍaka advises that after having learnt of the temporality of this universe and the worthlessness of actions, howsoever virtuous, the aspirant should approach a Guru who has himself achieved realisation.

"For knowing that Reality, he should go, with sacrificial faggots in hand, to a teacher, versed in the Vedas and absorbed in Brahman."[79]

Also,

"To him who approaches duly, whose heart is calm and whose outer organs are under control, that man of enlightenment should adequately impart that knowledge of Brahman by which one realises the true and immutable Puruṣa."[80]

No matter how learned the aspirant in the scriptures, he should not undertake the "search" on his own. Śaṅkara, commenting on Muṇḍaka I.ii.12, writes : "One though versed in the scriptures should not search independently after the knowledge of Brahman."[81]

The importance of a Guru has been pointed out time and again by the Upaniṣads. The Guru brings in his teachings not only guidance but grace.

Sadānanda says :

"Such a Guru through his infinite grace instructs the pupil by the method of de-superimposition of the superimposition."[82]

Śaṅkara in his commentary on the Muṇḍaka (1.2.12) referred to above, emphasises the absolute necessity of a Guru. In his Bhaja Govindam he writes :

"O Devotee of the lotus-feet of the teacher, may you become liberated soon from the Saṃsāra through the discipline of the sense-organs and the mind. You will come to experience (behold) the Lord that dwells in your own heart."[83]

The importance of the Guru lies in the fact that he inspires faith in his pupil. He gives him the power to Believe what he (the aspirant) does not see. Faith has been defined by St. Augustine in the following memorable words :

"Faith is to believe what you do not see, and the reward of faith is to see what you believe."[84]

Initiation forms not an unimportant part of mysticism. Formal initiation which forms part of ritual is of no importance. Satyakāma in reply to his teacher says :

"For it has been certainly heard by me from the venerable ones like you that, knowledge acquired from the teacher alone, surely becomes the best."[85]

Or take the two verses from Kaṭha :

"The Self is not certainly adequately known when spoken of by an inferior person; for it is thought of variously. When taught by one who has become identified with It, there is no further cogitation with regard to it. For it is beyond argumentation, being subtler even than the atomic quantity."[86]

"Of that (Self) which is not available for the mere hearing to many, (and) which many do not understand even while hearing, the expounder is wonderful and the receiver is wonderful, wonderful is he who knows, under the instruction of an adept."[87]

A rare soul becomes a knower, being instructed by a proficient teacher. (kuśalānuśiṣtaḥ). And why does the aspirant not become a knower when instructed by an inferior person, that is, a man of worldly understanding? With the latter, discussion centres round "It exists," "It does not exist," "It is the doer," "It is not the doer." In this dual talk the Self is not adequately known. But when instructed by one who does not see duality, there is no argumentation, *no* non-comprehension, no non-realisation.

The parable in the Chāndogya is a classic example of how a disciple is carried step by step to Realisation by his spiritual Teacher. This parable refers to a man who kidnapped by robbers, blind-folded, and taken away from his country, Gandhāra, and left in the forest to fend for himself. He runs in all the geographical directions asking for help.

"As somebody having removed the bandage on the eyes may say, 'The country of Gandhāra lies in this way. Walk in this direction,' (and) that intelligent man who has received instruction reaches the country of the Gandhāras indeed, by asking the way from village to village,' in this way indeed a man having a teacher acquires knowledge in the world."[88]

The purport of these two verses is given in the verse 2 : "A man having a teacher acquires knowledge." (Ācāryavān puruṣaḥ veda). This parable is reminiscent of the parable about the image of the cave in Plato' s Republic. It illustrates vividly how illumination comes to a benighted soul. The parable has two purposes to serve : to show the difference between knowledge and illusion, reality and appearance. Men, chained in a cave, facing a blank wall, with a fire burning behind them, can see only shadows, which they take for real objects. When one of them, who has been made to leave the cave, sees the real world by the light of the Sun, returns, it is difficult for him to adjust to the dim light in the cave. He is ridiculed for this by his former companions and is unable to convince them that what they see are but vague reflections of Reality. We quote from Plato's Seventh Book of the Republic :

"And you may further imagine that his *instructor* (italics mine) is pointing to the objects as they pass and requiring him to name them, — will he not be perplexed ? Will he not fancy that the shadows which he formerly saw are truer than the objects which are now shown to him?

"And suppose once more, that he is reluctantly dragged up a steep and rugged ascent, and held fast until he is forced into the presence of the Sun himself, is he not likely to be pained and irritated? When he approaches the light his eyes will be dazzled, and he will not be able to see anything at all of what are now called realities.

"Not at all in a moment, he said.

"He will require to grow accustomed to the sight of the upper world. And first he will see the shadows best, next the reflections of men and other objects in the water, and then the objects themselves; then he will gaze upon the light of the Moon and the Stars and the spangled Heaven ; and he will see the sky and the stars by night better than the Sun or the light of the Sun by day ?

"Certainly.

"Last of all he will be able to see the Sun, and not mere reflections of him in the water, but he will see him in his own proper place, and not in another; and he will contemplate him as he is.

"Certainly.

"He will then proceed to argue that this is He who gives the season and the years. . . . ."[89]

What Plato is driving at is that the soul in its *ascent* cannot go it alone. A guide is necessary.

Against the background of these comments Muṇḍaka I.ii.12-13 make a lot of sense. We quote from Paul Deussen's translation :

"The wise, critically pondering over the worlds brought about by their words, — they turn away (from disgust); the uneffected (Brahman) is not effected through works.

In order to attain knowledge, he should seek and visit with fuelsticks in hands,

The master who is proficient in scriptures and who is steady in Brahman."[90]

"He, who has approached in the proper way, who is calm in heart and restful, — to him the wise one then imparts the science (knowledge) of Brahman, just as it is, the knowledge of the imperishable, Of the intelligent spirit, of the Truth."[91]

What should one do after examining the world? One should turn away in disgust from it, renounce it, and go to a man who is not only knowledgeable (in scriptures) but is also a realised soul. Not only should the aspirant possess the requisite qualifications, but the Guru also should possess qualifications of a high order. Only a combination of these two can lead the aspirant to realisation. The reference to fuel sticks (samit-pāṇiḥ) signifies that a certain standard of discipline is expected of the aspirant. To such an aspirant whose mind is at rest (praśāntacittāya) and whose senses are subdued (śạmānvitāya) the Guru imparts the science of Brahman (brahmavidyām).[92]

SELF-REALISATION

What distinguishes the Hindu tradition from the other world mysticism is the former's constant repetition of the same truth in various forms. Hence the words uttered in the Muṇḍaka for instance, can be found in Chāndogya, Taittirīya, and several other Upaniṣads. This is inevitable. What mainly concerned the Seers was that Brahman is the mark that should be penetrated. Here again we notice the anxiety of the Guru when he repeats : "It is to be penetrated. O Good-looking One, shoot at it."[93]

How ?

"Taking hold of the bow, that is the great weapon familiar in the Upaniṣads, one should fix on it an arrow, sharpened with meditation. Drawing the string with a mind absorbed in Its thought, hit, O Good-looking one, that very target that is the Immutable."

"*Om* is the bow; the soul is the arrow; and Brahman is called the target. It is to be hit by an unerring man. One should become one with It just like an arrow."[94]

In their mystical ecstasies the seers often blended philosophy with poetry. The above two verses are sterling example of this. Here we quote a few enlightening words from Swami Chinmayananda :

"The method of penetrating the Truth-centre in us with our mind, is the theme of these two *mantras,* for which no better metaphor could have been employed than that of a bow and arrow. The bow here is the chanting of 'OM' with a knowledge and the significance of 'OM.' The arrow is the Life-centre in the individual. The Awareness in us, propelled by the motive force generated in voiceless ecstasy, during the thoughtless meditation, 'flies' to touch Total Awareness, the *Brahman*, the All-pervading Reality."[95]

Take again :

"When the Self, which is both high and low, is realised, the knot of the heart gets untied, all doubts become solved, and all one's actions become dissipated."

"In the supreme, bright sheath is Brahman, free from taints and without parts. It is pure, and is the Light of lights. It is that which the knowers of the Self realise."[96]

The reference to the bright sheath or golden sheath (pare hiraṇmaye kośe) is very significant. In order to achieve self-realisation, man has to go back to his source, to the primordial state. He has to cast off all superimpositions. He has to cast off the sheaths that cover his spirit — the five concentric circles of matter, the Food-sheath, the vital Air-sheath, the Mental sheath, the Intellectual sheath and the Bliss sheath. The seeker withdraws all attachment to the outer layers. In other words, he transcends them. Transcending the mind and the intellect he reaches the innermost realm which is closest to Pure Consciousness, (hiraṇmaya para).[97] The innermost Golden sheath is the closest to Awareness. The seer, as is common in the Upaniṣads (as also in mysticism of other traditions) employ all sorts of epithets to describe Brahman — Light of lights (jyotiṣām jyotiḥ)[98] etc. So powerful is the brilliance of this Light, that in comparison with its brilliance, the light of the Sun, the Moon and the Stars, fades into insignificance (na tatra sūryaḥ bhāti nachandratārakam).[99] Brahman is all pervading, above, below, in front, at the back, on the right, on the left. All this world is Brahman.

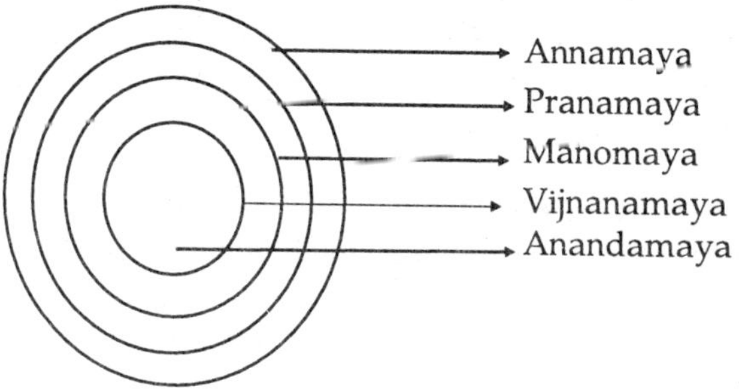

The aspirant has to acquire this knowledge. It is a stepping board to self realisation. He has to reach an unconditioned state where all other states of being find their place, that is, they are transformed and released from the special conditions that determine them as particular states. Once the aspirant gains this unconditioned state, it becomes his *permanent* acquisition. Nothing can deprive him of it. After all what he has acquired *is beyond time*. And what is beyond time cannot be snatched from him. This is a very important concept in Hindu mysticism. Perhaps it is the one major item that distinguishes Hindu from other mystical traditions.

When we say acquirement of knowledge, we also include theoretical knowledge. The reason is that all knowledge carries its own benefits. It cannot be separated from the benefits. It is not so with action. In the case of action there is a momentary modification of a being. Action is always separated from its effects. These effects, however, belong to the same order of existence as that which has produced them. Therefore, action cannot have the effect of liberating from action. Its consequence cannot reach beyond the limits of individuality considered in its fullest possible extension. It, therefore, follows that whatever may be the action, it cannot banish ignorance, which is the root of all limitation. Knowledge alone can dispel ignorance. The Seer would add, "As the light of the Sun dispels darkness" .

But on the way to this self realisation there are several dangers to be sedulously avoided. We only deal with one major danger at this point.

All phenomena are of the physical order. Higher knowledge is *not* phenomenal. It lies beyond the phenomenal world. Experimental science, for instance, deals with phenomena. In the process of self realisation, some phenomena occur in seemingly accidental manner. Depending on the stage the aspirant has reached, such phenomena are likely to give a sense of "power" to the aspirant. If he stops by the wayside to "taste" these powers, they will surely prove obstacles in the way of his self-realisation. He is likely to be halted or turned aside from his quest for self-realisation. An aspirant who falls a victim to such phenomena is like a maneater who has tasted blood. He wants more. He is likely to search for extraordinary "powers" . After he has reached this state, he has no chance of pressing on to self-realisation. The Western mystic would say that this is an aberration which takes the aspirant into the domain of the occult. In Hindu mysticism this is considered as a major obstacle in the way to self-realisation.

We are not concerned here with the wide ramifications of the problem except to point out that it is a serious obstacle against which the aspirant should guard jealously. Yoga calls it antarāyāḥ. Yoga is not the subject of this book though it has a bearing on mysticism. In fact even in Muṇḍaka the imagery of taking up a bow, has a reference to Yoga. The third and the final part of the Upaniṣad deals with this aspect. But one must not mistake for the end that which is no more than a contingent and an accidental aid.

A distinguishing factor in the Muṇḍaka is that it has for the first time introduced the problem of knowledge — Higher and Lower. In Advaita epistemology is inseparable from metaphysics. What the Advaitist says is that the cognizer, cognition and the object cognized are one non-dual consciousness. The Seeker has to arrive at this through knowledge. But for this purpose the Muṇḍaka excludes Lower knowledge. In an out of context verse (III.ii.3-4) it also excludes much learning, etc. The Muṇḍaka has a very definite purpose in doing this.

Lower knowledge is constructive and interpretative by nature. When knowledge is taken as constructive and interpretative, nothing can be known as it is, because the fact underlying knowledge is bound to remain ever hidden. Higher knowledge, on the other hand, being free from constructive and interpretative nature, helps in the attainment of Immutable Truth.

It is not enough to have higher knowledge. Knowledge and method must work co-jointly. There is a nice little parable in Tibetan. The Tibetans tell of two travellers, one lame and the other blind, proceeding towards the city of Nirvāṇa. They do not make much headway, because of the lameness of the one and blindness of the other. They worked out a plan. The lame traveller climbed on the back of the blind one. The blind one walked on with steady legs, while the lame one pointed the way. This is how they reached the city of Nirvāṇa. The man with the sound legs stands for the method. The blind man, for knowledge.[100] In Buddhism, for instance, wisdom and method, are shown as wife and husband in conjugal embrace.

Hence no self-realisation is possible without method. But does this mean that any aspirant who conforms to the prescribed method would reach self-realisation? Can anyone and everyone become a mystic? The answer is a categorical 'no.' Speaking generally, it would be more near the truth to say that some kind of initial vision of the truth, a first glimpse of Higher Knowledge, would be necessary before an aspirant can be impelled to alter the course of his life — a glimpse that would effect a 'conversion' in his life forcing him to turn his back on the world and its allurements.

This is a general question that touches all mystical traditions. If the aforesaid 'conversion' is to take place, it cannot just take place. It has to take place on account of some initial grace, thanks to which one suddenly becomes aware of the futility of one's present state, and by the same token, becomes aware of the possibility of reaching a better and happier state. And this grace can only be received because of faith. The initial awakening, the initial vision of truth, so necessary to embark an aspirant on his voyage of self-realisation, can, therefore, only come about as a result of Faith and Grace. It is when this grace descends on the aspirant that he asks himself the question : What must I do, or not do, to reach the goal I dimly discern in the distance? When the aspirant uses the word 'what,' he is automatically seeking for a method. So, in a way of speaking, the initial vision that comes to him combined with method, can take him to self-realisation.

When we study the Upaniṣads especially those falling in the genre of Muṇḍaka or Kaṭha, it is to be borne in mind that the Upaniṣad is not purely theoretical. That, a study of the Upaniṣad does not lead the student into an intellectual dead end. The Muṇḍaka conforms to tradition. And because it conforms to tradition the polar balance between theory and practice, between knowledge and its effective realisation through calling into play the appropriate spiritual means is maintained.

Take for instance :

"The bright and pure Self within the body, that the monks with (habitual effort and) attenuated blemishes see, is attainable through truth, concentration, complete knowledge, and continence, practised constantly."[101]

Here we have one part of the verse describing the self : Immediately followed by advice as to what should be done to attain it. The self is attained by veracity (satyena), by concentration (tapasā), by well knowing or complete knowledge (samyag-gñānena), and continence (brahmacaryeṇa). All these practised "for ever" (nityam). What is meant is that all these disciplines viz., veracity, concentration, complete knowledge and continence should be practised for ever, that is, unceasingly.

If, therefore, we describe knowledge as being concerned with *knowing*, then method will have to be described as that which is concerned with *being*. One can only *know* a thing by being *that* thing. It is here that philosophy differs from mysticism. To mistake merely a mental apprehension of knowledge is the classical trap of philosophers. This is not to berate philosophy. It is merely to point out that a mental appreciation of knowledge is *not* mysticism. There is mysticism or realisation only when *being* and *knowing* coincide. *Being* and *knowing* will coincide when *knowledge* and *method* go hand in hand. The Upaniṣads succeed as mystical text books because in them we see knowledge and method together. After the aspirant is told what Self is, he is not left to fend for himself. He is told about the method he should follow in order to realise this Self. Bṛhad Āraṇyaka says :

"The Self, my dear Maitreyī, should be realised — should be heard of, reflected on and meditated upon. By the realisation of the Self, my dear, through hearing, reflection and meditation, all this is known."[102]

Everything, says the Upaniṣad, (sarvam viditam) is known with the aid of hearing, reflection and meditation. A careful look will disclose the repetition of the same instruction. This is merely to point out the method, without which the former part of the verse remains ineffective. Such a meticulous way of describing "method" again and again is rarely found in mystical treatises of the West. Though it is found in abundance in The Cloud.

Broadly speaking, Advaita examines knowledge both in its empirical and metaphysical aspects. Pure consciousness being beyond the relativity of the knower and the known, is at the same time self-luminous, self-existent and, therefore, nothing can be said about it. It should not appear to be strange if we say that it shines even when there is no object to illuminate. This, which shines, when there is no object to illuminate is the Ultimate Reality, the non-relational, non-dual pure consciousness. But the moment we try to explain rational knowledge we enter into metaphysics and epistemology. When we view Pure Consciousness through the mental mode of knowing Self, the result is an object which is either psychological, like an inner cognition, or psychophysical, like a sense perception. What actually takes place is an effort to individualise the Pure Consciousness, to convert it into the Ego, the "I-ness." This I-ness can also be classified as a particular mode of the mind. It is this mixture, so to say, of the epistemological and metaphysical, that renders the experience ineffable. In fact, in the ultimate state, the question of ineffability does not arise, because in that state silence prevails and the mystic does not deem it fit to give any expression to what he has experienced. Between two mystics, both of whom have tasted Reality, the question of expressing would not arise. The problem arises only when such an experience is to be conveyed to a non-mystic or an aspirant. Hence the Upaniṣads. It would not be an exaggeration to say that there would be no Upaniṣads had the Seers, from time to time, not tried to convey their experience to the aspirant. This would be one way of explaining the problem of ineffability.[103]

Throughout the Upaniṣads, we come across the description of Pure Consciousness. It is self-shining. It is self-revealing, but in the process it reveals all objects. Sri Kṛṣṇa talked about the thousand Suns. What perhaps distinguishes the luminosity of Pure Consciousness and physical light, is that the latter is unaware of itself and every thing else. If we put this idea in Advaitic language we could say that physical light is marked by nescience. Psychologists and philosophers are not likely to accept this view. But then the question arises : Can that which is neither self-aware nor aware of anything else, make itself or any other thing known?

The Muṇḍaka introduces two verses rather abruptly and out of context. Verses (III. ii. 3-4). Verse 3 reads :

"This Self is not attained through study, nor through the intellect, nor through much hearing. By the very fact that he (i.e. the aspirant) seeks for It, does It become attainable! Of him This Self reveals It's own nature."

These oft-quoted lines emphasise that Intensity or intense desire on the part of the aspirant is a necessary prerequisite for self-realisation. What is demanded is earnestness. Erudition is not contra-indicated. In fact in Hindu mysticism the scriptures form a very important part of the aspirant's equipment. But the first and primary prerequisite is *intense desire*. Just as a preliminary vision, however partial and hazy, is necessary for the aspirant to embark on his voyage of self-realisation, so also an intense desire. To such a one the self reveals its true nature.

Does this not emphasise Grace? Well, hearing, contemplating and meditating by themselves, lead one nowhere. But, the seeker must be a 'chosen' one. By him only is IT attainable. Much learning, in itself has never been favoured by any mystical tradition. Christ preached that one had to become as a child before he entered the Kingdom of Heaven.

KENA UPANIṢAD

Kena is among the shorter Upaniṣads comprising of just thirty-five verses. But within the compass of these thirty-five verses it discusses both the philosophical and mystical aspects of Brahman. The third chapter in a delightful parable discusses the problem of Grace, the incapacity of the sense organs to give information about Brahman. This Upaniṣad is like a narrow window through which we look upon the vast and brilliantly lit sky.

At the very outset (verses 5 to 9) the phenomenal is dismissed as not Brahman. The constant refrain is : "Know that alone to be Brahman, and not what people worship 'as an object'."[104]

That by which the eye sees, the ear hears, by which breath is drawn, that is Brahman. In other words Brahman is unknown to those whose knowledge is confined to the empirical world. But it is not unknown to those who having polished their intelligence look upon it as the foundation of all states of consciousness.

"Since He is the Ear of the ear, the Mind of the mind, the Speech of speech, the Life of life and the Eye of the eye, therefore, the intelligent men, after giving up (self-identification with the senses) and renouncing this world, become immortal."[105]

The process of 'seeing' the Ear of the ear, the Mind of the mind and so on is merely the withdrawal of the senses, a sort of detachment leading to the transcendence of the aspirant's apparent nature. Only with this transcendence can man see the essence, which is invisible to the physical eye or ear or mind. In the empirical state these organs are unable to 'see' Brahman, because Brahman is unknowable to the physical senses. The Upaniṣads never assert that Brahman is unknowable. What they say is that It is unknowable to the finite nature. The mystic in the course of his disciplines and meditation develops a God-like nature which is different from his finite nature. In the ordinary states of consciousness, there are three states, waking, dreaming and sleeping. These states are the finite states, the states in which the aspirant is liable to error. Once the fourth state is reached the mystic enters a super conscious state where he is able to perceive the Divine. It is in the first three states that Brahman is unknowable. But the moment these three states are transcended, the mystic enters a region where potentially Brahman becomes knowable.

If at the ordinary levels God were knowable then the knowledge of God would be like any other knowledge. Therefore, mind is to be distinguished from mind as ordinarily understood. In common parlance mind has the meaning of a sense organ. But when it is illumined it becomes 'Mind of the mind,' the Mind that the Upaniṣadic Seers always talk about — the Mind that can apprehend Reality.

If we compare the Kena with the Īśa, we notice that the Kena is more restricted in its scope. As Aurobindo writes : "It (Kena) concerns itself with only the relation of mind-consciousness to Brahman-consciousness and does not stray outside the strict boundaries of its subject. The material world and the physical life are taken for granted, they are hardly mentioned."[106]

The Kena thus attempts to relate mind-consciousness to Brahman-consciousness. Its preoccupation is with knowledge. When statements like the following are made they should not be considered as pure rhetoric.

"He truly knows Brahman who knows him as beyond knowledge ; he who thinks that he knows, knows not. The ignorant think that Brahman is known, but the wise know him to be beyond knowledge."[107]

It will be observed that for the ignorant the word 'think' is used. For the wise, 'know.' Says the Teacher :

"If you think, 'I have known Brahman well enough,' then you have known only the very little expression that It has in the human body and the little expression that It has among the Gods. Therefore, Brahman is still to be deliberated on by you. (Disciple), I think (Brahman) is known.[108]

This verse displays both Vanity and Ignorance on the part of the disciple. To declare : 'I have known Brahman well enough' is tantamount to saying that the knower can be known by himself. It is as good as saying that fire which is the consumer can be burnt by fire.

The Bṛhad Āraṇyaka[109] illustrates this position with unsurpassed clarity. Uṣasta asks Yājñavalkya to explain "to me the Brahman that is immediate and direct — the Self that is within all."

"This is your self that is within all."

"Which is within all, Yājñavalkya?"

"That which breathes through the Prāṇa is your self that is within all."

Not satisfied with the answer Uṣasta says

"You have indicated it as one may say that a cow is such and such, or a horse is such and such. Explain to me the Brahman that is immediate and direct — the Self that is within all. This is your Self that is within all."

"Which is within all, Yājñavalkya?"

"You cannot see that which is the witness of vision; you cannot hear that which is the hearer of hearing; you cannot think that which is the thinker of thought; you cannot know that which is the knower of knowledge. This is your Self that is within all, everything else but this is perishable."[110]

In other words Pure Consciousness is Brahman. But even this Pure Consciousness can assume concrete form in order to impart knowledge to an earnest seeker. Brahman once won a victory for the Devas. The Devas thought it was their victory and were inflated with vanity. To teach them humility and impart knowledge, Brahman appeared before them as a mysterious form. Agni was deputed to find out who this mysterious form was. He returns crestfallen, unable to burn even a straw he was asked to burn. Similarly, Vāyū was unable to blow away the straw. As a last resort, Indra is deputed, but the mysterious form disappears and, "In that very space, he approached the superbly charming woman viz. Umā Haimavatī."[111] Haimavatī, the superbly fascinating, is knowledge of Brahman. What is significant in this verse are the words, 'in that very space.'[112] The adjective 'superbly fascinating' is employed here as it applies to knowledge which, of all the things in the world is the most fascinating. Umā appears exactly where (that is in the space) the Yakṣa was before. It vanished after revealing Itself, and where Indra also was at the time of the disappearance of Brahman. Here we have an example of the subtle manner in which the Upaniṣad brings out the difference between the Absolute and personal aspects of Deity. The Upaniṣad also tries to drive home the point that in mysticism there is no place for pride. Brahman does not even grant an audience to Indra. In mystical parlance this could be explained by saying that one cannot 'see' God until such time as every vestige of pride is eradicated. No doubt the approach of Indra to Brahman was different from that of Agni and Vāyu. But Indra was aware and knew that he was Indra. Despite this, Indra stood his ground and displayed his sense of devotion. The result was that knowledge of Brahman appeared to him in the form of a woman, Umā.

So long as man is under the sway of the Ego, he tends to identify himself with the body, mind and senses. This identification inspires a sense of arrogance. Man fails to take into account the 'X' factor which is Brahman. The lesson of the parable is that there is no real power and no real doer except Brahman. He is the Eye of the eye and the Ear of the ear. The point of transcending death and attaining immortality is reached when we realise that all our faculties are dependent on Brahman, inasmuch as It is the underlying Reality.

And finally purification of the heart, which is brought about by the requisite disciplines, is necessary. The Kena says : "Concentration, cessation from sense objects, rites, etc., are its legs, the Vedas are all its limbs, truth is its abode."[113]

It is to be meditated upon with the help of the name *tadvanam.*[114] This is reminiscent of The Cloud where the unknown author advises meditation on a short word like 'Love' or 'God.' In this connection the following quotation from Radhakrishnan is interesting :

"The Upaniṣads sometimes suggest that we can induce the trance condition by control of breath, though more often they speak to us of the method of concentration. Mystic words such as Aum, Tadvanam, Tajjalān, are the symbols on which we are asked to fix attention. The way to reach steadiness of mind is by concentration or fixing the thought for a time on one particular object by effacing all others."[115]

The special purpose of this Upaniṣad is thus to give us the knowledge of the Real. While imparting this instruction the Upaniṣad does not deflect from its path.

REFERENCES

1. BṚ. I. iii. 28.
2. The Upaniṣads, Sri Aurobindo Ashram, Pondicherry, 1985, p. 1.
3. Ibid, p.1.
4. Radhakrishnan, Brahmā Sūtra, Harper and Bros., New York, p. 246.
5. The Hindu View of Life. Blackie & Sons Publishers Pvt. Ltd., Bombay, 1983, p. 24.
6. Nāyamātmā pravacanena labhyo
   na medhayā na bahunā śrutena
   Yamevaiṣa vṛṇute tena labhyaḥ
   tasyaiṣa ātmā vivṛṇute tanūm svām (I. ii. 23)
7. Satchidānandam
8. Time and Eternity, Princeton University, 1952, p. 98.
9. Yadā sarve pramucyante kāmā ye'sya hṛdi śritāḥ atha martyo'mṛto bhavatyatra brahma samaśnute (Kaṭha vi 14)
10. Encyclopaedia of Indian Philosophy, Ed. Karl H. Potter, Motilal Banarasidass, Delhi, 1981, p. 321, Verse 91
11. yadā yadā hi dharmasya
    glānir bhavati bhārata
    abhyutthānam adharmasya
    tadā' tmānaṁ sṛjāmy aham (B.G. IV. 7)

12. Īśa, 15.
13. The Upaniṣads, Sri Aurobindo Ashram, Pondicherry, 1985, p. 71.
14. Selections from Sri Aurobindo's Savitri, Sri Aurobindo Ashram Trust, Ed. Mary Alderidor, 1975, p. 111.
15. Vedānta-Sāra, Swami Nikhilananda, Advaita Ashrama, Calcutta, 1987, p. 2.

    "Vedanta is the evidence of the Upaniṣads, as well as the Śāriraka Sūtras, and other books that help in the correct expounding of its meaning."
16. 'jñānayajñena cā'py anye

    yajanto mām upāsate

    ekatvena pṛthaktvena

    bahudhā viśvatomukham

    (B.G. IX.15)
17. pūrṇamadaḥ pūrṇamidaṁ pūrṇāt pūrṇamudacyate

    pūrṇasya pūrṇamādāya pūrṇamevāvaśiṣyate
18. Quoted in Ten Classical Upaniṣads, Vol. 1, General Editor P.B. Gajendragadkar, Bharatiya Vidya Bhavan, Bombay, 1981, p. 76.
19. Śaṅkarācārya : Māyā and Brahman,—a Mathematical Interpretation, Centre of Advanced Studies, Madras, pp. 1-2.

    Idea of the Inexpressible, A.R. Mohapatra, Cosmo Paperbacks, New Delhi, 1984, p. 15.
20. "Cette Invocation lui convient si bien qu'elle en forme une partie intégrante."

    The Invocation suits it so well that it forms an integral part of it. (of the Upaniṣad). Six Upaniṣads, Majeures, Le courrier du Livre, Paris, 1971, p. 118.
21. saḥ brahmavidyām sarvavidyā — pratiṣṭhām (1.1.1.)

    That knowledge of Brahman that is the basis of all knowledge.
22. Vedā' haṁ samatītāni

    vartamānāni cā 'rjuna

    bhaviṣyāṇi ca bhūtāni

    māṁ tu veda na kaścana

    (B.G. VII.26)
23. Six Upaniṣads, Majeures, p. 119.
24. See The Upaniṣads, Sri Aurobindo Ashram, Pondicherry, 1985, p. 63, Note 2.
25. Pandurang, Pandurang, Mohan Mudranalaya, 1965, p. 12.
26. Ibid, p. 52.

27. The Upaniṣads, p. 134.
28. Ibid, p. 68.
29. Ibid, p. 68, Note I.
30. Ibid, p. 68.
31. Kaṭha I.11.4.
32. Hindu Mysticism, Motilal Banarsidass, Delhi, 1983, pp. 34/35.
33. Kaṭha l.i.4 : tāta kasmai māṁ dāsyas iti
34. Ibid, I.i.4 : mṛtyave tvā dadāmi iti
35. Complete Works, Vol. IV, Mayavati Memorial Edition, Advaita Ashrama, Calcutta, 9th Edition, 1966, pp. 177/178.
36. The Message of the Upaniṣads, Bharatiya Vidya Bhavan, Bombay, 1968, p. 267.
37. Kaṭha, l.i.10.
38. Kaṭha. l.i.13.
39. Ibid, l.i.16.
40. Ibid, l.i.20.
41. Ibid, l.i.22. Any other instructor of this principle is not to be had even by searching.
42. Ibid, l.ii.3.
43. Kaṭha, l.ii.5.
44. Bṛ. IV.iv.ll.
45. Īśa. 3.
46. Kaṭha. I.ii.7.
47. Ibid, I.ii.7.
48. Kaṭha. I.ii.23.
49. Ibid, I.ii.23.
50. Ibid, I.ii.8.
51. Ibid, I.ii.8.
52. Vedānta-Sāra of Sadānanda, Advaita Ashrama, Calcutta, 1987, pp. 17-18.
53. Vivekacūḍāmaṇi, 60, Commentary, Swami Chinmayananda, Central Chinmaya Mission Trust, 1981.
54. The Upaniṣads, Part II, Motilal Banarsidass, Delhi, 1969, p. xxi.
55. Kaṭha. l.l.4.
56. Ibid, l.i.20.
57. Ibid, I.i.6.
58. Bṛ. II.iv.13.
59. Ibid. II.iv.14.

60. Gotama The Buddha, Presented by Ananda K. Coomaraswamy and I.B. Horner, Cassell, London, 1948, p. 213. Quoted from Samyutta-Nikāya, V. 218.
61. Kaṭha. I.ii.20.
62. Ibid, I.ii.22.
63. Ibid, I.ii.20.
64. Ṣir John Woodroffe, The Serpent Power, p. V and p. 188.
65. Hindu Mysticism, Motilal Banarsidass, Delhi, 1983, pp. 47/48.
66. Kaṭha. I.ii.20.
67. Bṛ II.i.20. "satyasya satyam."
68. Ibid, satyam.
69. See Kaṭha. I.iii.3-4.
70. Quoted by Swami Ranganathananda, in The Message of The Upaniṣads, Bharatiya Vidya Bhavan, Bombay, 1968, p. 407, from The Book of The Kindred Saying (Saṁyukta-Nikāya), Part I, I.V.6 Pali Text Society Edition.
71. Kaṭha. II.iii.15.
72. Ibid, II.iii.18.
73. Muṇḍ. I.i.3.

    kasmin nu Bhagavaḥ vijñāte sarvam idam vijñātam bhavatiti.
74. Chānd 6.I.2.
75. Muṇḍ. 1.1.5.

    atha parā yayā tat akṣaram adhigamyate
76. The Cloud of Unknowing and The Book of Privy Counselling, Ed. William Johnson, Image book, New York, 1973, p. 149.
77. Muṇḍ. I.i.6.
78. B.G. XI.12.
79. Muṇḍ. 1.ii.12.
80. Ibid. 1.ii.13.
81. Sadānanda, Vedānta-Sāra, Advaita Ashrama, 1987, pp.17-18

    śastrajnopi svātantryeṇa brahmajñānānveṣaṇam na kuryāt
82. Ibid, pp. 18-19.
83. Swami Chinmayananda, Sri Śaṅkarācārya' s Bhaja Govindam, Central Chinmaya Mission Trust, Bombay, 1986, (31), p. 72.
84. Quoted by Swami Chinmayananda in Bhaja Govindam, p. 72.
85. Chānd. IV.9.3.
86. Kaṭha. I.ii.8.
87. Ibid, I.ii.7.
88. Chānd. VI.14.1-2.

89. The Dialogues of Plato, Trns. B. Jowett, Vol. I, Book VII, 18th Printing, Random House, New York, pp. 774-775.
90. Muṇḍ. I.ii.12, Nirvedam āyāt Can also be translated as 'One should arrive at detachment' or renounce.
91. Ibid, I.ii.12-13. Paul Deussen, Sixty Upaniṣads of the Veda, Trs. V.M. Bedekar and G.B. Palsule, Part II, Motilal Banarsidass, Delhi, 1980, p. 576.
92. Ibid, I.2.13.
93. Ibid, II.ii.2.
94. Ibid, II.ii.3-4.
95. Muṇḍakopaniṣad, Central Chinmaya Trust, Bombay, p. 85.
96. Muṇḍ. II.ii.8-9.
97. Ibid, II.ii.9.
98. Ibid, II.ii.9.
99. Ibid, II.ii.10.
100. This is Sāṃkhya parable also.

     The congress of both these is like that of a lame man and a blind man.
101. Muṇḍ. III. i. 5.
102. Bṛ. II. iv. 5.
103. *Buddhism* :

     (i) naitad Buddhena bhāṣitam

     This is not said (spoken) by the Buddha.

     (ii) avachanam Buddha vachanam

     Not saying is the (eloquent) say of the Buddha

     (iii) paramārtho hi āryaṇām tuṣṇibhāvaḥ

     The best (connoted) meaning for the noble ones is silence.

     Vedānta:

     (iv) śanto ayam ātmā

     This Ātman is quiescent.

     (v) gurostu maunam vyākhyānam śiṣyastu chinna sanśayah

     Silence is the discourse of the preceptor and the disciple has (all) doubts dispelled.
104. Kena. 1.5.

     tad eva Brahmā tvaṁ viddhi nedaṃ yad idam upāsate
105. Ibid, I. 2.
106. The Upaniṣads, Sri Aurobindo Ashram, Pondicherry, 1985, p. 155.

107. The Upaniṣads, Trs. Swami Prabhavananda and Frederick Manchester, A Mentor Religious Classic, New American Library, 1964, p. 31.
108. Kena. II. i.
109. Ibid, III. iv. 1-2.
110. Ibid, III. iv. 2.
111. Ibid, III. 12.
112. Ibid, III 12 tasminn evākāśe
113. Ibid, IV. 8.
114. Ibid, IV. 6. tadvanam

     Note : tadvanam is derived from the words *tasya*, his, and *vanam*, adorable Brahman is *tadvanam nāma*, one to be adored by all beings.
115. Indian Philosophy, Vol. I, George Allen and Unwin Publication, Reprinted in India, 1985, p. 263.

CHAPTER III

Christian Mysticism : The Cloud of Unknowing

The study of the Cloud takes us from Eastern to Western mysticism : More specifically, from Hindu to Christian mysticism. Broadly speaking we could categorise mystical experience along the lines Prof. Zaehner has done in his various books on the subject :

(1) Pantheism or Nature Mysticism (as seen in Rimbaud and several poets).

(2) Monistic Mysticism (Advaita of Śaṅkara).

(3) Theistic Mysticism (as in the Christian tradition, the Bhagavad Gītā, etc.).

We have said enough about (2) that is Monistic mysticism, in the foregoing Chapters. In this Chapter we are concerned with Christian mysticism and with The Cloud of Unknowing, which is a Christian classic on mysticism.

The Advaitin would believe that he has realised the oneness of the Ātman with the Divine Being or Brahman. The question then arises : Does the Advaitin make his claim simply on the basis of an inner contemplative experience? Definitely not. This Ātman-Brahman identification in fact brings together different strands of religious thought and life, a sort of a derivation from the extension of the idea of the Sacred Power implicit in Pre-Upaniṣadic sacrificial ritual. It cannot be said to be something that is thrown up by contemplative experience *alone*, even though this contemplative experience is highly relevant to it. In the same way, the Theistic mystic, in our case the Christian mystic, while thinking that he has achieved a sort of union with God must already have the concept of God, whether as a personal Being, or Creator, or author of revelation, and so on. So when the Christian mystic mentions God as part of his mystical experience, he does not derive this concept from a mere inspection of an interior state, but co-relates that interior state to beliefs which he already has. Later, in the following chapter, we shall notice that these remarks apply to Jewish mysticism also.

These remarks also indicate that some distinction must be made between experience and its interpretation; that a particular tradition must be examined within the genius of that particular tradition. For instance, a mystic reared in a Christian environment and sedulously following the Christian life may have a contemplative experience which he views as a union with God. In other words the complete spirit of his interior quest will enter into the experience. For him the historicity of Jesus is assured by the New Testament and other written records, just as for the Buddhist mystic, *Nirvāṇa* assumes the Truth of the doctrine of rebirth and once attained will free him from further births.

We have in the preceding Chapters examined Hindu and Buddhist mysticism within the Hindu and Buddhist traditions. In the opinion of some writers on mysticism, some creeds have proved more helpful to the mystic than other creeds. This is no doubt true of the Hindu and Buddhist creeds. Both these mystical traditions have arrived at a vast synthesis, because of the Catholocity of their outlook and absence in them of cheap electicism.

Our study of Christian mysticism should, therefore, be in accordance with the genius of Christianity. In other words we have to remain in the axis of the Christian perspective. Incorrect conclusions will be drawn if we judge and assess Christian mysticism by the yardstick and terminology prevalent in Hindu mysticism. Words like "truth," "sin" in Christianity have totally different meanings from those they have in Hinduism. To the Christian truth has a religious sense. To the Hindu it has an extra-religious sense. The words "sin" and "Incarnation" appear frequently in the Hindu scriptures, yet it would be a grave mistake to take them to have the same meaning as they have for the Christian. For instance one thought that is central to the Christian understanding of the CROSS, is that the crucifixion of Jesus Christ was a sacrificial offering of Himself to his Divine Father on behalf of sinful man, as a remedy for man's sin. The Christian believes in original sin. It would be a folly and an error to persuade the Christian to give up the idea of original sin because that idea forms the very basis of his religion and the coming of Christ has direct bearing on it. In Christian mysticism, therefore, words like "SIN" and "Incarnation" are interconnected. Christ came for a definite purpose to rescue mankind from the original sin. Adam and Eve's disobedience polluted mankind and it was necessary for God to send his Son to redeem mankind. Christ had to come and sacrifice himself on the CROSS in order to show the way of establishing a new alliance between man and God. This was done once and for all by Christ. In Christianity thus there is only one incarnation. In fact asking for another incarnation is a sacrilege. The scriptures had foretold of such a coming and by asking for another incarnation the validity of Christ's sacrifice on the CROSS is put in jeopardy. By asking for another incarnation the very foundations of Christian theology is put in doubt. To the Christian the idea of original sin is all important. To rob him of this idea is to rob him of all the beliefs and to leave him destitute.

As opposed to this, Hinduism welcomes many incarnations and makes it the foundation of the Hindu Scriptures. Connected with this is the question of Time. The notion of time is static in Judaic theology (which also includes Christian theology). For the Christian time is created and must have a stop. With the result that man has only one life-time in which to fulfil his destiny. For the Hindu, time is dynamic. He, therefore, has innumerable lives in which to fulfil his destiny. For the Hindu there is neither creation nor stoppage of time.[1] In Māyā, with which it is identified, time functions in infinite fields of consciousness. Whereas on the human plane, the personality does not cease or terminate in history when the incarnated consciousness in a body ceases to exist in death. It repeatedly comes back to earth to work out its Karmas. This constitutes the upward movement of consciousness. Similarly there is in Māyā a downward trend and movement. It is in this that the Divine, stripped of Karma, takes human form with a view to set free those who are enslaved by Karma. This is arrival of incarnations which descend to this world at various periods of history. Such a belief is foreign to Christianity in the same way as the idea of original sin is alien to Hinduism.

Both traditions have "SIN" occurring in their scripture. The idea that God comes to earth to take away sin also occurs with regularity. But the conception of "sin" differs in the two traditions and this exercises a direct influence on the respective mystical traditions. For the Hindu even if sin is a deviation from the path of righteousness it is merely an error which depends on man's awareness of different levels of consciousness. In empirical life there are grades of truth which are viewed from the various levels depending on the awareness of the viewer. This viewing thus becomes relative. So long as the "ego" persists, absolute truth is not realised. The moment "ego" is completely renounced, truth is realised. It is at this stage that truth and reality become one, they become interchangeable. Truth passes into intuition, which is the achievement of the fourth stage of consciousness—the Turīya stage. Technically it can be said : The Eternal Is. Instead of expressing this knowledge in the way the Hindu does, the Christian would use the word "faith" instead of the word "Intuition" and in the ultimate analysis the two words would mean one and the same thing.[2]

If for the Christian redemption from sin is the path towards realisation, for the Hindu it is the removal of ignorance. For the Christian what stands between liberation and man, is sin, for the Hindu it is ignorance. If on the one hand the Christian scriptures repeatedly refer to sin, the Hindu scriptures repeatedly refer to ignorance. For the Christian breach of spiritual authority constitutes Sin. For the Hindu it is *ignorance* of spiritual authority that is the cause of deviation from the path of righteousness.

To conceive more than one incarnation is unthinkable to the Christian. To the Hindu it is natural. In fact it is not unnatural for a Hindu to think of Christ as one of the incarnations. By so doing he does not mix up traditions. In this regard we have the example of Sri Rāmakṛṣṇa, who after his Vedic experience also had the Christian experience without in the least doing violence to the Hindu experience. If we understand this rightly and interpret it dispassionately, we come to the conclusion that Hindu mysticism has the ability to absorb all the good traditions (or atleast all the good in such traditions) of the world. This is not possible for the

Christian. He cannot reach God without the mediation of Christ. Thus for him there is only one way open. For the Hindu there are several paths. The paths shown by Śaṅkara, Rāmānuja, Madhva are equally honoured. And so also the paths shown by others. Even the Buddhist mystical traditions allowed bifurcations. In short, there was considerable toleration shown to the aspirants who set out on their paths of realisation. The path of the Christian mystic on the other hand is hedged in by dogmas and creeds. He pays dearly if he infringes or deviates. The Christian lacks the freedom that the Hindu enjoys in the matters concerning realisation. The reason for the anonymity of the author of The Cloud will perhaps remain a mystery, but some writers on mysticism speculate that the author remained anonymous to avoid censure from the Church authorities.

The latitude given by Hinduism to its mystics is given by no other religious tradition in the world. The least by Christianity and Judaism. Śaṅkara, Rāmānuja and Madhva differed from one another in the interpretation of the Upaniṣads and the Bhagavad Gītā. But not one of them failed to defend these scriptures. The Christian mystic has to work within the framework of Christian dogmas and Church authority.

The highest state the Christian mystic can attain in this life is "Union" or what is technically called "Spiritual marriage." Even this spiritual marriage is not perfect. It is transitory. Perfect union comes about only after death, in Heaven. (In Hindu theology this is one of the ways, represented by Videhamukti). The notion of original sin keeps the Christian mystic away from the final goal, as the possibility of falling into sin again while living on this earth, cannot be ruled out. The Hindu does not believe in original sin and, therefore, can gain his goal while living on this earth. Once "ignorance" has been banished the mystic sees the truth. Alongwith the disappearance of ignorance, relativity also disappears and the possibility of a relapse, as believed by a Christian, does not arise.

Coming back to the conception of incarnation we see that for the Hindu this also explains the theory of Karma. Successive lives afford an opportunity to the soul to work out its Karma. We need not go into the various theories on this subject except to mention that some theories attribute the coming of the incarnation of great mystics for the purpose of vicarious suffering for mankind. Here we notice a very important and significant difference between the two traditions. The mysticism of the Hindu is centred around the *life* of the mystic. How he dies is of little consequence. Rāmakṛṣṇa for instance died of cancer and Sri Kṛṣṇa of an arrow wound. Their deaths are not made central to the issue. In Christian mysticism the way Christ died on the CROSS is of paramount importance.

This brings us to another very important aspect of Christian mysticism. To the Christian, man is the centre of the created universe. Thus the Christian view is anthropocentric. As against this the Hindu view is cosmocentric. Here we come to an area which borders on science. In passing, it can be said that the East has dealt with its mystical phenomena scientifically, inasmuch as person or personality is not viewed as having any intrinsic or durable reality. One of the aspects of science is being totally impersonal and it has to be admitted that the Hindu mysticism is impersonal. If physical nature is the subject of study of Western science the East studies human nature. Physical nature and human nature may as well constitute the outer and inner universes. And what does Eastern mysticism do but study consciousness? In fact a certain "Coldness" in Hindu mysticism can be explained by this scientific approach. The lyricism of Western mysticism is conspicuous by its absence in Hindu mysticism. Vairāgya (detachment or passionlessness) is the key word for Hindu mysticism.

One thing, however, stands out clearly in the Hindu tradition. Though the incarnations are many yet back of them all stands one unique person. Says Kṛṣṇa :

> " Many are the births taken by Me and You, O Arjuna.
>
> I know them all while you know not, O Parantapa."[3]

It is significant that the mystic is not an anarchist. History of mysticism testifies to this fact. The religious tradition in which he is born and reared influences him and rarely, if ever, he departs from it when giving expression to his experience. We shall have much to say on this when we discuss Jewish mysticism. In the meantime a few lines from Evelyn Underhill will illustrate the point :

"Thus St. Teresa interprets her ecstatic apprehension of the Godhead in strictly-Catholic terms, and St. John of the CROSS contrives to harmonise his intense transcendentalism with incarnational and sacramental Christianity. Thus Boehme believed to the last that his explorations of eternity were consistent with the teaching of the Luthern Church. The Sufis were good Mohammedans, Philo and the Kabbalists were orthodox Jews. Plotinus even adapted—though with what difficulty'—the relics of paganism to his doctrine of the Real."[4]

One more quotation from the same author will clinch the point :

"Whether the dogmas of Christianity be or be not accepted on the scientific and historical plane, then, those dogmas are necessary to an adequate description of mystical experience—at least, of the fully developed dynamic mysticism of the West. We must, therefore, be prepared in reading the works of the contemplatives for much strictly denominational language; and shall be wise if we preface the encounter by some consideration of this language, and of its real meaning for those who use and believe it.

"The two chief features of Christian schematic theology are the dogmas of the Trinity and the Incarnation. They correlate and explain each other : forming together, for the Christian, the 'final key' to the riddle of the world."[5]

Many theological and moral criteria were involved in deciding whether or not the mystical God-seeker could find his or her place in the life of the Church. As they directly affect the Christian mystic and as they illustrate vividly the marked difference between the two mystical traditions (Hindu and Christian) we sum them up briefly below.

IN CHRISTIANITY

First, the ontological distinction between God and the Soul has to be left intact. Any hint or suggestion that the mystical union involves a total annihilation of personality or absolute passivity, is to be avoided. Some recognised Christian mystics arguably failed to meet this criterion.

Secondly, the traditional rules of conduct had an over-riding and paramount place. A mystic may never use contemplation as a pretext for disregarding these rules. The mystic is subject to the supervision of his confessor like anybody else and even if he claims to have been given orders by God that run counter to the standard of obedience, it is the rules laid down by the Church that prevail. The mystic is forbidden to make any statements relating the issues of dogmas and he is not entitled to claim a special source of wisdom. If he utters a judgement unacceptable to the Church he has, upon the latter's verdict to retract without hesitation.

Thirdly, a mystic's experience, if genuine, strengthens his common virtues of humility, charity and chastity. Indifference to others or breach of conduct are signs of diabolic temptation. The Hindu mystic will be fully in agreement with this. Spiritual pride has always been distasteful to him. It acts as an obstacle in his effort for realisation.

The historical visissitude of mysticism is not central to our discussion. But in the context of what has been said above we may conclude that the phenomenon of mysticism was much more tolerated by the Church when it flourished in the monasteries where the rules could be enforced easily and where the tendency to comply with the rules was high. When, however, laymen and secular priests took to it, it aroused suspicion. And when it assumed collective shape it attracted condemnation.

In point of fact almost all the traditions with the exception of Hindu tradition, viewed mysticism with distrust. As we shall see later Jewish mysticism gained momentum and thrived during the time of crisis, unlike Hindu mysticism which thrived in time of prosperity (with rare exceptions). History tells us how Sufis and Christian mystics have paid dearly for their audacity. It is not necessary to stress on this point any more.

This is, in short, a comparison between Hindu and Christian mysticism. Before proceeding to the mysticism of The Cloud we shall discuss the chief characteristics of Christian Mysticism. Christian mysticism displays unique features which require to be emphasised. For instance no one will say that Buddha was not a mystic. But writers like W.T. Stace hesitate to give the description of mystic to Jesus Christ, though Stace does not rule out the possibility of Christ having had mystical experience. He writes :

"It is a fair question to ask whether the founder of Christianity was a mystic in the strict sense of having in himself the mystical consciousness and living and speaking out of it as a basis for his teachings and his life, as the Buddha did. Perhaps Jesus was a mystic, but I cannot find that there is any real evidence of it. There is nothing of it in the synoptic gospels. In the Gospel of St. John we find several times repeated certain statements about union with God and onenese with God. In view of the negative evidence of the synoptic gospels, there is no reason to suppose that these phrases were ever uttered by the historical Jesus. Possibly they show that the author of St. John's gospel was a mystic or perhaps no more than that he was familiar with a few mystical phrases.[6] "They show nothing about Jesus."[7] In his The Teachings of the Mystics, Stace writes :

"It is quite possible that he himself had mystical experience, but his use of these phrases does not constitute sufficient evidence of it. We do not have here, as we do in the Upaniṣads, in Plotinus, in Eckhart, in St. Teresa, any sort of specific and detailed descriptions of the mystical consciousness. Christian mysticism, then, does not begin either with Jesus or with the author of the fourth gospel."[8] Prof. J.B. Pratt's comment on this view will throw light on the issue. He says :

"Plotinus' description is obviously based upon his own personal experience; and this experience seems to have been (so far, at least, as we can see) uninfluenced by imitation but quite spontaneous in its nature. As such it set an example for all Neoplatonic mysticism and served as a text for Neoplatonic writers. Through 'Dionysius the Areopagite's and Scotus Erigena, his translator, the torch was passed on into Christianity; so that Plotinus may in some sense be called the father of Christian Mysticism."[9]

The foregoing is a brief comparison between Hindu and Christian mysticism. Only the salient features have been brought out. In order to appreciate this comparison and the differences it has brought forth, and in order to see the whole comparison in its proper perspective it is also necessary to appreciate the historical factors that influenced early Christianity and its mystical tradition. In dealing with this we will restrict ourselves to the mediaeval period to which the Author of The Cloud belonged. We have not made any attempt to pinpoint exact dates, because by and large it is difficult to fix dates, and in any case they do not affect the study of mysticism of The Cloud. Generally speaking, The Cloud is considered to be a 14th Century mystical classic, belonging to mediaeval European Thought. Terms like mediaeval thought are loose terms, as loose as the term modern thought. So we had better let the definition of it alone. It would, however, not be wrong to say that the hegemony of Christianity was not distinctive trait of mediaeval thought. But what characterised mediaeval thought was the tendency of mediaeval thinkers to explain the natural and the human by reference to such tenets of faith as God, creation, the incarnation, employing philosophical and logical arguments to do so. As a result of this, the dependence of reasoning upon the dictates of faith became central to the whole of mediaeval thinking. When discussing Christian mysticism (as we have shown above while comparing Hindu and Christian mysticism), it is very vital to note that the dictates of faith was an ultimate yardstick by which to judge the validity of an argument irrespective of the impeccability of reasoning, it had to conform to the tenets of revelation. Thus for example to deny God's existence, or the creation of the world or the necessity of Grace, was simply to fly in the face of Christian authority. Such philosophical errors were classified as heresy. This only meant that the last word on any question rested with the Church as the final arbiter. Great mystics stopped short of the final step and often used modified language to express their mystical experience in order to conform to the authority of the Church. Eckhart is one such mystic. The author of The Cloud got out of the situation by remaining anonymous. Thus mediaeval Christian thought (Philosophy and mysticism included) was born out of a juxtaposition of faith and reason.

What then were the main sources of mediaeval thought? The main sources were the Bible (both the Old and New Testaments), the philosophy of Greece, Plato, Aristotle, Neoplatonism as it developed in the third and fourth century A.D., Jewish and Arabian thinkers of the 10th, 11th and 12th century A.D. The position very briefly was as under.

Heraclitus on the one hand held that reality was change and Parmenides held it to be stability. We thus find Plato and Aristotle trying to escape from these two alternatives. For Plato there was an ultimate reality of pure unchanging Forms or Ideas and there was the sensible world where everything was transitory. The latter was a pale reflection, a manifestation of the true unchanging structure of the Ideal. The object of knowledge was to penetrate to the universal principles which lay beyond the particular objects. The Forms or Ideas alone provided certainty, they existed in their own right. Their first principle was the Good, the source of all other Forms and the means by which they were known. So far as man was concerned his soul had originally pre-existed as a spiritual substance in which state it had been able to grasp the intelligible directly. Now, however, it could only reach the truth by disentangling it from its material setting in individual things. Accordingly, the way to truth lay in contemplation of the Ideas by which the soul could recover the knowledge that it used to possess. Thus Plato was a good part of the way in seeing an immaterial source of reality. But this did not approach the Christian position; because it accorded no place to a creator. How the Forms came into being was not explained, nor was it explained wither they led. There was merely a timeless process without *raison d'être.* There was no eschatology; the soul itself pre-existed and migrated to different bodies but it never met a last judgement or an eternal life. Thus the most distinctive aspect of Platonism for Christian thought was its approach to reality; its acceptance of the need to transcend this world to reach the ideal and the eternal. B. Jowett in his introduction to the Dialogues of Plato writes :

"Just as for Aristotle, art was not a mere esthetic pleasure, but a purgation of the soul by pity and terror, so, for Plato, philosophy was not merely an intellectual exercise but a cleansing of the mind from error and the freeing of the soul from conceit . . . . ..The highest rapture possible to man is the rapture of the contemplation of the Ideas . . . . . His thought is both technical and mystical."[10]

The student of comparative mysticism will not fail to detect the influence of Hindu mysticism on Plato. In the final analysis, it was this mystical aspect of Plato's philosophy, through the refraction of Neoplatonism, that influenced the author of The Cloud. Contemplation became central to The Cloud. Aristotle could hardly have influenced Christianity directly. Aristotle's

God is not a creator, but a self-contemplating Being, pure actuality, the thought of thoughts, a Thinking Theoria.

When we come to Neo-Platonism, especially Plotinus, we approach the Christian outlook. These philosophers and mystics built up Plato's hierarchy of Forms into a more cohesive structure. If they did not succeed in formulating a theory of creation, they at least saw a procession of being from the One to the lowest spiritual being, the human soul. This they did by translating Plato's Good into ONE. Though it was above being, it was the principle of all existence. But it was above being, immaterial and indefinable. From the self-knowledge of ONE emanated the first Intelligence (The Logos or the word) containing the immaterial Ideas (Plato's forms) of all beings. The Logos in turn gave rise to a Second Intelligence, the World Soul from which individual intelligences were derived, passing down in a hierarchy from intelligence to intelligence until the Moon and the sublunar world was reached. The human soul was the last in the hierarchy of spiritual beings.

Christian thought was from the first greatly influenced by four fundamental Neoplatonic concepts : (a) the hierarchy of spiritual beings or Intelligences (which Christians in their thinking regarded as angels) with God at the summit, (b) the spiritual nature of reality which was accessible to the human soul, (c) the return of the soul to the One through contemplation which enabled it to regain the state it had formerly possessed as an Idea in the Logos and (d) the belief in the goodness and fullness of being. It came from God or the ONE, and, therefore, that which had it in the fullest measure was participating most fully in the One.

The application of Plato, Plotinus and others to Christian revelation was fraught with difficulties. Yet these pagan notions made Christian philosophy and Christian mysticism possible. It was not necessary for our study to point out in detail the difference between the philosophy of the pagans and that of Christianity. In any event philosophy does not play a major role in Christianity. Even mysticism is looked upon with suspicion. One of the reasons for this is that the approach of the mystic to religion is so different from that of the New Testament and left no real place for Jesus Christ as Saviour.

Despite all this the fourteenth century has been called the classical age of mysticism. But there was a great problem faced by the mystics. In Christianity there exists a gulf between God's necessary being and the contingency of all creation. The mystic was, therefore, faced with the problem of finding means by which the created could reach the Divine. For the Greeks as for Śaṅkara there was no difficulty. The Greeks tended to see only a progressive separation of the image from the source. For Śaṅkara it was the removal of ignorance. For the Christian, as for Rāmānuja and Madhva, Grace was the saving factor.

Contemplation and various other disciplines are merely a starting point and cannot claim to reach God. God remains transcendent and it is only by a true condescension on His part that man can be united to Him by Grace. The disparity between the created and Divine was bridged by Grace, which in a way was the measure of this disparity.

Christianity did take over Neoplatonism, but modified it to suit Christian thought. Hence, the part played by reason in Greek thought was different from that played in Christian thought. The Greek could reach truth by reason. The Christian had to temper reason with faith to reach the Truth.

Christian mysticism was thus influenced by Greece. The mysticism of Plotinus was perhaps the most important factor in this. And if this was the case it will also have to be admitted that Christianity was influenced by Hindu thought. Aldous Huxley writes :

"Plotinus was interested in oriental thought and as a young man accompanied the Emperor Gordian's expedition to the East, in order to pick up first hand information on the subject of Persian and Indian Philosophy. His One, Ultimate Reality, which cannot be understood except through a direct mystical experience bears a close resemblance to the Brahman which is also Ātman, the 'That' which is at the same time 'Thou.' During the fourth and fifth centuries, neo-platonism and along with it, at several removes, the most valuable elements of Hindu religion, entered Christianity and became incorporated, as one of a number of oddly heterogeneous elements, into its scheme of thought and devotion."[11]

The mysticism of The Cloud is to be understood and interpreted within the context of what we have stated above.

THE CLOUD OF UNKNOWING

The transition from Hindu to Christian mysticism, from the Upaniṣadic mysticism to the mysticism of The Cloud, may leave us a little confused at the *outset. Inter alia* language is responsible for this confusion. The English language is not as well equipped to express mystical thoughts, as Sanskrit is. The second reason is that Upaniṣadic mysticism is purer as compared with Christian mysticism. This is because the latter has gone through the refractive medium of other cultures, other religions and mysticisms belonging to the traditions of other civilizations.

Christian mysticism, like Christian religion, has been influenced by Greek, Jewish and Arabian philosophy. No evidence exists to show that Upaniṣadic mysticism has been influenced by other civilizations. And finally the former, that is Christian mysticism, has developed under restrictions and fears, from both of which Hindu mysticism was free.

Besides The Cloud, the unknown author wrote a few other books. It is in The Cloud that he expresses "his experiment with Truth" most articulately. Ostensibly the book is written for a twenty-four year old young man intending to take to the contemplative life. The author perhaps intended the book to be a guide for the young man, pointing out to the disciples the difficulties that beset the contemplative life. But it is more likely that this method was used as a literary device, a sort of a frame of reference to get his teaching across. But, as we shall see below, the book is more than a guide. In it are to be found passages that are definitely of a confessional nature.

Complete withdrawal from the world is necessary, if one were to lead a life of a contemplative. Such a rigid qualification would disqualify and also discourage most of the aspirants desiring to embark on a contemplative life. To reassure such people he hastens to add that there are several levels of contemplative life and that withdrawal from the world does not necessarily mean physical withdrawal. What is of paramount importance is psychological withdrawal—what the Vedāntist would refer to as 'detachment.' The whole burden of the Upaniṣads and the Gītā is to insist that man remain unattached to the world—individual entities, objects, relationships—to be completely detached from all these if he aspires to self-realisation.

A life in the monastery has its advantages. But only a microscopic minority can follow it. For the majority of the aspirants what is important is to cultivate a spontaneous love of God. Grace will follow naturally.

We must not forget that The Cloud has to be studied in the context of the mediaeval times. Ritual played a very important role in Christian religion at that time. Despite this, the author of The Cloud does not consider the formal observance of ritual to be of great importance. This did not mean that complete indifference was to be shown to ritual. As we have already seen in the study of the Muṇḍaka Upaniṣad, ritual has its own place in the scheme of things. The Cloud says almost the same thing. He writes :

"Just as the meditations of those who continually labour in this grace and in this work appear suddenly without any preparation, their prayers come in the same way. I mean their own, personal prayers, not the prayers that are ordained by the Holy Church. Those who truly practise this work do not worship by prayer very much. They pray according to the form and the law that has been ordained by the holy fathers before us ; but their special prayers always rise spontaneously to God without having been planned in advance, and without any particular techniques either preceding them or accompanying them."[12]

The framework of the Bible — Jesus, Mary, Moses, Aaron, the doctrines of the Church concerning the nature of God, and so on, is to be used in the initial stages. These are just preliminary teachings — scaffoldings. Once momentum is gained, all dependence on these is left behind. The whole object of the teaching is to lead the disciple beyond theological conceptions and doctrines, and beyond all attachment to religious objects and observances. The following passage sounds as if it has been taken from a book on Vedānta :

"Indeed, if it will be considered courteous and proper to say so, it is of very little value or of no value at all in this work to think about the kindness or the grat worth of God, nor of Our Lady, nor of the saints or angels in Heaven, nor even of the joys in Heaven. It is of no value, that is to say, to hold them intently before your mind as you would do in order to strengthen and increase your purpose. I believe that it would not be helpful at all in accomplishing this work. For, even though it is good to think about the kindness of God, and to love Him and to praise Him for it, nevertheless it is far better to think about His naked being and to praise Him and to love Him for Himself."[13]

The last sentence is significant. The God that is to be sought after is not God as thought of, or God as imagined to be, but as God *is* in His nature. This may appear as an absolute attitude. But it is not so. Here we have a parallel between Advaita and The Cloud. Just as the removal of Ignorance makes a man see that all the time he was Brahman, which he realises he is, once the veil of Ignorance is removed, so also, says The Cloud, union with God *is* in His nature, refers to an experience in which man feels that he is transcending himself. What is actually happening is that man is actually discovering himself *as he is.* He is coming into contact with his own 'naked being.' This in turn makes it possible for him to come into contact with *God* as *He is*. But this is easier said than done. There are certain factors that separate man from his eternal self. Memory is one such factor. Memory has a special meaning for the author of The Cloud. Memory does not mean that faculty or force by which something is remembered. It is for him a dynamic force in the mental make up of man that binds or even roots it in something observed in the past. Memory in this sense becomes the cause of man's attachment to something. It is what Śaṅkara called *Adhyāsa* (also known as Adhyāropa). Śaṅkara called it the apparent recognition of something previously observed in some other thing.[14]

In both Śaṅkara and The Cloud, memory plays a very significant role in keeping the aspirant away from self-realisation. The comparison, of course, is not on all fours. The attachment of memory in the case of The Cloud refers mainly to the individual experience in respect of, say, past pleasure and pain. It may even be a group memory like the attachment to some symbol or doctrine or image. Śaṅkara, on the other hand, would cite the instance of the silver in the mother of pearl or water in the mirage. But in both the instances memory plays the major role and deludes the mind. What the author of The Cloud wants to impress on the disciple is that pleasures, pain (where memory is individual) and symbols, images doctrines (where memory is collective) should not be stopping places on the way to self-realisation. *No attachment* should be shown to them. The most sacred and hallowed things are mere stepping stones to self-realisation. Our goal is God as He is in Himself. Notice :

"Memory is a type of power which, properly speaking, cannot be said to work of itself. Reason and Will, however, are two working powers, and Imagination and Sensuality are two more. All these four powers and their works are contained in memory and are comprehended in it : Other than this we cannot say that the memory works, unless this quality of containing can be called a work."[15]

"Reason and Will are called the principal powers, for they work altogether in the spirit without anything of a physical nature. Imagination and Sensuality are classed as secondary because they work in the body, using the bodily instruments that are called our five senses. Memory is called a principal power because there is contained within it spiritually not only all the other powers but all the things with which they do their work."[16]

A little later the author of The Cloud says :

"Whenever the Memory is occupied with any physical thing, no matter how good the purpose may be, you are beneath yourself in that act and you are outside your soul."[17]

This idea could not be expressed more strongly than in the Zen words : "When you have spoken the name of Buddha, wash your mouth out." It would be puerile to think that these words are sacrilegious. What is sought to be emphasised is that Buddha or Christ are merely symbolic. Attachment to them would prove to be an impediment in the path of Realisation. Spiritual energy which is required to be conserved for the final assault is wasted by outward diffusion.

The author cautions the disciple that the path to self-realisation had side effects which initially may prove to be highly disturbing and even frustrating. His contemplative activity necessitating withdrawal from his environment and cutting him off from contact with fellowmen would lead to distractedness. This distractedness is likely to be interpreted most unfavourably by his fellowmen, referring to him in terms likely to disturb him. A similar state is described by Vedānta while talking about Jīvanmukta. Once the Jīvanmukta has attained self-realisation his contact with the outside world is the minimum required by him to work out the rest of his worldly life — to exhaust the unspent part of his Karma. This misleads his fellowmen, who think of him in unfavourable terms. It is not uncommon to label such Jīvanmuktas as ones who have lost balance of their mind. The distracted condition of the Christian aspirant is no different. However, it is very significant that the Christian mystic after a temporary period during which his distracted condition lasts, returns to normal life to carry on good work in this world. Says the author :

"He would be well able to bring himself into harmony with all those who come into contact with him, whether they are habitual sinners or not; and he would not fall into sin himself. Drawing the admiration of all who saw him, he would be able to lead others by the help of grace to work in the same spirit in which he works himself."[18]

Incidentally, this also has its psychophysical aspect. The withdrawal of psychic ego into the subliminal depths of the unconscious naturally results in very little energy being available for outer life. The result is that the energy available for conventional life is so depleted that the behaviour of the contemplative appears (even is) erratic. This is in fact a spiritio-psychological problem.

CENTRAL DOCTRINES

The little book, The Cloud, has been written in LXXV chapters. Each chapter consists of a few paragraphs. Several chapters consist of just three or four paragraphs. Each paragraph is carefully and lucidly written. No wonder, writers on mysticism consider it to be a mystical classic.

Despite the outspokenness of the author, he is guarded in his choice of expressions and words. He ensures that his language does not flout the tenets of Christianity. In fact in the middle ages no one, mystic or otherwise, would have flouted the Christian tenets with impunity. It would be unthinkable to imagine the author of The Cloud using words like That Art Thou (tat tvam asi). The Hindu mystic never shrank from establishing complete identity between the spark and God Himself. The Christian mystic was cautious. As the Author says, the soul of man could be 'oned with God' but it is not for that reason of the same substance as God. The mystic is 'oned' only in Grace. In nature he is far beneath.

The author of The Cloud, and for that matter any Christian mystic, would not have dared to utter : By knowing Brahman, you become Brahman (Brahmavid brahmaiva bhavati). This Christian attitude has been explained in many ways. One of them is that in the flesh men are not strong enough to bear the plenary experience of God, without physical injury or even death. For the Christian mystic God is not only infinitely desirable, but also infinitely insupportable. For the Hindu mystic, too, beyond a certain limit, Samādhi is fatal to the body.

The author of The Cloud derives his inspiration from Dionysius. For Dionysius human nature is divinised in three ways: Purgation, illumination and union. These three steps were also taught by Plotinus. God is a mystery and can never be fully known by finite man. Both positive and negative statements are made about Him. Dionysius adopted the negative method, wherein the mystic is plunged into the "Darkness of unknowing." Dionysius, like Plotinus, wrote of the union of the soul with God, and of the gradual divinisation (*theosis*) of man. He says that by exercise of mystical contemplation the mystic will rise by 'unknowing' (*agnosia*) towards the union. It was this mystical agnosticism, unknowing, that influenced some writers and mystics, among whom the most prominent is the annonymous author of The Cloud of Unknowing.

Rarely, if ever, does one come across a book on mysticism, so lucidly and systematically written. Besides, the style in which it is written, it has both facility and felicity. At the outset in the Prologue he writes :

"Whoever you may be who comes into possession of this book, whether as your own property or by borrowing, that you neither read it nor write it not permit it to be read, written or spoken by any one who has not, as far as you can judge, a full desire and intention to be a perfect follower of Christ not only in his active life but in the ultimate degree of contemplation to which it is possible to attain by grace in this life by a perfect soul still dwelling in a mortal body."[19]

In this connection Evelyn Underhill writes :

"Nor was this warning a mere expression of literary vanity. If we may judge by the examples of possible misunderstanding against which he is careful to guard himself, the almost tiresome reminders that all his remarks are 'ghostly, not bodily meant,' the standard of intelligence which the author expected from his readers was not high one. He even fears that some 'young presumptuous ghostly disciples' may understand the injunction to 'lift up the heart' in a merely physical manner ; and either 'stare in the stars as if they would be above the moon,' or 'travail their fleshly hearts outrageously in their breasts', in the effort to make literal 'ascensions' to God.''[20]

Of all the 14th century mystics, the author of The Cloud makes the most emphatic distinction between the physical and the spiritual. He follows the negative way of contemplation most rigorously claiming Dionysius as the chief inspiration for his method of contemplative prayer and the only authority he wished to quote :

"It was for this reason that Saint Denis said, 'The best knowledge of God is what is known by unknowing.' Truly, whoever will read Denis' books will find that his words clearly affirm all that I have said or shall say from the beginning of this treatise to the end."[21]

His basic symbol, The Cloud, has been drawn from Dionysius tradition of scriptural exegesis. In this Moses typifies the contemplative and his ascent of Mount Sinai a progressive purification not only from Sin but also from the attachments of the soul to what is not God. When Moses had climbed to the limit of his own powers, his normal consciousness being finite, could comprehend only finite things and, therefore, in itself it formed a barrier to the way to God. It was in the thick cloud at the summit when Moses could see nothing, that God spoke. When further progress is impossible to the human intelligence, the contemplative must be prepared to plunge into the cloud. He clarifies :

"When I speak of darkness, I am referring to a lack of knowing. It is a lack of knowing that includes everything you do not know or else that you have forgotten, whatever is altogether dark for you because you do not see it with your spiritual eye. And for this reason it is not called a cloud of the air but rather a cloud of unknowing that is between you and your God."[22]

The author of The Cloud, however, modified the Dionysian concept by characterising the 'plunge' as an act of 'Grace' and

'Love.' As in Vedānta so in The Cloud, the aim was essentially psychological, to break the chain that bound the individual to the world of his senses and discursive reason, thereby holding him from his external nature. It may be well to remind ourselves that, in The Cloud, 'knowledge' does not carry the meaning it would carry in Vedānta. It should generally be taken to carry the meaning it would convey in common parlance. This is how it should be read in the following passage :

"He accords with our soul in terms of the limits of His Godhead; and our soul accords to Him because of the high worth of our having been created in His image and in His likeness. And He by Himself alone is more than sufficient to fulfil the will and desire of our soul ; and none but He may do so. Our soul by virtue of this transforming grace then becomes altogether capable of comprehending God by love; and this, like knowing an angel or a man's soul, is beyond the comprehension of all man's created powers of knowledge. I mean by knowing and not by loving, and that is why I refer to them here as powers of knowledge, with another main effective power referred to as the loving power."[23]

"With respect to these powers, God is the creator of them. The first is the power of knowledge, and to this, God is incomprehensible. The second is the loving power, and by means of this, God may be comprehended fully by each person. . . . .Whoever has the Grace to see this, see it; for the feeling of this endless bliss, and the contrary is endless pain."[24]

The aspirant must begin his contemplative life in faith, and only in response to a special and unmistakable prompting of grace. This is defined as an activity of the will directed by love, and attainment is shown to be possible through God's condescension to his creation :

"But now you put a question to me asking, 'How shall I think about Him, and what is He?' And to this I can only answer you, 'I do not know.'"[25]

"He may be well loved, but he may not be thought of. He may be reached and held close by means of love, but by means of thought never. And, therefore, even though it is good occasionally to think of the kindness and the great worth of God in particular aspects, and even though it is a joy that is a proper part of contemplation, nevertheless in this work it should be cast down and covered with a cloud of forgetting."[26]

But nothing is loved unless it is first known. There is a close relation between love and knowledge. However, the word knowledge here is not to be taken in the sense to which it is taken in Advaita. There knowledge dawns after Ignorance is destroyed. In Christian mysticism the initiative is always with God. Love is not something that one drums up by personal effort. It is called forth by God who takes the initiative. It is God who is in search of man. But then the aspirant cannot just sit with folded hands, waiting for God's love to fall into his lap.

"You are to strike that thick cloud of unknowing with a sharp dart of longing love; and you are not to retreat no matter what comes to pass."[27]

Thus the cloud symbol recurs throughout, varied sometimes by "darkness" and its meaning accumulates as the work unfolds. It is paradoxically a means of separation and a way of union. At first it connotes a painful state, when the contemplative denies the mind, feelings, their customary satisfaction :

"For, when you begin it, you will find that there is at the start but a darkness ; there is, as it were, a cloud of unknowing. You know not what it is except that you feel in your will a naked intent toward God."[28]

"Try as much as you can to behave as though you are not aware that these thoughts are pressing so strongly upon you between you and your God. Try to look, as it were, over their shoulders, as though you were looking for something else; and this other thing is God enclosed in a *cloud of* unknowing."[29]

This is the method of repression, and inattention, a sort of a tredding down under the cloud of forgetting. But such a thing cannot be done with the vehement effort of the will. Such a vehement and deliberate effort would only end in defeating its own purpose. On the contrary such an effort of the will is likely to strengthen the force of distraction. What is necessary is to turn away gently towards the object of contemplation. Ignore the distractions. Thus deprived of its chief nutrition (attention) the distraction dies of inanition.[30]

But should this method prove ineffective the aspirant should "take but one short word of a single syllable. This is better than two, for shorter it is the better it accords with the work of the spirit. Such a word is the word GOD or the word LOVE. Choose whichever one you prefer, or if you like, choose another that suits your taste, provided that it is of one syllable. And clasp this word tightly in your heart. So that it never leaves it no matter what may happen.[31]

"This word shall be your shield and your spear whether you ride in peace or in war. With this word you shall beat upon the cloud and the darkness, which are above you. With this word you shall strike down thoughts of every kind and drive them beneath the cloud of forgetting."[32]

The Hindus call it a mantra — or word or short phrase constantly repeated so that it fills, so to speak, the whole conscious and subconscious background of the personality, leaving the something that exists in the background, free to beat with its blind stirring of love against the cloud of unknowing.[33]

Aldous Huxley writes :

"The shortest *mantram* is OM a spoken symbol that concentrates within itself the whole Vedānta philosophy. To this and other *mantrams* Hindus attribute a kind of magical power. The repetition of them is a sacramental act, conferring grace *ex opere operato* . . . .. And meanwhile the constant repetition of this word 'GOD' or this word 'LOVE' may, in favourable circumstances, have a profound effect upon the subconscious mind, inducing that selfless one-pointedness of will and thought and feeling, without which the unitive knowledge of God is impossible. Furthermore, it may happen that, if the word is simply repeated, 'all whole, and not broken up or undone,' by discursive analysis, the Fact for which the word stands, will end by presenting itself to the soul in the form of an integral intuition. When this happens, 'the doors of the letters of this word are opened' (to use the language of the Sufis) and the soul passes through into Reality."[34]

The author of The Cloud offers other alternatives. Should the methods suggested so far fail, then yield to the distraction and allow them to swarm over the mind like conquering hordes. In The Cloud is to be found a description of a technique which aims at the exploitation of distraction by acceptance. Man's extremity is God's opportunity, would be the theological way of expressing this fact of self surrender. William James in his lecture on

'Conversion' summarises the position of employing the mind and the relaxing of worry as a means of preparing for the mystical entry of the desired God by 'getting so exhausted with the struggle that we have to stop — so we drop down, give up and *don't care* any longer. Our emotional brain-centres strike work, and we lapse into a temporary apathy. Now there is documentary proof that this state of temporary exhaustion not infrequently forms part of the conversion crisis. So long as the egoistic worry of the sick soul guards the door, the expansive confidence of the soul of faith gains no presence.'"[35]

The Cloud would advise :

"There is another method, and you may test it if you wish. When you feel that you are altogether unable to press down your thoughts, cower beneath them cringing as a coward overcome in battle. Think them that it is foolishness for you to strive any longer with them, and yield yourself, therefore, to God in the hands of your enemies. Regard yourself then as one who has been lost forever."[36]

Rāmānuja would have categorised this attitude as the attitude of self-surrender (*śaraṇāgati*). When man cowers before God in helplessness, it results in meekness.

"And this meakness results in God Himself coming down with great strength to avenge you on your enemies, to raise you up and with loving care dry your spiritual eyes, as the father does to his child about to perish at the mouths of wild beasts."[37]

The author never tires of repeating that in this work, the remembrance of the holiest of things will prove to be a hindrance. Such remembrance is bad for the health of the soul. Mere 'unity' or 'union' and 'marriage' is not enough. What Ira Progoff says in his introduction is illuminating :

"What the author of The *Cloud of Unknowing* seeks is thus not an experience or feeling of unity with God; but rather the establishment of a fact of existence, a condition of life, in which the individual is God —and vice versa—in actuality even if only for the briefest atom of a moment."[38]

THE DARK NIGHT OF THE SOUL

The mystic has to pass through the 'dark night of the soul.' No matter to what tradition he belongs, he cannot escape it. The Cloud, however, does not make a direct reference to it. Unlike many other Christian mystics, the author, from the very outset assumes that God is impersonal. This is perhaps the reason why he makes no mention of any phase of spiritual distress. He is preoccupied with God the Father, rather than God the Son. Aldous Huxley feels that this is the reason why there is no mention of the 'Dark night.'

But as we pointed out above the author does refer to the distracted state in which the mystic finds himself. This distracted state is common to mystics of all traditions, leading to considerable and embarrassing misunderstanding. J.B. Pratt, in his great study, *Religious Consciousness,* has this to say :

"It would be a mistake to suppose that the ecstasy is an experience of mere sweetness . . . . It is, however, a very real and intense joy. This cannot be said of the periods of dryness. The sufferings of the ecstatics during these times are of many sorts. St. John of the Cross classifies them as of three kinds : loss of delight in any creature, the feeling of one's distance from God and the memory of the joy of ecstasy which is no longer to be had, and thirdly inability to 'meditate' or to excite oneself to pious emotion by the use of the imagination. This triad, however, fails to exhaust all the ills reported by many of the mystics during these times of dryness."[39]

Pratt also refers to a mystical classic, Theologia Germanica, written about the same time as The Cloud (14th century) also by an unknown German mystic. It throws much light on the subject of this aspect of spiritual suffering. The unknown author says :

"Christ's soul must needs descend into hell, before it ascended into heaven."[40]

The dark night and what follows could not have been expressed better than by the author of Theologia Germanica when she adds :

"Now God hath not forsaken a man in this hell, but He is laying His hand upon him, that the many may not desire, nor regard anything but the Eternal Good only, and may come to know that this is so noble, and passing good, that none can search out or express its bliss, consolation and joy, peace, rest and satisfaction. And then, when the man neither careth for, nor seeketh, nor desireth, anything but the Eternal Good alone, and seeketh not himself, nor his own things, but the honour of God only, he is made a partaker of all manner of joy, bliss, peace, rest and consolation, and so the man is henceforth in the Kingdom of Heaven."[41]

We have stated above that no mystic, however great, can escape 'The Dark Night.' But there is a marked difference in this regard between the Eastern and Western traditions. The Dark Night, even though it constitutes the most striking stage of the mystical process, its emotional expression, appears by and large, in the Western tradition, where of course, it has taken its name from the evocative phrase of St. John of the Cross. In the Dark Night there is total negation and rejection of the joy of the preceding stage. The person feels totally removed and alienated from his previous experiences and feels very much alone and depressed. So powerful is the purgation that, in the process, the mystic has to purge himself not only of all social attachments, but also of his experiences of self. For this, his will has to be completely extirpated, because, so long as he asserts his will, he will continue to maintain a distance or separateness from what he feels to be the ultimate. The Dark Night thus is a death of everything, not excepting God. The saving hope resides only in grace, with the help of which the mystic can survive the Dark Night. Hence the importance of grace in mysticism. That contemplation is successful which is accompanied by solitude, aridity and the Dark Night. In the Christian tradition we find, for this reason, the desert playing a very important part.

"Then was Jesus led up of the Spirit into the wilderness to be tempted of the devil."[42]

And, "But when it pleased God, who separated me from my mother's womb, and called me by his grace, to reveal his Son in me, that I might preach him among the heathen, immediately I conferred not with flesh and blood; neither went I up to Jerusalem to them which were apostles before me; but I went into Arabia, and returned again unto Damascus."[43]

The geographical desert is the symbol of an attitude of self-emptying and going to God without any illusions. It is an attitude that combines in itself both physical and spiritual poverty. It is an attitude that can attract grace and consequent relief from spiritual distress.

Thus we see that spiritual distress, which has been termed as The Dark Night, can be relieved by grace. The prayer of the Christian mystic was always for being raised by grace to a mystic knowledge of God in contemplation. For him this is a state of simplicity, in which the normal faculties of knowing are stilled, and the mind is consequently dark, in a state of not-knowing. The use of the epithets 'blind,' 'naked' to describe this activity is the central theme of his teaching.

Whether it is Christian or Hindu or Jewish mysticism, God or Brahman is considered to be above all thought. So to contemplate and see Him, we must, like Moses, enter into the darkness of the Cloud. That is, we must shed all the thoughts we have of Him as unworthy of Him, and regard with the eyes of faith the Supreme Being who surpasses all our conception of Him. We shall, a little later, discuss what 'shedding' means. For the present we will talk of the three practices an aspirant should undergo, viz., reading, thinking and praying. He writes :

"There are methods, however, which a student in contemplation may practise, and these are Lesson, Meditation and Orison, or you may call them : Reading, Thinking and Praying."[44]

He adds :

"Reading and hearing are essentially the same : the clergyman reads in books, while illiterate men read by means of the clergyman, when they hear him preach the word of God. But prayer[45] may not be achieved, neither in beginners nor in advanced students, unless thinking comes first."[46]

This is reminiscent of Hindu mysticism :

ātmā vāre śrotavyaḥ

"Till such realisation of the consciousness which is one's own self, it is necessary to practise hearing, reflection, meditation and absorption."[47]

The author writes : (This is again reminiscent of the Upanisads : śrotavyo mantavyo nididhyāsitavyah). "In this context, God's word whether written or spoken may be compared to a mirror. Spiritually, the eyes of your soul are your reason, your consciousness is your spiritual face. And just as it is so that if you have a dirty spot on your physical face your eyes cannot see that spot nor know where it is without a mirror or someone else to tell you; so it is spiritually in the same way that without reading or hearing God's word it is not possible for a soul blinded by habitual sin to see the foul spot upon his consciousness."[48]

There is a certain order in which these practices are to be carried out. This again bears a striking resemblance to the disciplines of Vedānta.

"You can see from this that good thinking cannot be achieved, neither by beginner nor by advanced students, without their first reading and hearing. And, in the same way, praying cannot come before thinking."[49]

But, "with those who continually carry out the work of this book, their meditations come as though they were spontaneous thoughts and unguided feelings concerning their own wretchedness or the goodness of God. They come neither from reading nor from listening, nor are they beholden to any special thing under God."[50]

The author continues :

"These spontaneous thoughts and unguided feelings come to one much more from God than from man. It is not necessary for you ever to have meditated on your wretchedness nor on the goodness of God, assuming that you are a person who is stirred by grace and works with spiritual guidance. It is necessary only that you meditate on the word SIN or on the word GOD, or on any comparable words that you may prefer, not analysing or interpreting them with refinements of learning, but simply considering the qualities of the words with earnest intention of increasing your devotion."[51]

The foregoing two paragraphs are of considerable interest, inasmuch as they state that for those continuously occupied with mysticism, the preliminary steps are not necessary. The mystical experience comes to them spontaneously. All that is necessary is to meditate on words like 'God' or 'Sin'. This again reminds us of 'Aum.' A further condition is imposed : There should be no "analysing or interpretation." Similarly, "Those who truly practise this work do not worship by prayer very much. They pray according to the form and the law that has been ordained by the holy fathers before us; but their special prayers always rise spontaneously to God without having been planned in advance, and without any particular techniques either preceding them or accompanying them." "When these prayers are in words, as they very seldom are, they are only in very few words ; in fact, the fewer the better. Indeed, if it is but a little word of one syllable it seems to me to be better than a word of two syllables or more. This is in accordance with the work of the spirit, for a spiritual worker should always be at the highest and ultimate point of the spirit."[52]

The quotations above illustrate how close the disciplines prescribed by The Cloud come to the disciplines prescribed by Vedānta. Both Christianity and Judaism are more or less institutionalised religions. The prayers recited by devotees are standardised. In many cases these prayers are recited with a ferver that raises them to mystical heights. Prayers in this sense do not exist in the Hindu tradition. So when the author recommends a prayer consisting of "few words" he is departing from the Christian traditional prayer. Here the author has mildly criticised the long and lengthy prayers recited in places of worship. And why does a prayer of one small syllable prove effective? The author answers :

"And why does it pierce heaven, this little short prayer of one small syllable ? Surely because it is prayed with a full spirit, in the height and in the depth, in the length and in the breadth of the spirit of him who prays it. It is in the height, for it is with all the power of the spirit. It is the depth, for in this one little syllable all the knowledge of the spirit is contained. It is in the length, for no matter when it would feel as it does feel it would cry just as it cries. It is in the breadth, for it wills to everyone the same that it will to itself."[53]

In the following paragraph the author says :

"The everlastingness of God is His length. His love is His breadth. His power is His height. And His wisdom in His depth."[54]

Mystical prayer is in a class by itself. Psychology plays such an important part in our lives today that we tend to look upon mystical prayer as a technique, losing sight of the other important aspects. No doubt even in the mediaeval Christian mysticism, technique was not unknown, though it was not so highly developed as in the orient. This technique consisted of emptying the mind of all images as a prerequisite for the development of mystical prayer. The prayer recommended by the author was no doubt revolutionary when viewed from the Church's point of view. The author somehow feels that his prayer is unacceptable to the theologians. What we have to remember, however, is that what the author had in mind while recommending the prayer was that it requires a metaphysical background. Also a theological background. The postulant using such a prayer should not only have a mastery over the words he is using in his prayer but should know what ends to use them for. There is a faint hint at this in The Cloud. Prolonged repetition aims at the exhaustion of the ego; such an effort wears out the ego, pulverises it, and its place is taken by divine reason. This is similar to the study of the Koan in Zen. Simply emptying the mind of thoughts and images is of no use, is even dangerous, unless that same mind is filled with a very special love of God.

UNION

And this brings us to the question of union. Throughout The Cloud the author is preoccupied with a 'oneing exercise,' an exercise in seeking union with God. How is this union to be effected? The argument, strikingly, is similar to that used by the Advaitist. The Advaitist advises the removal of ignorance. The Christian advises the removal of all that is not-God. Both, in principle, are one and the same thing. For the Christian, not-God is the superfluous material surrounding God.[55] Plotinus used the illustration of a statue to explain this. (Ennead 1.6.9) : "Withdraw into yourself, and if you do not find yourself beautiful as yet, do as does the sculptor of a statue . . . cut away all that is excessive, straighten all that is crooked, bring light to all that is shadowed . . . do not cease until there shall shine out on you the Godlike splendour, until you see the Final Goodness surely established in the stainless Shrine."[56]

What is this 'union'? This is a problematic question common to all mysticism. Generally speaking the most distinctive characteristic of Christian mysticism is Grace. The second such characteristic is drawn from the states of union. Grace we have already discussed from time to time. It is, therefore, worthwhile to examine the problem of union as it is understood within the framework of the Christian tradition.

At the outset we should get one thing clear. Within the Christian tradition, the doctrine of union absolutely excludes all substantial unification between the Divine Being as such, and the human being as such, and vice versa. That is, never, in any event can the substance of the mystic himself become the substance of God. Christianity also rules out the tendency to conceive the union as a sort of an annihilation. Like Hinduism, Christianity too gives examples of glowing iron, or air illumined by the Sun or drop of water diluted in wine. What actually takes place in union, the mystic argues, is transformation and *not* abolition of the creature. If the transformation seems to be an abolition, it is, to the mystic, merely an appearance.

What then is the nature of this union ? The Christian mystic would reply : While respecting the distinction between Divine Substance and human substance, between the Will of God and the will of man, there is a perfect accord—a coincidence of two substances and two wills. They coincide with such perfection that one is a perfect image of the other. The author of The Cloud mentions a 'loving union.' This means that the concurrence of wills is bound together by love. In other words, this unity results rather from concurrence than from the union of essence. The will of one substance coincides with the will of the other. Union, therefore, is this accord, the metaphysical gulf between the two being bridged by love. The only union conceivable is thus a unity of spirit. There is no identity of substance but an accord of their structure and lives. In both Christian and Jewish mysticism this is expressed by the word 'likeness,' that is resemblance. Both God and man thus maintain their identity without being diminished in any manner. Aldous Huxley commenting on The Cloud writes :

"Man's final end, the purpose of his existence, is to love, know and be united with the immanent and transcendent Godhead. And this identification of self with spiritual not-self can be achieved only by 'dying to' selfness and living to spirit."[57] Huxley adds a few pages later :

"The third, best and hardest way is that which leads to the divine Ground simultaneously in the perceiver and in that which is perceived."[58]

Ecstasies are *not* union. They have physical and psychical accretions that exclude them from the scope of union. Evelyn Underhill writes : In Ecstasy "the contemplative, losing all consciousness of the phenomenal world, is caught up to a brief and immediate enjoyment of the Divine Vision . . . They cannot, therefore, be regarded as exclusively characteristic of the Unitive way .... Union must be looked upon as the true goal of mystical growth, that permanent establishment of life upon transcendent levels of reality, of which ecstasies give a foretaste to the soul."[59]

'Union' is a concept peculiar to Christian mysticism. It can never be applied to Hindu mysticism. R.C. Zaehner brings out this fact as follows :

"A distinction must be drawn between the Christian experience in which the individual soul is united or 'oned' with God, to use the expression of *The Cloud of Unknowing*, and the Vedāntin experience which is one of absolute identity with Brahman— 'I am Brahman' and 'What thou art, that am I'."[60]

The difference is not merely of terminology, but real. Zaehner remarks :

"Are we entitled to class the experience of the *Advaita*, that is, the strictly non-dualist, Vedāntins as mystical? The difficulty is that in this case it is not strictly proper to speak of union at all; for according to the proposition 'I am Brahman,' which means that I am the sole unqualifiable Absolute, One without a second, I cannot logically speak of being united to Brahman, since I am already He (or It)."[61]

We shall see later while dealing with Kabbalah, that in Jewish mysticism, too, on an ultimate level, there is no plurality. And if there is no plurality then we are also one with God. But what is to be borne in mind is that union is to be interpreted within the framework of each tradition. For the author of The Cloud the union is spiritual, that is, the mystic can become one with God in spirit. He writes :

"You are beneath your God. And why is that ? It is true that in a sense you and God at this time are not two but are one in spirit. In fact, you are any other person who by such an act of unification has reached the perfection of the work may certainly on the testimony of Scriptures be called a God. But you are beneath God all the same. The reason is that He is God by nature without beginning. You on the other hand, were nothing at all at one time and after you had been made into something by His might and His love, you wilfully with sin made yourself worse than nothing. And now only by His mercy and not because of your merit you are made a God in grace, united with Him in spirit without separation, both here and in the bliss of Heaven without any end. Thus it is that although you are completely one with Him in grace, you are nevertheless very far beneath Him in nature."[62]

What conclusion can we draw from all this discussion? We can say that when the Christian mystic talks of 'union' he implies that the union does not involve identity but some kind of relation like resemblance. Hence among the Christian mystics (we have repeatedly noticed this in The Cloud) words like 'darkness,' "nakedness,' are frequently used : In darkness distinctions disappear, 'Nakedness' is the absence of adornment and so on. In this context W.T. Stace's remarks are significant. He writes :

"The almost universal use of these negative metaphors among Christian mystics points to the fact that their experience is always an undifferentiated unity although most of them prefer to use concrete metaphors rather than the literal abstract description."[63]

Elsewhere in the same book, Stace describes 'union' as "a theistic interpretation of the undifferentiated unity."[64]

Therefore, no general conclusion can be drawn. Mystics, with rare exceptions, are not philosophers or metaphysicians who analyse concepts. So, in Christian mysticism we have to be satisfied with the interpretation that union with God is the coincidence of the will of the individual with the Divine Will.

In our discussion of the various traditions we have hardly, if ever, allowed religion to intrude upon mysticism. Judged by this standard The Cloud represents Christian mystical teaching at its best. In its short span it covers every aspect of Christian mysticism, maintaining at the same time an undercurrent of Christian balance. In the fourteenth century when The Cloud was written, a comparative study would have caused a stir, perhaps a misunderstanding. But today anthologies on mysticism include extracts of The Cloud, that rub shoulders with the Upaniṣads, the Vedānta, Zen and the Kabbalah. Truth remains Truth, no matter in what traditional language it is expressed.

REFERENCES

1. Time am I to those who reckon and measure.
   kālaḥ kalayatām aham (B.G.X. 30).
   I alone am the imperishable time.
   aham evā' kṣayaḥ kālo (B.G.X. 33).

2. *Note* : There have been many apostles of Intuition. Germany's P.H. Jacobi (1743-1819) sometimes known as "faith-philosopher" was a great advocate of intuition. Says William Earnest Hocking : "It seemed to him that the unaided intellect must necessarily lead to atheism and fatalism, because in its own nature it can only deal with finite and partial objects, putting them into systematic connection, but is unable to get the raw material of truth, particularly the truth about the whole of things. A God who could be proved would be no God at all : for intellectual knowledge is a sort of mastery or taking possession, and the Supreme Being cannot be thus mastered. Metaphysical truth must be reached, not by the 'Mediate' knowledge of ideas, but by immediate perception. Jacobi called this direct knowledge *Glaube* (faith). It is what we mean by intuition'. Types of Philosophy, Charles, Scribner's Sons, New York, 1930, p. 185.
3. bahūni me vyatītāni
   janm ̄ani tava c ̄a' rjuna
   tāny ahaṁ veda sarvāṇi
   na tva ṁvettha para ṁtapa (B.G. IV. 5).
4. Mysticism, Methuen and Co. Ltd., 1967, p. 96.
5. Ibid, p. 107.
6. "I and my Father are one," "He who has seen me has seen the Father.' etc.
7. Mysticism and Philosophy, Macmillan; 1972, p. 342.
8. A Mentor Book, 1960, p. 125.
9. The Religious Consciousness, Note 2, The Macmillan Co., 1951, New York, p. 365.
10. Jowett, Vol. I, Random House, New York, pp. X/XI.
11. Aldous Huxley, Grey Eminence, Heron Books, London, pp. 58-59.
12. The Cloud of Unknowing, translated by Ira Progoff, A Delta Book, New York, 1978, Chap. XXXVII (1).
13. Ibid, Chapter V/3.
14. Smṛti rūpah paratra pūrva dṛṣṭāvabhāsah.
15. Ibid, Chapter LXIII (1).

    Note : The term 'memory' is used here in a sense that is much more extensive than in modern usage. It refers to the dynamic quality of the conscious mind as a whole. The direct source of this conception is St. Augustine and a close equivalent to it in modern philosophy would be the *memoire* of Henri Bergson

(Note by the translator, Ira Progoff). Dynamism characterised Bergson's Philosophy.

16. Ibid, Chapter LXIII/4.
17. Ibid, Chapter LXVII/2.
18. Ibid, Chapter LIV/2.
19. Ibid, Prologue, p. 53.
20. The Cloud of Unknowing, John M. Watkins, London, 1912, pp. 15-16, Edited from the British Museum Mss. Hare, 674.

    Quotations are all from The Cloud of Unknowing, translated by Ira Progoff, unless otherwise specified.
21. Ibid, Chapter LXX/6.
22. Ibid, Chapter IV/18.
23. Ibid, Chapter IV/5.
24. Ibid, Chapter IV/6.
25. Ibid, Chapter VI/1.
26. Ibid, Chapter VI/3.
27. Ibid, Chapter VI/4.
28. Ibid, Chapter III/4.
29. Ibid, Chapter XXXII/2.
30. *Notes* : (i) Patañjali recommends positive helpful thoughts to counter thoughts hostile to self-realisation. This is reminiscent of the doctrine, *contraria contraris curantur*. An impure thought, for instance, is to be countered with thoughts of chastity, anger with kindness.

    "To be free from thoughts that distract one from Yoga, thoughts of an opposite kind must be cultivated" (2/33).

    (How to Know God, The Yoga Aphorisms of Patañjalī, translated by Swami Prabhavananda and Christopher Isherwood, New American Library, 1953, p. 101.

    (ii) vitarka bādhane pratipakṣabhāvanam

    "The trouble arising from doubt is the most dangerous of the obstacles that bar the road of concentration."

    (Mircea Eliade, Immortality and Freedom, Bollingen Series, Princeton, 1969, p. 51).

    Mircea Eliade translates the word "vitarka" as 'doubt,' 'uncertainty,' and not as 'guilty thoughts,' as some translators do.

    tasya v̄achakah pra ṇavah

    tajjapa ḥtadarha bh̄avanam

    Kolhatkar comments thus :

We should repeat the word 'OM' which is the symbol of God, that is, we should pronounce the word correctly. One should feel that God who is symbolised as 'OM' resides in one's heart as the internal regulator and, therefore, one should feel that 'oneself' and God are not different but one and the same.

Bharatiya Manas-Shastra, Yoga-Darshan,

Keshav Bhikaji Dhavale, 3rd Edition, p. 81.

31. Chapter VII/7.
32. Chapter VII/8.
33. *Notes* : (I) This can be compared to the Oṁkāra Japa of Hindus. What is significant is that there is no special requirement for the use of this mystical technique. Constant repetition of the word without adding any speculation regarding it, is all that is called for. It is, however, necessary to repeat the word with meditation upon its meaning.

"OM (Aum) is the (symbolic) sound of God."

"By meditating on the meaning of God, one should repeat that symbol OM." (Patañjali Yoga, I/27-28).

(II) 'Ekāgratā,' continuous single pointed concentration is another method. In this the diffused attention is brought together and integrated. A diffused mind is a mind that is circumscribed by Time and Space, cause — effect. Such a mind cannot reach the Absolute. It is a mind that goes out into objects, things and persons. Unless all these are shut out, *ekāgratā* is not possible. Hence commenting on 'ekāgratā' Mircea Eliade writes :

"The immediate result of *ekāgratā,* concentration on a single point, is prompt and lucid censorship of all the distractions and automatisms that dominate — or, properly speaking, *compose,* profane consciousness."

(Immortality and Freedom, Bollingen Series, Princeton, New York, 1973).

34. Perennial Philosophy, Chatto and Windus, London, 1946, pp. 319-320.
35. The Varieties of Religious Experience. The Modern Library, New York, 1929, p. 208.

Note : The Yoga gives us the first discipline for 'Citta Vṛitti Nirodha' the method abhyāsavairāgyābhyām tannirodhaḥ 'This is difficult.' Well, Iśvara praṇidhānād vā or aṣṭāngayoga or maitri karuṇā mudita upekṣā etc.

36. The Cloud of Unknowing, Chapter XXXII/3.
37. Ibid, Chapter XXXII/4.

38. The Cloud of Unknowing, p. 37.
39. Pṛatt, The Macmillan Company, New York, 1951, pp. 431-432.
40. Translated by Susanna Winkworth, Stuart and Watkins, London, 1966, p. 50.
41. Ibid. p. 51.
42. Mathew, 4 : 1.
43. St. Paul : Epistle : Galatians I : 15-17.
44. Cloud, XXXV/1.
45. *Note* : "Prayer was a recognised vehicle for speculative enquiry. Augustine had begun one of his first philosophical works, the *Soliloquia,* with a prayer." (Peter Brown, Augustine of Hippo, Faber Paper covered, 1968, p. 166)
46. Cloud, XXXV/2.
47. śravaṇa manana nididhyāsana samādhyanuṣthānam (181) Vedānta-Sāra of Sadānanda, Advaita Ashrama, Calcutta, 1987, p. 105.
48. Cloud, XXXV/3.
49. Ibid, XXXV/4.
50. Ibid, XXXVI/1.
51. Ibid, XXXVI/2.
52. Ibid, XXXVII/1-2.
53. Ibid, XXXVIII/1.
54. Ibid, XXXVIII/2.
55. Something like ignorance veiling Brahman.
56. Quoted from The Mystical Theology of Dionysius the Areopagite, Pub. Shrine of Wisdom, London, 1923, p. 8.
57. The Perennial Philosophy, Chatto and Windus, London, 1946, p. 48.
58. Ibid, p. 69.
59. Mysticism, Methuen and Co. Ltd., London, 1967, p. 170.
60. Mysticism, Sacred and Profane, Oxford University Press, London, 1961, p. 33.
61. Ibid, p. 32.
62. The Cloud, LXVII/6.
63. Mysticism and Philosophy, Macmillan, London, 1972, p. 100.
64. Ibid, p. 104.

CHAPTER IV

Kabbalistic (Jewish) Mysticism

"O taste and see that the lord is good."— Psalm 34(8)

In the foregoing chapters we have already discussed the characteristics of mysticism. In this chapter we are concerned with the nature of Jewish mysticism. In general it can be stated that Jewish mysticism is that form of the Jewish religion which like the mysticism of other religions seeks especially to foster personal communion between the worshipper and God. There is a peculiar intensity, which on occasions rises to ecstasy giving to it a dynamic form which is not present in ordinary religion. There are two aspects of this mysticism. The practical or devotional and speculative or intellectual. The former relies on prayer. The latter on Jewish religious philosophy which inquires into the relationship between God and the universe. But there is an important difference between the two approaches. The one is intuitional, the other logical. The one proceeds from the known to the unknown. The other, being intuitional, visualises the unknown by means of some inner insight granted only to the mystic ; and works from that to the known.

At the outset we quote Gershom Scholem, from his famous book, Major Trends in Jewish Mysticism. This quotation from a great scholar of the Kabbalah and Jewish Mysticism clarifies the Jewish way of looking at mysticism :

"The point I should like to make is this—that there is no such thing as mysticism in the abstract, that is to say, a phenomenon or experience which has no particular relation to other religious phenomena. There is no mysticism as such, there is only the mysticism of a particular religious system, Christian, Islamic,

Jewish mysticism and so on. That there remains a common characteristic it would be absurd to deny."[1]

Reduced to simple terms this means that the mystic is not a religious anarchist but a faithful adherent of his religion. Religious adherence is thus central to Jewish mysticism.

Secondly, if by mysticism is meant a direct and immediate union with God, then there is *no* Jewish mysticism within the framework of Jewish tradition. If, however, we define mysticism as knowledge or experience of Divine matters, then many and various forms of Jewish mysticism exist in all their nuances. Scholem writes :

"Jewish mysticism in its various forms represents an attempt to interpret the religious values of Judaism in terms of mystical values. It concentrates upon the idea of the living God who manifests himself in the acts of Creation, Revelation and Redemption. Pushed to its extreme, the mystical meditation on this idea gives birth to the conception of a sphere, a whole realm of divinity, which underlies the world of our sense-data and which is present and active in all that exists. This is the meaning of what the Kabbalists call the world of the 'Sefirot'. "[2]

Literally, Kabbalah stands for the Jewish mystical tradition in general and in particular, the system whose classical text is the Zohar. The Zohar is the fundamental book of Jewish Kabbalah. The Zohar is in form a commentary on the Pentateuch. (The first five books of the Old Testament). Legend has it that it (the Zohar) is a record of discourses carried out between Rabbi Simon ben Yohai, who lived in the second century of the common era and certain contemporary Jewish mystical exegetes. With the mystical literature as ancient as the Zohar or Upaniṣads, legends are bound to spring up. However, modern Jewish scholarship has brushed aside these legends. They consider the Zohar to be a well knitted anthology of texts, extracts and fragments, of texts of mystical literature. But two things distinguish these extracts :

1. Their anonymity
2. These extracts resemble one another in their approach to the mystical interpretation of the Pentateuch.

Another distinguishing feature is that the extracts are both Jewish and non-Jewish. They cover several centuries. The sacredness of the Zohar lies in the fact that it mirrors Judaism as an intensely vital religion of the spirit. Like the Upaniṣads it appeals because, even more than the Bible, it gives them a conviction of an inner unseen spiritual universe. But in the final analysis, the Zohar professes to be more than a commentary on the Pentateuch. It purports to show that the Bible is not a simple narrative and ordinary words. Commentaries are interspersed with quotations from the Psalms. It is not necessary for us to discuss the Zohar. A specimen will suffice.

Psalm XXXIII (6) says :

"By the word of the Lord were the heavens made and all the host of them by the breath of his mouth."

Here for instance "By the word of the Lord" would refer to Genesis l(6) : "And God said, Let there be a firmament in the midst of the waters."

"Host of them" refers to Sun, Moon and Stars.

Such a verse gives rise to a whole series of mystic axioms to show that the world rests on Divine spirit. "The upper universe"resembles "the lower universe" and both find their unity in God. Earth is a copy of Heaven. Heaven a copy of earth. In other words, they constitute not a duality but an absolute unity. We could sum up by saying that the Zohar attempts to combine in one single concept the transcendent and the immanent aspect of the Deity. This brings us to the Kabbalah.

The historical aspect does not concern us except insofar as it is incidental to the context. It may, however, be clarified at the outset that whenever use of the word theosophy is made it is to be taken to mean that which was generally meant before it came to mean a modern pseudo-religion. It should be taken to mean a mystical doctrine which purports to describe the mysterious workings of the Divinity. It is in this sense that theosophy is to be taken in the following quotation from Scholem :

"Theosophy postulates a kind of divine emanation whereby God, abandoning his self-contained repose, awakens to mysterious life; further it maintains that the mysteries of creation reflect the pulsation of this divine life. Theosophists in this sense were Jacob Boehme and William Blake, to mention two famous Christian mystics."[3]

It is this theosophical concept of God that influenced Kabbalah and Kabbalists. Divine emanation forms the very basis of Kabbalah. The approximate term for 'emanations' would be "sefirot." The word sefirot (singular Sefirah) has several other meanings like "spheres" or "regions." It even means "numbers." However, as mystical terminology evolved, the term went on acquiring new meaning, till it came to mean the birth or emergence of divine powers and emanations. It is in this sense we shall use it. To start with we shall use the chart below.

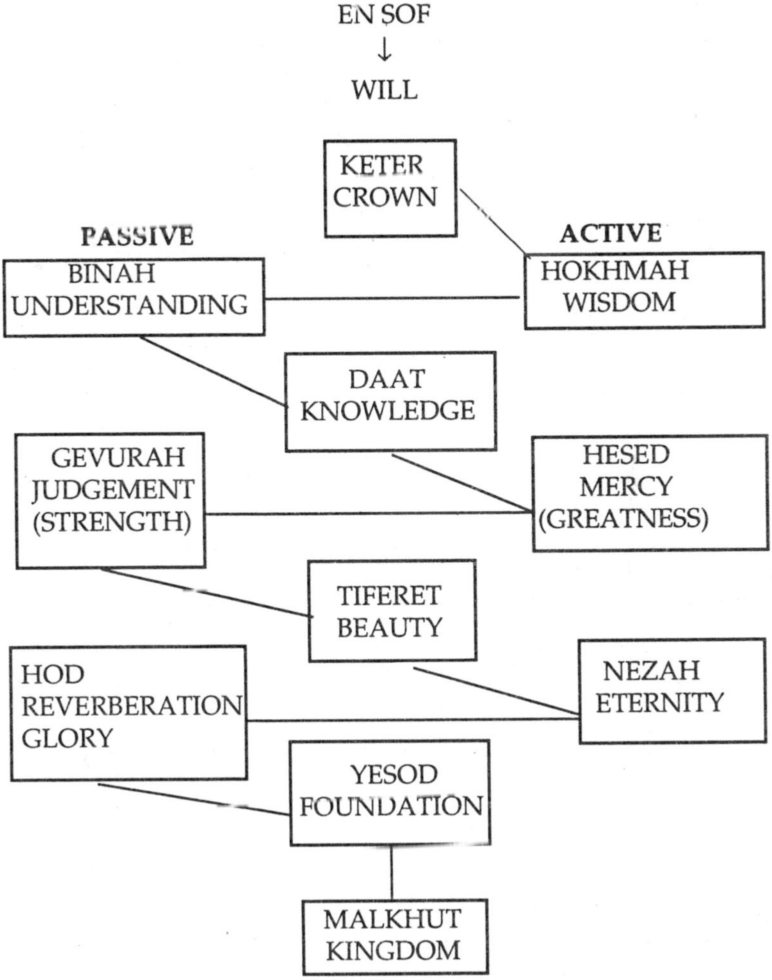

The Kabbalists make a distinction between God as He is in Himself and God as He becomes manifest to His creatures, between *deus absconditus* and *deus revelatus*. For the Kabbalists God is revealed to others through the 'instruments' or 'powers' which emanated from Him, the Ten Sefirot. God as He is in Himself is called En Sof, that which is without limit. The Kabbalists make every effort to avoid the faintest suggestion of a dualistic doctrine. The concept of two Gods (as in Gnostic theories) one hidden, the other revealed is repugnant to them. *En Sof* and the Sefirot, the Kabbalists insist are one. They also stress the impersonal nature of *En Sof*.[4]

We will now discuss briefly the Ten Sefirot. The Kabbalists' picture of the divine totality as an emanated fulness of Ten Sefirot is reminiscent of the Gnostic System. *Inter alia*, the Gnostic system consists of hundreds of divine *aeons* or powers, the Kabbalistic world of Sefirot is reduced to a manageable ten. That there are some points of resemblance between the two cannot be ruled out. In a sentence it could be stated that in Gnosticism direct contact with the godhead may be impossible, but the soul reaches out through a series of intermediaries, dieties, demi-urges, or other celestial beings. The notion of the cosmos as a series of descending emanations from a divine source is a familiar neo-platonic motif. It would be absurd to deny the influence of neo-platonism on the Kabbalah, though the statement that the doctrine of Sefirot is a combination of Gnostic and neo-platonic motifs, will have to be accepted with some modifications. The cosmos as a hierarchical structure of successive emanations is neo-platonic part : But the idea that this emanated cosmos is divine or, to be more exact, constitutes the fulness of the divine realm and that the entities making it up are divine forces, is thoroughly Gnostic. Will Durant has put this admirably and succinctly. He says :

"Jewish mysticism is as old as the Jews. It received influences from the Zoroastrian dualism of darkness and light, from the neo-platonist substitution of emanation for creation, from the neo-pythagorean mysticism of number, from Gnostic theosophies of Syria and Egypt, from the apocrypha of early Christianity, from poets and mystics of India, Islam, and the mediaeval Church. But its basic sources were in the Jewish mentality and tradition themselves."[5]

For the present we will let the matter rest here and proceed to the Ten Sefirot. The Kabbalists were not interested in an absolutely abstract approach to the concept of divine unity. This gave rise to the doctrine of *En Sof* and the Sefirot. God as He is in Himself, is *En Sof* (That which is without limit). This aspect is entirely unknown and unknowable. But God in manifestation, God as He reveals Himself to others, emerges from concealment in ten emanations known as *Sefirot*. The Ten Sefirot are :

1. *Keter*, 'Crown,' the divine will to create.
2. *Hokhmah*, 'wisdom,' in which all God's creative activity is contained potentially (*potentia*).
3. *Binah*, 'Understanding,' the unfolding in the divine mind of the details of creation.
4. *Hesed*, 'Loving Kindness,' the divine goodness in its uncontrolled flow.
5. *Gevurah*, 'Power,' the divine judgment which arrests the flow of loving kindness so that creation can endure and not be engulfed in the splendour of the divine grace.
6. *Tiferet*, 'Beauty,' the harmonising principle affecting the necessary balance between Hesed and Gevurah.
7. *Nezah*, 'Victory.'
8. *Hod*, 'Splendour,' the two supporting principles.
9. *Yesod*, 'Foundation,' the generative principle.
10. *Malkhut*, 'Sovereignty,' the governing principle, the prototype of God's rule over his creatures. Malkhut is called 'The Shekhinah.'

Man by his deeds can influence the highest worlds and help to bring down the flow of divine grace, if he is virtuous. When this happens there is harmony and balance in the Sefirotic realm. Otherwise the Shekhinah is in exile. In and outside the Kabbalah, the Shekhinah occupies a very important place in Judaism. Malkhut is the complement to 'Keter' the crown. In it, so to say, the Divine Lightening Flash is earthed. It constitutes the Shekhinah, the presence of God in matter. To put it in philosophical terms, the Shekhinah is the presence and immanence of God in the whole of creation. It is the point where man, in attaining the deepest understanding of his own self becomes aware of the presence of God. If the emanations are considered as a tree, then the Shekhinah's nature is four-fold encapsulating the four levels inherent within the tree as a whole (the root, trunk, branch and fruit as it grows down into existence). In ourselves the four levels of Malkhut appear as body with its traditional four elements : earth, water, air and fire : the solids, liquids, gases and radiations whose interactions keep us alive.

CLEARING THE GROUND

Before proceeding to discuss each Sefirah and its interrelation, let us examine briefly what does not fall within the purview of Jewish Kabbalah. There is no book of the Kabbalah, no manuscript called 'The Kabbalah,' in the sense in which there are The Upaniṣads, The Vedas or Bhagavad Gītā. In either case the mystical element has to be extracted by the scholars and saints. The exoteric side is there for them to see. The esoteric side is to be extracted. If a definition of the Kabbalah is to be attempted it can be said that the many manuscripts and books written upon the Kabbalistic knowledge are known collectively as the Kabbalah. Hinduism being broad based, in which there is no demarcating line between religion and mysticism, a separate term for collective mystical knowledge was not necessary. Looked at from practically any angle, in Hinduism, one stumbles upon mystical thoughts everywhere. The Kabbalists too see mysticism in The Torah. It forms the basis of the Kabbalah. But unlike Hinduism, Judaism separates mysticism from religion, in the same way as Christianity and Islam separate mysticism from religion.

Unfortunately when one talks of origins one tends to forget that all cosmic Truth could have had no actual beginning, but must be as eternal as Truth. Truth can never change. There were always men who knew such doctrines and they were continually giving them out to the world in different lands at different epochs as required—sometimes in one form and at other times in another, but ever it was the same Truth. Truth is eternal for it is the means of manifesting the knowledge stored up in the memory of Nature—in the collective unconscious of mankind.

But there must have been a time when the wisdom was first promulgated. When were these Kabbalistic doctrines, for instance, first given out to the world? Can history take us back far enough into the time stream? The answer could hardly be in the affirmative. Hidden away in ancient writings and monuments and temples all over the world, in Sanskrit, Greek, Hebrew, Latin and Chinese we see illustrations of esoteric knowledge waiting to be untangled. Suffice to say that the Zohar is attributed to Simeon ben Yochai who lived at the time of the destruction of the Second Temple (See Note).[6] The Kabbalah is not a book. It is Jewish mysticism containing the teachings of the Zohar.

Kabbalah is often referred to as magic. This word is apt to be misleading. Magic can be both 'white' and 'black.' Kabbalah is also of two types : Theoretical and Practical. Here again there is room for misunderstanding. The view is likely to be taken that practical Kabbalah means putting into action. Theoretical Kabbalah, in the same way as Sāṃkhya and Yoga, are sometimes treated as theoretical and practical sides of the same system. Yoga mostly accepts the metaphysics and epistemology of Sāṃkhya. We could define practical Kabbalah in Kabbalistic parlance as simply magic (as distinct from black magic which uses demonic powers and delves into sinister regions). Though there is no religious ban on magic meaning practical Kabbalah, it is not approved, inasmuch as it makes use of names and incantations, which are not approved methods. Numerous theurgic, magical and superstitious practices clustered around practical Kabbalah.

Generally speaking practical Kabbalah stressed the wonder working powers of controlling nature through a knowledge of the names and functions of angels; speculative or theoretical Kabbalah held that all things exist as a result of ten emanations which graduate from God to the universe and serve as mediators. In the lower reaches of all mysticism the aspirant is likely to succumb to his feeling of power acquired by meditative contemplation of Holy Names, by sliding imperceptibly and insensibly into unsavoury magical practices aimed at external objects. They thus expect from the inward path the power to change the outer world. All aspirants are cautioned to guard against succumbing to this temptation.[7]

Thus the chief aim of true mysticism is to be completely detached. In Patañjali once *Citta Vṛtti Nirodha* is achieved, paradoxically the desire/craving/yearning for it must also be given up. The higher religious traditions, especially those of

Hinduism and Buddhism are explicit in stressing the need to be completely detached. The moral is that those who identify themselves with anything outside their true self or soul, will be shattered as life cruelly, yet beneficially, takes away from them all false objects of attachment and identification. Kabbalah does not lag behind Hinduism or Buddhism. As practical Kabbalah does not stand this test, it is excluded from Kabbalah proper. Of course this does not detract from the merit practical Kabbalah may otherwise possess.

Similarly, what came to be known as Christian Kabbalah, is also excluded from Kabbalah or Jewish mysticism. Beginning with late 15th century a movement arose in certain Christian circles (of mystical and theosophical persuasion) which tried to harmonise Kabbalah doctrines with Christianity. What they tried to demonstrate was that the Kabbalah doctrines actually pointed in the Christian direction. One of the reasons for this was the Christian speculation of a number of Jewish converts in the 13th century upto their expulsion from Spain.

A lot of literature was produced on the subject and Christian Kabbalah occupied not an unimportant place in the Christian world. For instance in 17th century Christian Kabbalah received impetus from the theosophical writings of the great mystic Boehme. "If," says Boehme, "thou conceivest a small minute circle, as small as a grain of mustard seed, yet the Heart of God is wholly and perfectly therein : and if thou art born in God, then there is in thyself (in the circle of thy life) the whole Heart of God undivided."[8]

Underhill tersely comments : "The idea of Immanence has seldom been more beautifully expressed."[9]

Jewish scholars, as they participated in the intellectual life of Europe could no longer withhold the Kabbalah from their Gentile Colleagues. Christian Kabbalah was primarily concerned with the development of certain religious and philosophical ideas for their own sake. If the desire to evangelize among Jews was at all present, it was negligible. In fact even this negligible activity was to justify a pursuit which was otherwise suspect in many eyes. It could be termed as a sort of facade. But in the course of time the knowledge, which formed the basis of their Kabbalah, from the Jewish sources, diminished among the Christian Kabbalists, with the result that the Jewish element diminished. In the place of the original Christian Kabbalah, esoteric and Christian speculation far removed from Jewish motifs appeared. Besides this, conversion became rampant. Judaism, like Hinduism, is not a religion given to proselytizing. There was no quarrel with Christian scholarship, which was sometimes of a very high order. But with major divergences in thinking, it could hardly be possible that Christian Kabbalah could form part of Jewish Kabbalah.

And finally occultism does not form part of Kabbalah. Irrespective of the merits or demerits of occultism, it neither forms part of the Kabbalah in particular nor mysticism in general. Unfortunately, more than any other subject, Kabbalah has been made use of in occultism and black magic, in the West. In their writings on the Kabbalah the French and English occultists have added nothing to the advancement and understanding of the Kabbalah. Excepting books written by Dion Fortune and some others like her, authors like Eliphas Levi (actually Alphonso Luis Constance 1810-1875) and Aleister Crowley (1875-1946), have written books wherein they have distorted facts. Despite his genius, Aleister Crowley who acquired an unsavoury reputation has rightly been ignored by the scholars of Jewish Kabbalah. In fact, Dion Fortune was at pains to declare in her book[10] that she was never associated with Aleister Crowley, though she quotes from his books.

In our study we exclude what falls within the purview of the above, except for incidental references. We now turn to the central issue, The Sefirot.

THE SEFIROT

Neo-Platonist influence is seen in several modes of mystical traditions. In Kabbalah, however, it does not function, as in the philosophy of Plotinus and his successors, primarily as an explanation of the process, whereby the wholly spiritual One is linked through a series of intermediaries to the multiplicity of the material world. Emanation in Kabbalah is intended rather to describe the emergence of God out of his concealed state as *Ayin* or nothingness into the *pleroma* or plentitude of Divine Being. The *alam ha-azilut* or world of emanation is divinity itself conceived as an organism consisting of the ten interrelated Sefirot, which are aspects or manifestations of God's self-revelation of his moral and intellectual character. Some Jewish scholars did not accept this view and even showed their dissatisfaction vehemently. Some raised the perennial problem of how could a perfect God produce an imperfect and incomplete world. As a matter of fact the question of the origin and nature of evil was one of the principal motivating forces behind Kabbalistic speculation. In the importance attached to it lies one of the basic differences between Kabbalistic doctrine and Jewish Philosophy, which gave little original thought to the problem of evil. Various Kabbalistic solutions were proffered. One of them was the conventional neoplatonist position that evil has no objective reality and is merely relative. (Reminiscent of Śaṅkara and Advaita). Man is unable to receive all the influx from the Sefirot, and it is this inadequacy which is the origin of evil which has, therefore, only a negative reality.

The determining factor is the estrangement of created things from their source of emanation, a separation which leads to manifestations of what appears to us to be the power of evil. On the other hand the Sefirah Gevurah is categorised as the left hand of the Holy one and as an attribute whose name is evil and which has many offshoots in the forces of judgement, the constricting and limiting powers in the universe. The existence of evil is a very major problem in Kabbalistic speculation. We shall, therefore, revert to it later while dealing with the respective Sefirah. We may, however, observe that 'evil' as part of 'sin' forms a very major problem in Christianity, though, there the problem is tackled by religion and philosophy not by mysticism as in Judaism.

How the Infinite could bring forth the finite without a damaging subtraction from Himself is again not a new problem, both to mysticism and religion. In Advaita, as we have seen Śaṅkara distinguishes two kinds of knowledge and truth, the lower, conventional, practical, relative knowledge and truth (*vyāvahārika satya*) and the higher, absolute knowledge and truth (*pāramārthika satya*). The lower knowledge is the product of the senses and intellect. It is the knowledge of the changing, finite objective world of our empirical experience. It is the knowledge of the world of appearance. On the other hand the higher knowledge is non-perceptual, non-conceptual and, therefore, non-propositional. It is the knowledge of Brahman. But this does not mean that the former knowledge is false. Such knowledge is perfectly valid in the realm of phenomena. A lower truth is not false. It is merely conditioned by other truths. It is not absolute Truth. Just as the advaitists postulated two levels, the Kabbalists went back to the Boundless (*En Sof*). From Him, as light springs from a Sun, proceeded various emanations called the Ten Sefirot. Upaniṣads, too, speak of emanation[11]—for yathorṇābhiḥ sṛjate gṛhṇate ca—even as a thread comes out of navel of a spider, and is withdrawn, so does the universe emanate and return to the Brahman.

For the Kabbalist as for the Advaitist "knowledge is power," but in the transcendent scheme of things there is no greater power than being one's *self*. If it is false power, disconnected from one's essence, then all that we touch, as in the King Midas myth, turns to meaningless gold, incapable of sustenance.

The diagram[12] shows *En Sof* (also written Ein Sof, Ayin Sof) at the top. It is not a Sefirah. The diagram should not give the impression that the Sefirot flowed from *En Sof* automatically. Such a view could be too simplistic. Views on the emanation theory swung from one point to another. Some scholars held that the Kabbalah was a pure emanation system, which they considered to be identical with the pantheistic approach. This means that in the opinion of the scholars emanation was the going forth of the substance of God and not simply the power of the emanation. Other scholars claimed that the Zohar and early Kabbalah in general contained nothing of the theory of emanation. They believed in the free creation of primaeval substance *ex nihilo*. In fact they interpreted *ex nihilo* literally. Without going into the merits of the former view, it can be stated that Pantheism is against the very genius of Judaism. Taking the second view first, it should be clear to the students of philosophy, that the trend of philosophical thinking the world around, both modern and ancient, has not favoured *creatio ex nihilo*. Even orientalists cannot accept what is probably the greatest objection to *creatio*, if it is taken, as we think it must, to mean some alteration in the being of God. A very peculiar situation arises. If whatever is considered ultimate, be it God or space, etc. changes, what would cause the alteration? An ultimate, after all, is introduced to give final intelligibility to all observed change. Both these views were not acceptable to the Kabbalists, for the simple reason that early Kabbalists needed a theoretical foundation in the building of which it was largely influenced by neo-platonism. So, though it proposes a definite process of emanation,—(the theory of the emanation of Sefirot)—this was the kind of activity which took place within the Divine itself. In this connection we quote : "The God who manifests Himself in his Sefirot is, the very same God of traditional religious belief, and consequently, despite all the complexities such an idea involves, the emanation of the *Sefirot* is a process within God Himself. The hidden God in the aspect of *En Sof* and the God manifested in the emanation of Sefirot are one and the same, viewed from two different angles."[13]

EN SOF

We begin by reviewing briefly the background for the Theory of Emanation of the Ten Sefirot. *En Sof* is central to Kabbalah as Brahman is central to Advaita. As we shall see a little later, the similarity is striking. Z'ev ben Shimon Halevi writes thus on *En Sof* : "In Kabbalah, God the Transcendent is called *AYIN*. AYIN means in Hebrew 'No-Thing,' for God is beyond Existence. AYIN is neither below nor above; not is it in movement or in stillness. There is nowhere AYIN is. God is absolute Nothing. (Infinite, unlimited boundless, indestructible undecaying).

"AYIN SOF means 'Without End.' This is the title of God Who is everywhere. AYIN SOF is the One to the Zero of AYIN. This is the totality of what is and is not. AYIN SOF is God the Immanent, the Absolute All. AYIN SOF has no Attributes, because they can manifest only within existence and existence is finite."[14]

The glossary of the Zohar defines *En Sof* as "That of which nothing can be predicated and which yet must be postulated."[15]

These definitions are more or less like attempting a definition of Brahman. Over the centuries the mystics of all traditions have used such language. In the abstract one can think of God Himself, that is, God with reference to His own nature alone. But God can also be thought of in His relation to His creation. Most Kabbalists are agreed on both these views, but they hold that no religious knowledge, even of the most exalted kind can be gained without contemplation of the relation of God to creation. The reason for this is that God in Himself (that is in His abstract Essence) lies beyond ecstatic or speculative contemplation. The relation, in other words, with creation, is of paramount importance. In this respect the Kabbalistic view comes very close to neo-platonism. For the Kabbalist, therefore, there was an unknowable aspect. It was to put into words this unknowable aspect of the Divine that early Kabbalists of Provence and Spain coined a term, *En Sof*. From the outset there were divergent views on the interpretation of the term. The views were reminiscent of the views on 'Brahman.' While discussing *En Sof* the feeling cannot be suppressed that Brahman is being discussed. At best the terms used for describing are negative, very often confusing and contradictory. But where a concept like Brahman or *En Sof* is concerned this is unavoidable. *En Sof* is absolute perfection without distinction and without differentiation. It is not possible to know it directly but only through creation by deduction. *En Sof* is often identified with Aristotelian "cause of all causes" or with neo-platonism as "root of all roots." The way of describing in apparently categorical terms carries also at the same time overtones of negativism. *Deus absconditus* cannot be an object of religious thought. In Judaism, as also in Islam and Christianity, such a concept would be repugnant and invite the wrath of constituted authority. The Kabbalists are ever on guard against the faintest hint of anything approaching the idea that any but God is in control of the universe, that there are two Gods, one hidden, one revealed (as in Gnostic theories). *En Sof* and the *Sefirot*, the Kabbalists hold are One. How this is possible remains for them a profound mystery. (We are faced with this problem also while defining *Brahman*).

But where the practice of religion was concerned positive affirmations are helpful. Hence positive attributes are permissible in speaking of God as He makes Himself manifest and these are provided by the doctrine of the *Sefirot*. It was permissible to ascribe even emotions and not alone acts to God in manifestation. But of God as He is in Himself, of *En Sof*, not even negative attributes are allowed. The distinction is no longer between two types of attributes but between two aspects of Deity.

Despite this we find that there were some attempts to use positive expressions to designate *En Sof* as Nine Lights of Thought that shine from the Divine Thought. This brought *En Sof* out of its concealment into the humbler level of emanation.

The Zohar is the chief spokesman on this. However, the technical language used in it makes it difficult reading. The translators have, therefore, in anticipation of this difficulty, added a clarification. We quote :

"One of the most characteristic ideas of the *Zohar* is that God, while essentially one, is yet found, in various grades or degrees. These 'grades' turn out on examination to be degrees of creative power, arranged in descending or ascending order according to the sphere in which each one functions and the stage of development which it postulates in the created universe, and which thus constitutes, so to speak, its 'opposite number.' Thus the highest grade corresponds to sheer nothingness, and the lowest grade to the conscious soul of man (*the neshamah*). The creative power in itself is conceived as 'thought,' which in the process of creation becomes 'light' or 'illumination.' The primal light is utterly beyond human (or even angelic) comprehension.

"But as the grades descend the 'lights' (which form, as it were, a vestment to one another) swim into human ken, until between the lowest grade and the conscious soul of man, a close communion is established."[16] Writing further : "The first grade — the 'Most Mysterious and Recondite'— indistinguishable from the '*En Sof* '(limitless, uncharacterisable), and corresponding to absolute nothingness in the work of creation — is not directly mentioned in the scripture, unless it is alluded to by the letter *beth* (= in) of the word *bereshith,* implying that it went, so to speak, into itself, and so made, a start. This start consists in a 'flash'(Z*ohar*), which thus releases the creative powers of the 'limitless' ."[17]

The question arises : Is there a necessity for *En Sof* to emerge from concealment? In other words, as a consequence of the essence of *En Sof,* does a necessity for emergence exist? The Kabbalist says that the decision to emerge was free and did not depend on the essence of *En Sof.* It is a free decision, which cannot be explained and, therefore, remains a mystery. Most Kabbalists feel that the question of the ultimate motivation of creation is not a legitimate one. The assertion that God revealed Himself in order to exhibit the measure of his goodness, is merely an expedient. Gershom Scholem writes :

"These first outward steps, as a result of which Divinity becomes accessible to the contemplative probings of the

Kabbalist take place within God Himself and do not leave the category of the Divine."[18] As in other religious traditions there was difference of views with regard to the first step. Scholem continues :

"The first problem, which from the start elicited different answers, was whether the first step was one toward the outer world at all, or rather a step inward, a withdrawal of *En Sof* into the depths of itself. Early Kabbalists adopted the former view which led them to a theory of emanations close to the neo-platonic, although not absolutely identical with it. But Lurianic Kabbalah, which took the latter position, speaks not only of a return of created things to their source in God, but also of a return (*regressus*) of God into the depths of Himself preceding creation, a process identifiable with that of emanation only by means of interpreting it as a mere figure of speech."[19]

The concepts that are most often associated with the description of the first step are mainly two : Will and Thought. Both the concepts of Will and Thought form a very profound part of Kabbalah, because both have important bearing on the Sefirot. In some parts of the Kabbalah, *En Sof* + Will = Infinite Will and their joint manifestation in the first Sefirah is called the "Holy Ancient One." Some Kabbalists accorded sole status to Thought, thereby emphasising the intellectual rather than the volitional creational process. Besides these two concepts about the first step in the manifestation of *En Sof* was the concept of *Ayin* ('Nothingness'). To the student of Hinduism this is not a new concept. In fact mysticism of the higher religions have, at one time or another, been confronted by this concept. Once the human intellectual power reaches its capacity, it had to confess that there is a realm beyond which it cannot proceed and has, therefore, to label it 'Nothingness'. Of course this would appear to be a very simple way of explaining such a complicated concept. This apart, for Kabbalah this theory carried great importance because it is a transformation of the *Creatio ex nihilo*. It runs contrary to it. They are reminiscent of the famous words of The Chāndogya Upaniṣad: "He said, 'O good looking one, by what logic can existence verily come out of non-existence? But surely, O good looking one, in the beginning all this was Existence, One only, without a second."[20] In the very next verse we have : "That (Existence) saw, 'I shall become many'. "[21] It contemplated, It thought "Let me be many, Let me procreate."

Let us now proceed to discuss the three concepts referred to above : WILL, THOUGHT and NOTHINGNESS.

THE WILL AND THOUGHT

The early Kabbalists considered the Divine will as that aspect of Divine Essence which alone was active in creation. It was implanted there by the power of *En Sof*. The final aim of prayer was thus communication with this Supreme Will, because it was the source of life.

Another concept basic to the problem of first emanation was Thought : some Kabbalists allotted to Thought a status above Will. Thought was sometimes referred to as Pure Thought to distinguish it from human thought. An analogy could be drawn here :

"Brahman is vijñāna (consciousness or intelligence) and Bliss."[22]

Unless the Self is ever-conscious, such perception as "I am the knower" can never arise. The apparent consciousness of the phenomenal objects, is in reality, the reflected consciousness of Brahman.[23] These two themes represented the volitional and intellectual acts of creation. It is not necessary for us to go into the historical development of these theories. It could, however, be mentioned that at one stage 'they'were considered identical. But a third concept, considered more daring in Kabbalistic speculation was the concept of Nothingness (*Ayin*). G. Scholem writes :

"Essentially, this nothingness is the barrier confronting the human intellectual faculty when it reaches the limits of its capacity. In other words, it is a subjective statement affirming that here is a realm which no created being can intellectually comprehend, and which, therefore, can only be defined as 'nothingness.' This idea is associated also with its opposite concept, namely, that since in reality there is no differentiation in God's first step toward manifestation, this step cannot be defined in any qualitative manner and, can thus, only be described as 'nothingness.' *En Sof* which turns toward creation manifests itself, therefore, as *ayin ha-gamur* ('complete nothingness') or, in another version : 'God who is called *En Sof* in respect of Himself is called

Ayin, in respect of His first self-revelation."[24] This statement is reminiscent of Advaita's Brahman and Iśvara. No doubt the comparison is not on all fours, but the echo, however faint, is unmistakable. What is striking is the fact that there is an all out effort to keep the source of manifestation intact, notwithstanding any contradiction or paradox in the process : There should be no damage or subtraction as a result of the emanation. We quote a line which perhaps symbolises the whole Upaniṣadic thought. Had the Kabbalist a language like Sanskrit at his command, he would have expressed the concept of the first emanation in similar words :

"From the whole when the whole is negated, what remains is again the whole."[25]

We discussed this line when we dealt with mysticism of the Īśā. For the Kabbalist, as for the Advaitist, it is of paramount importance to defend the integrity of the whole. There are, as we have seen before and as we shall continue to notice from time to time, psychological reasons *also* for this. In fact, metaphysical concepts are *not possessed* but the concept *possesses*. The mystic is jealous of his concepts and ensures that no harm comes to the Absolute. But are we to brush aside such concepts because they cannot stand the arbitrary tests prescribed by empiricists ? Carl Jung, one of the greatest psychologists of this century writes : There is, he says, "the strange supposition that a thing is true only if it presents itself as a *physical* fact . . . . Physical is not the only criterion of truth; there are also *psychic* truths which can neither be explained nor proved nor contested in any physical way. If, for instance, a general belief existed that the river Rhine had at one time flowed backwards from its mouth to its source, then this belief would in itself be a fact even though such an assertion, physically understood, would be deemed utterly incredible. Beliefs of this kind are psychic facts which cannot be contested and need no proof.

"Religious statements are of this type. They refer without exception to things that cannot be established as physical facts. If they did not do this, they would inevitably fall into the category of the natural sciences . . . . The fact that religious statements frequently conflict with observed physical phenomena proves that in contrast to physical perception the spirit is autonomous, and that psychic experience is to a certain extent independent of physical data. The psyche is an autonomous factor, and religious statements are psychic confessions which in the last resort are based on unconscious, i.e., on transcendental processes. These processes are not accessible to physical perception but demonstrate their existence through the confessions of the psyche. The resultant statements are filtered through the medium of human consciousness; that is to say, they are given visible forms which in their turn are subject to manifold influences from within and without. That is why whenever we speak of religious contents, we move in a world of images that point to something ineffable."[26]

This fairly long quotation raises one or two vital questions. We cannot deal with them at length. But what concerns us is : Do we know how clear or unclear our concepts are? Taking the concept of 'God' in general, we give expression to a concept which has undergone change in the course of time. Can we say with any degree of certainty the extent to which it has changed? Admitting for a moment that it has undergone change, the question is whether there is a change in the concept or image of God or the unknowable itself. We are faced with the following two alternatives :

(1) We can imagine God as vital energy which eternally flows and changes shape endlessly.

(2) We can imagine an eternally unmoved and unchangeable essence.

Looking at this position rationally we find that we can be somewhat sure of one thing and that is, that our reason is capable of manipulating ideas and images which are dependent on human imagination. It is for this reason that these ideas and images have changed in the course of their long history : But when we look at these changes and examine these ideas and images, we find a striking similarity. The religious statements over a period of ages and across geographical regions do not vary much, nor do they exhibit much change. Carl Jung would explain this similarity by saying "no doubt (that) there is something behind these images that transcends consciousness and operates in such a way that the statements do not vary limitlessly and chaotically but clearly all relate to a few basic principles or archetypes. These, like the psyche itself, or like matter, are unknowable as such. All we can do is to construct models of them which we know to be inadequate, a fact which is confirmed again and again by religious statements."[27]

Here we have the Jungian theory that every unconscious was in one way or another somehow linked with every other. All human beings have in common a set of deep rooted motivational and behavioural patterns carried over from generation to generation which form a part of our evolutionary heritage. Jung called this the Archetype. *En Sof*, therefore, (as also Brahman) and also the Vedas, scriptures, could in the final analysis, belong to this collective unconscious. We can draw two tentative conclusions from the foregoing discussion :

(a) It can *only* be assumed that the *En Sof* remains intact after the first emanation, in the same way as the Brahman remains after the appearance of the phenomenal world.

(b) We can also presume that ultimately these concepts can be traced back to a common source, the collective unconscious. Here we could qualify the statement by adding that there could be a collective unconscious for *each* nation or region, say India, Africa, Europe and so on.

This (b) calls for an explanation lest it be taken to be too simplistic. It should be borne in mind that the archetype corresponds to the parent word, or to the flexible mould. In other words it corresponds *not* to the actual manifestation, as produced by any particular culture. Yet it underlies all manifestations produced by all cultures. The nearest we could come to this is the thing-in-itself. This will always escape precise definition. In this behalf we will let Jung speak for himself :

"Again and again I encounter the mistaken notion that an archetype is determined in regard to its content. In other words, that it is a kind of unconscious idea (if such an expression be permissible). It is necessary to point out once more that archetypes are not determined as regards their content, but only as regards their form, and then only to a very limited degree. A primordial image is determined as to its content only when it has become conscious and is, therefore, filled out with the material of conscious experience."[28]

We thus inherit a predisposition, not an idea, a predisposition to create significant myths. And myths form a very vital part of mysticism. We are not concerned with the theories of Jung except insofar as they pertain to our subject. The mythical character of Kabbalistic theology is most clearly manifested in the doctrine of the ten *Sefirot*, the potencies and modes of action of the living God. God emerges from his ineffable Being and hiddenness to stand before us as the creator. "The stages of this process can be followed in an infinite abundance of images and symbols, each relating to a particular aspect of God. But these images in which God is manifested are nothing other than the primordial images of all being. What constitutes the special mythical structure of the Kabbalistic complex of symbols is the restriction of the infinitely many aspects under which God can be known to ten fundamental categories, or whatever we may wish to call the conception underlying the notion of the *Sefirot*. In the *Book of Creation*, where the term originates, it means the ten *archetypal* numbers (from *safar* to count)."[29]

As we have already stated before the concepts of *En Sof*, Brahman, in the ultimate analysis cannot escape the archetype. It is precisely for this reason that at some stage psychology has to be brought in, in the study of religion and mysticism. Psychology helps in explaining concepts which are not amenable to the standards prescribed by logic.

It is common knowledge that certain psychological schools make use of comparisons between the most varied types of civilisations to gain a better understanding of the structure of the psyche. It is for this reason that we need to have a good knowledge of the religious values of other cultures and to look at ourselves as others see us. In this regard it becomes very interesting and instructive to see how India for instance viewed Nothingness. We would not be far wrong if we state that Being and Non-being is a speciality of Indian thought. India has never given philosophic importance to History, inasmuch as its preoccupation was with Being. History was just a form of Non-being, as it was created by becoming. But in the immediate sense of the words, the world is not a mirage or illusion. In fact "Māyā" could be referred to as an image — formula representing an ontological unreality of the world and human experience. Being ontological both the world and human experience do not participate in absolute being. None-the-less both exist in Time. In his perpetual optimism the Hindu thinks that if not tomorrow, a hundred million years hence, these two will cease to exist. In such thinking consists the Māyā, which ultimately represents a special kind of experience of non-being and Nothingness. The European, the Christian, and to a certain extent the Jew, rest content with the discovery of evil in this world and the futility of it all. He adopts, what the psychologist would call the pessimistic attitude. The Hindu on the other hand, having come to grips with the dialectic of Māyā (which includes evil, etc.) tries to deliver himself from it. Herein lies the difference between the Hindu and the Western world. Herein also lies a very major difference between the Hindu way of thinking and the European (both Christian and Jewish) in regard to salvation. To the Christian it is life everlasting : For the Hindu it is a state of being that does not last at all. Time itself is transcended.

Having said this we will proceed to discuss the problem of evil, which constitutes a major problem for Kabbalah as also for the Hindu tradition.

THE PROBLEM OF EVIL

The problem of evil forms an integral part of Kabbalah. While Christianity had the original sin to fall back upon, and Advaita, explained that the world and everything in it was phenomenal and that once the veil of ignorance was removed, Evil with all that it implies would disappear, the Kabbalist had to rely on the theory of emanation to explain Evil. In other words, the problem of Evil was made a part of Jewish mysticism. Herein lies, in a way, its uniqueness. In fact, Kabbalah speculation made Evil part and parcel of the process of creation. Back of Kabbalistic speculation acting as a principal motivating force was the question of the origin and nature of Evil. While the philosophers of other traditions gave due importance to the problem of Evil, Jewish philosophy accorded to it a short shrift.

We will not go into the long history of the problem. We shall only discuss two or three positions that pertain to our study. The moral view, for instance does not concern us. One of the views is that evil has no objective reality and is merely relative—clearly a neo-platonic position. The Kabbalist explains this position i.e.

relativity, by saying that man is unable to receive the complete influx of the *Sefirot.* This deficiency in the capacity to receive is the cause of the relative Position and of evil. The shortfall in the receipt of the full influx of the *Sefirot* causes a separation between man and his source, giving rise to a manifestation which is termed the power of evil, but this power has no metaphysical reality. In other words, it has no existence outside the 'structure' of the *Sefirot.* It is associated with *Sefirah Gevurah.* It is the left hand of the Holy One. Its offshoots are in judgement. Judgement is the power that limits and constricts in the universe. There is, as we have said before, a balance among the *Sefirot.* This balance is likely to be disturbed. We quote Scholem : "The doctrine gradually developed which saw the source of evil in the superabundant growth of the power of judgement, which was made possible by the substantification and separation of the attribute of judgement from its customary union with the attribute of loving kindness. Pure judgement, untempered by any mitigating admixture, produced from within itself the *Sitra ahra* ('the other side'), just as a vessel which is filled to overflowing spills its superfluous liquid on the ground. This *Sitra ahra,* the domain of dark emanations and demonic powers, is henceforth no longer an organic part of the World of Holiness and the *Sefirot.* Though it emerged from one of the attributes of God, it cannot be an essential part of Him."[30]

The Zohar has allotted a Sefirah to each day of creation. Turning to the opening verses of the Genesis we read :

"And God said, Let there be light and there was light. And God saw the light, *that it was good* . . . . and the evening and the morning were the first day. And God said, Let there be a firmament in the midst of the waters, and let it divide the waters from the waters . . . . And God called the firmament Heaven. And the evening and the morning were the Second Day."[31]

The story of creation proceeds in this manner. In the creation of all the six days, *except the second day,* God found that it was good. This is very vividly explained as under :

"The material of creation was of two qualities, and correspondingly the product was of two qualities. From the 'spirit of God hovering over the waters' issued light, characterised as 'good,' and forming the content of the first day under the aegis of the divine attribute of *Hesed* (kindness or mercy), from the 'darkness on the face of the deep,' issued the firmament, *not* characterised as good, and forming the content of the second day under the aegis of the divine attribute of *Gevurah* (force, or rigor). Though luminous in itself, the firmament is dark by the side of the primordial light; and the fact that the formula 'God saw that it was good' is omitted from the account of the second day may be taken as a sign that the work of that day was not devoid of evil."[32]

There will perhaps be other explanations for the omission of the formula 'it was good' in the creation of the second day. But we will not go into that. It can only be observed that from the point of view of the Zohar the omission is significant especially when "it was good" appears for the first, third, fourth, fifth and sixth day.

Several theories were propounded to explain the problem of Evil. The more important among them revolved around *En Sof.* Just as in Advaita Brahman is the frame of reference in explaining the accretions of problems, so also *En Sof* is the frame of reference in Kabbalah. For instance the implications in the Zohar are that evil was the result of the left overs of the worlds that were destroyed. Perhaps the most famous is that which is associated with The Tree of Knowledge and the Tree of Life. Notice : "Of every tree of the garden thou mayest freely eat : but of the tree of the knowledge of good and evil, thou shalt not eat of it : for in the day that thou eatest thereof thou shalt surely die.[33]

Eve is tempted by the serpent. He tells her that it is forbidden because God knows "that in the day ye eat thereof, then your eyes shall be opened, and ye shall be as Gods, knowing good and evil."[34]

Adam and Eve eat, their eyes are opened and they know for the first time that they are naked. God expels them from the garden of Eden. God then sets an angel with a flaming sword at the gates of Paradise to guard.

"So he drove out the man; and he placed at the east of the garden of Eden Cherubims, and a flaming sword which turned every way to keep the way of the tree of life."[35]

By eating of the Tree of Knowledge, Adam gave substance to Evil. The Gerona Kabbalists explained that it came about in this manner. G. Scholem writes :

"The Tree of Life and the Tree of Knowledge were bound together in perfect harmony until Adam came and separated them, thereby giving substance to evil, which had been contained within the Tree of Knowledge of Good and Evil and was now materialised in the evil instinct (Yezer ha-ra). It was Adam, therefore, who activated the potential evil concealed within the Tree of Knowledge by separating the two trees, and also by separating the Tree of Knowledge from its fruit, which was now detached from its source. This event is called metaphorically 'the cutting of the shoots' (*kizzuz-ha-neti'ot*), and is the archetype of all the great sins mentioned in the Bible, whose common denominator was the introduction of division into the divine unity."[36]

Evil was, according to the foregoing passage, the result of separation — Separation of the Tree of Life from the Tree of Knowledge and the separation of the fruit from the Tree of Knowledge. Unity forms the very basis of man's aspirations. Any disturbance leads to disharmony. In Kabbalistic terms the Tree of Knowledge contains the power of judgement and the Tree of Life contains loving kindness. With the separation, the salutary effect of the latter is mitigated or completely lost resulting in the release of Evil.

SABBATEAN DOCTRINE OF EVIL

Sabbatai Sevi (1626-1676), aroused a messianic movement that engulfed the whole of Jewery. In this he was helped by Nathan Levi of Gaza. In the Sabbateans we come to the final development in the speculation about the problem of evil. According to them *En Sof* contained two lights, one with Thought and the other without Thought. The one with Thought had the desire of creating the world. The other (without Thought) did not have such a desire. It wanted to remain concealed in the *En Sof,* resting within itself. Thus the former was active, the latter passive. The light with Thought contracted[37] to make room for creation. The light without Thought, however, remained in its place, offering, so to say, passive resistance. Its very essence was to resist any creation. The light with Thought had created a vacuum by its contraction. It had also built an emanation in the vacuum. The passive resistance of the thoughtless light affected the structure of this emanation giving birth to evil. In other words the light without Thought became the source of Evil in the work of creation.

"According to Nathan it is unthinkable that the infinite light of *En Sof* should contain only such lights as were focused (and, as it were, limited) on the purpose of creation, for this would be tantamount to saying that the act of creation exhausted the contents of *En Sof*. Hence another force or principle must be present in *En Sof* : the thoughtless light, that is, a light devoid of any thought or 'idea' that would be prefigurative or constitutive of a cosmos. The thought-some light had withdrawn in the act of retraction in order to penetrate again into the *tehiru* and there to build the cosmos. After the retraction and until the 'shining forth of the straight line' (that is, the penetration of the thought-some light). The *tehiru* contained residual lights only, most of which were thoughtless light, resisting by their very nature the coming into being of the cosmos."[38]

The interpretation that can be placed on this is that by nature the thoughtless light is not evil, but it is a desire to keep *En Sof* intact, that is, to ensure that nothing should exist besides *En Sof*.

The struggle between these two lights continues at every stage of creation and will only come to an end at the time of redemption when the light with Thought penetrates the light without Thought and manifests in its holy form. Most of the Kabbalists were agreed on the view that evil exists, even if it exists negatively. What they were not agreed on was on the eschatological problem of how it would be finally terminated. But generally speaking most Kabbalists held the view that all things would return to their original holy state. Of course, such a standpoint would lead to a contradiction. 'Does not it exist' — (negatively) — really means it does not exist at all. Being (negative), the question of its final termination does not arise. 'Evil' is only a partial view of things. In a whole which is a harmony with the right thing in its right place there is no Evil. (Leibnitz — Ex. of Symphony).

Incidentally it may be mentioned that Leibnitz (1646-1716), in one of his lesser works Theodicee comes very close to the Kabbalistic view. The period is significant, because Sabbatai Sevi passed away in 1676 (1626-1676). Good and Evil exist together in the supreme mind of God. There is nothing that can be done about it, because there is no other possible logical solution to the problem.

SEFIROT

Let us briefly examine the following two paragraphs from a book on Kabbalah. The book has been written by Z'ev ben Shimon Halevi, a Jewish writer. He says :

"In Kabbalah, God the Transcendent is called AYIN. AYIN means in Hebrew 'Nothing,' for God is beyond Existence. AYIN is neither below nor above; nor is it in movement or in stillness. There is nowhere AYIN is. God is Absolute Nothing.

"AYIN SOF means 'Without End.' This is the title of God who is everywhere. AYIN SOF is the One in the zero of AYIN. This is the totality of what is and is not. AYIN SOF is God the immanent, the Absolute All. AYIN SOF has no Attributes, because they (Attributes) can manifest only within existence, and existence is finite."[39]

A look at this quotation will show how close it comes to the description of One given in the Upaniṣads.

We quote another paragraph from a non-Jewish writer, Richard Cavendish also writing on Kabbalah. He says :

"This (knowledge) is not gained by rational enquiry or argument about the nature of God, which are rejected as useless. The knowledge of God comes through a direct divine inspiration or through sacred traditions which are themselves divinely inspired. This knowledge transforms the man who acquires it by making him a sharer in the divine being — to *know* God is to *be* God. The elect are not those who lead good lives, but those who are enlightened, who possess the knowledge of the divine. The sin which cuts man off from God is not any form of moral backsliding, but ignorance."[40]

Were these paragraphs, taken from books written by Jewish and non-Jewish writers, to appear in books on Vedānta, they would easily pass muster, without the reader suspecting that what is being written is about Kabbalah. All that would have to be done would be to change a word here or there. Were passages to be culled from the various major mystical traditions of the world and placed side by side, it would be impossible to say to which tradition they belonged. All that would have to be done would be to delete a few tell-tale words that would give an indication to the source or tradition. Mystics are the free masons of the world. Today it is not uncommon to see writers on the Kabbalah quote from the Upaniṣads or the Bhagavad Gītā to illustrate their points of view. S.L. Mac-Gregor Mathers, a great writer on Kabbalah, belonging to this century, quotes the Bhagavad Gītā, Chapter IX to substantiate his point :

"In the Bhagavad Gītā (Ch. IX) it is said, 'I am immortality and also Death; and I, O, Arjuna! am that which is and that which is not'. "[41]

Such writings only go to show that there are large areas of similarity, between the various mystical traditions of the world.

Like most major mystical traditions the Kabbalah seeks to explain the essence of the Supreme Being, the origination of the universe, the creation of man, the destiny of man and the universe and the profound significance of the sacred Torah. It seeks to explain the 'transition' from the Infinite cause of causes (*En Sof*) to the finite tangible universe by means of the graded emanations (*Sefirot*).

The major mystical traditions have diverse paths by which the aspirant can approach God. The Hindu tradition for instance has the paths of karma, devotion, knowledge, tantra. Similarly Jewish mysticism also prescribes three paths — devotional, ethical and the philosophical. Of course, like all paths, they are not separated into airtight compartments.

"It is possible to distinguish three strata in the Zohar, regarded as a theological work, which we may designate, the devotional, the ethical and the philosophical, and which address themselves primarily to the imagination, the emotions and the intellect respectively. Each of these strata is, so to speak, dominated by its own designation for the Deity, representing God under a distinct aspect — in one case as both personal and local, in the second as personal but not local, in the third as neither personal nor local. But the Zohar is not content to leave these aspects side by side . . . . A great part of it — perhaps the most important — is taken up with an endeavour to correlate them by expressing each in the terms of the others. This involves a wide extension of the designations of God . . . ."[42]

So, in this manner, man can communicate with God :

1. by appeal to sentiment of prayer and devotion (Bhakti),

2. by appeal to his ethical impulse (Karma),
3. by appeal to his philosophical spirit (Jnānā).

Those acquainted with Hindu, Buddhist and even Christian mysticism will find the terminology in Jewish mysticism to be strange. For instance, God as the recipient of prayer and as the object of devotion, in Zoharic mysticism, is referred to as "Community of Israel." For the Kabbalist this is not a community in the ordinary sense of the word. On the contrary it has divine significance. The modern writer would perhaps translate the term as "national" or "tribal" God of Israel.

It is terms such as these that sharply distinguish Jewish mysticism from all other mystical traditions. When prayers are offered to such a God, belief is placed in Him on purely historical grounds. When God is designated as the "Community of Israel," God becomes the protector and guardian of Israel in this world. That is to say, God, for this purpose becomes both personal and local. This is tantamount to saying that God is with the children of Israel no matter where they are. This is considered to be a union between the people and God. This union first took place on Mount Sinai. It was consummated by the building of the Temple. Even though the Temple was destroyed, the union was never broken. The question then arises : How does God manifest His presence in Israel ? The answer is : Through Shekhinah, the Divine Light.[43]

Just as God is designated "Community of Israel" as the recipient of prayer, similarly, He is designated by the Zohar as "The Holy One, blessed be He" as the promoter of man's moral strivings, 'As the Holy One, blessed be He,' God, is the Creator of species and the vitalising force of the universe. Mystically speaking, man knows God in this aspect, — this, his own consciousness (*Neshamah*), which is based on breathing power (*Nishimah*) the super soul, that is the deeper Self which transcends his spirit, or intellectual faculties (*ruah*). Thus man through his consciousness is able to establish direct communion with the 'Holy One, blessed be He.'

For the Jew the Torah is the guiding Spirit. The term Torah is primarily applied to the Five Books of Moses or Pentateuch, but may also include the whole body of Judaism's religio-ethical literature. The word Torah is sometimes incorrectly translated as Law,[44] when actually it includes every facet of Jewish culture —

ethics, justice, religion, education. Consciousness (*Neshamah*) is rewarded or punished after death, depending upon how much it has complied with the Torah. The place for reward is Garden of Eden and of punishment Gehinnom. God, as the dispenser of reward and punishment after death is called "Holy King." The Kabbalah also refers to God in this behalf as, Tree of Life, in the branches of which the souls of the righteous rest. This part of the Zohar appears no doubt to be emotional and imaginative, but it is the part around which the Zoharic doctrine of moral life revolves, as also, as we shall soon see, the theory of the Sefirot, perhaps the German philosophical word; *Lebensanschauung* would correctly describe this aspect — the basing of religious life on the emotional side of man's nature.

However, the Zohar seeks to approach God, not only introspectively from the starting point of *Lebensanschauung*, but also extrospectively, taking the starting point as *Weltanschauung*. When looked at from this extrospective point of view, God is called the Ancient Holy One. He is also known as 'That Hidden and Undisclosed.' In this aspect God is regarded as the First cause of all movement and existence. As against God being personal when he is approached through prayer and devotion, he is impersonal when he is approached in his aspect as Ancient Holy One. The Zohar says :

"It is a postulate of the *Zohar* that this First Cause is a kind of algebraical *x*, which for the sake of Intellectual satisfaction must be sought for, but which can never be found . . . . In order, therefore, to find a beginning we posit an 'Ancient One' who differs from the 'Ancient Holy One' in being not absolutely absolute, so to speak, but containing the possibility of producing or becoming the non-absolute."[45]

We thus have 'The Community of Israel,' 'The Holy One, blessed be He' and the First cause. The question that naturally arises is : How does the Zohar unify the First cause with the Community of Israel and The Holy One, blessed be He ? The answer is through the doctrine of the Sefirot.

The Sefirot are ten in number. DAAT (knowledge) which is shown in the diagram is not manifested. The Zohar speaks of the Sefirot as "grades." In Hindu mysticism they would have been referred to as 'levels.' Whatever the term used, these 'grades' or 'levels' could only mean grades of the Godhead, specifically of the Godhead regarded as the First Cause. It would follow, therefore, that there are ten First Causes — a situation that would result in contradiction in terms. The Kabbalists, however, consider this to be a unity in diversity. The favourite manner in which the Zohar explains this, is by comparing them to the members of the human body or to a luminary shining on to a reflecting mirror, which in turn shines on another and so on. Other traditions, including the Hindu tradition, have also used similar metaphors to explain such diversities.

EQUILIBRIUM

Unlike the Upaniṣads, where metaphors and similes are used to explain emanations, the Sefirot are governed by the Principle of Equilibrium. This principle also explains the analogy of contraries. This principle is a sort of stabilising factor between the opposing forces. We must not confuse these two terms, equilibrium and balance. The balance consists of two scales (opposing forces), the equilibrium is the central point of the beam. S.L. MacGregor Mathers writes :

"What is here meant by the terms 'equilibrium of balance'? Equilibrium is that harmony which results from the analogy of contraries, it is the dead centre where, the opposition of opposing forces being equal in strength, rest succeeds motion. It is the central point. It is the "point within the circle" of ancient symbolism. It is the living synthesis of counter-balanced power. Thus form may be described as the equilibrium of light and shade; take away either factor, and form is viewless. The term balance is applied to the two opposite natures in each triad of the Sefirot, their equilibrium forming the third Sefirah in each ternary. This doctrine of equilibrium and balance is a fundamental Qabalistical (Kabbalistical) idea."[46]

If we look at the diagram (page 159) we notice that the left side is the Passive side and the right side, Active. Z'ev ben Shimon Halevi writes :

"The relationship between the Sefirot are governed by three unmanifest Divine principles, the 'Hidden Splendours' (*Zahzahot*) of Primordial Will, Mercy and Rigour (or Justice). Will holds the balance, while Mercy expands, and Rigour constrains the flow of Emanation, and so they organise the ten Divine Attributes into a specific archetypal pattern. The pattern thus called forth is the model on which everything that is to come into manifestation is based. It has been named the Image of God, but it is more generally known as the Tree of Life. Each Sefirah in turn manifests under the influence of one of the Zahzahot in particular, and for this reason the flow which manifests the ten Sefirot can be visualised as Zigzagging in a 'Lightening Flash' from a central position (Balance) to the right (Expansion) and across to the left (Constraint). Thus the Zahzahot give rise to the three vertical alignments in the Tree of Life diagram known as the Pillars : that of Equilibrium (Grace, Will) in the centre; that of Mercy (Active Force, Expansion) on the right, and that of Severity (Passive Form, Constraint) on the left."[47]

The diagram also shows an additional unmanifested, non-Sefirah, DAAT (knowledge). "This, we are told, is where the Absolute may enter at Will to intervene directly in existence, which is now eternally held until Divine Will allows it to vanish like the image it is. In human terms DAAT is the Knowledge that emerges out of nowhere and comes direct from God. It is quite different from the revelation of Wisdom (Hokhmah), DAAT is not only seen but known. It is different, too, from what comes of Understanding (Binah) or deep pondering. DAAT, the child of the Supernal Sefirot, is not only observation but becoming."[48]

Thus perfect harmony prevails. The general plan of the Sefirot is as follows. There are in all ten Sefirot. On the active right hand pillar of Mercy three Selfirot are aligned : Three on the left hand Pillar of Severity. This is passive. And on the Central Pillar we have four, in addition to the non-Sefirah DAAT. This is the Pillar of Grace or Equilibrium. The lightning Flash establishes their relationship. This relationship is further realised by twenty-two paths (Twenty-two Hebrew letters).

The diagram (page 188) gives an idea of this relationship. These twenty-two paths form triads (triangular configurations) active on the right, passive on the left. The horizontal and central triads, linking all three pillars, are concerned directly with consciousness.

Man is under physical and psychological bondage. It is not easy for him to shake off this bondage. Just as the Israelites required a leader (*Guru* or *Maggid*) to come out of the Egyptian

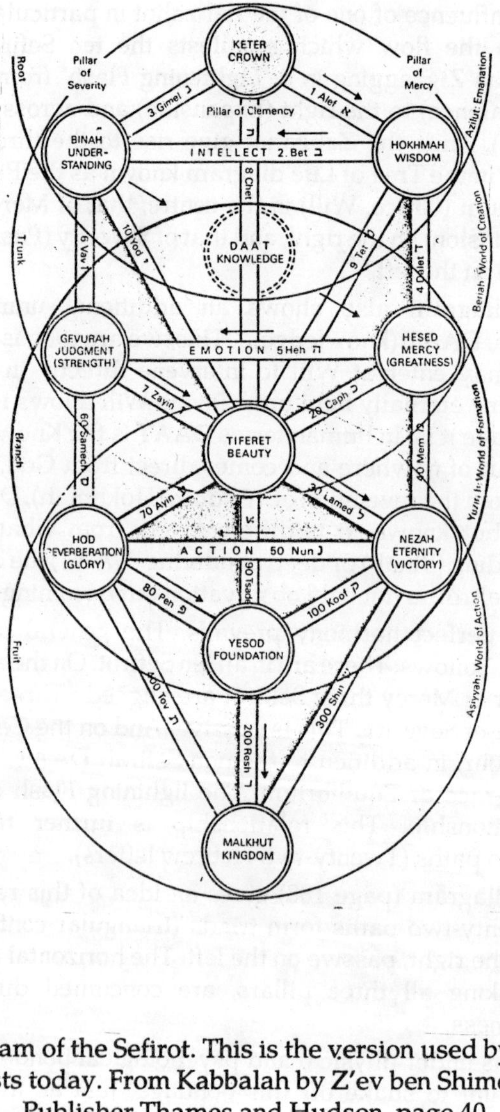

Diagram of the Sefirot. This is the version used by many Kabbalists today. From Kabbalah by Z'ev ben Shimon Halevi, Publisher Thames and Hudson, page 40.

bondage, so also a Maggid or Guru is necessary to come out of the physical and psychological bondage. Let us examine and see how this takes place.

When the Tree of Life comes into existence, it is made up of a Divine world of Emanation (*Azilut* or proximity). This Azilut is at the stage of Pure Will. It is complete in all respects, that is, though all dynamics and laws are complete in It, nothing can take place unless there is movement in time and space. In fact It could have remained in this position of Its pristine glory all through Eternity, but for the fact that God willed the beginning of Days, the unfolding of creation of great cosmic cycles. In Isaiah we read :

"Even every one that is called by my name : for I have created him for my glory, I have formed him; Yea, I have made him."[49]

These four levels which occur again and again in the scriptures and the Kabbalah, viz. calling, creating, forming and making, we see within the primordial Tree of Life, Azilut. Symbolically they are the root, trunk, branch and fruit. They are in the four elements of the lowest Sefirah, Malkhut. They stand for the four stages of separation from the Source of All. These are fire, air, water, earth. In this "The first level, associated with fire, is closest to the Crown (Keter) and is seen as symbolic of pure Will (the Divine 'Calling').

"The second associated with air, is symbolic of Intellect (the Divine 'Creation'). The third level, associated with water is seen as an expression of Emotion, in ever changing forms (the Divine 'Forming'). The fourth and last, associated with earth, speaks of Action, the practical implementation of all that has gone before (the Divine 'Making'). Each level contains the qualities and activities of the one above, so that each descending level in turn is under more laws, is more complex and is further from the Source."[50]

These are the subtle bodies of Vedānta. Except for reference to Ether the similarity is striking. The Azilut is perfect in all respects, except that it is at the conception stage. When these four levels inherent in the Azilut unfold themselves in four great stages, each stage is a world in itself. Talking in terms of the Sefirot, the position is as follows :

"The origin of this conception, and of the understanding of the dynamics of the relationship between one World and the next, lies in the Hebrew text of the Bible. The Divine 'Calling by My Name' which is the essence of Azilut means that each Sefirah has attached to it one of the Names of God. Keter, the Crown, has the Name EHYEH ASHER EHYEH.

I AM THAT I AM : the beginning and end of all Existence. The Sefirot of Wisdom and Understanding, Hokhmah and Binah, have been given the names of YHVH and ELOHIM respectively, which ancient belief associates with the Merciful and just aspects of the Deity. At Tiferet which is the focus of the Paths from these three Sefirot, is God the Creator, known by the composite name of YHVH ELOHIM. The rest of the Sefirot have Divine Names of their own, and are understood by some Kabbalists to be the ELOHIM referred to collectively in the opening sentence of the Genesis, *Bereshith bara* ELOHIM, in the beginning the ELOHIM created".[51]

If we take the first two Books of the Old Testament, the Book of Genesis which deals with Worlds of Creation, Formation and Action describes how man came *to descend* into the natural realm. The second Book, Exodus, describes the ascent, back towards the Source. It is not necessary for us to go into the details of the Bible Story. Suffice it to say that the Story of Jacob's family descending into Egypt (Misraim in Hebrew) is symbolic of the description of the incarnation of the Soul, whereas the incident of the Burning Bush (Exodus 3) is the culmination and signifies the State of Grace granted to a person who through severe discipline has reached the pinnacle of inner accomplishment. Halevi writes :

"Moses's initial reluctance to go back to Egypt and fulfil his mission (Exodus 4) is likewise typical of the initial opposition of Self Will to Divine Will, before the state of submission 'Not my will but Thy Will be done.' On accepting his destiny Moses, returns to his people to help bring them up out of the house of bondage and into the land flowing with milk and honey or into the higher worlds. In personal terms, this means inwardly to educate the undisciplined parts of oneself and outwardly to teach others seeking initiation."[52]

This 'work' (Avodah-Hebrew) also means 'service' or 'worship'and is centred around the Sefirah Malkhut. Here acute awareness is developed, There is a saying in this regard of an 18th century Kabbalist. It sounds like a Zen master's saying. 'I come to observe how my teacher ties up his boot laces.' In Kabbalah such intensity of observation results in the realisation that all the four worlds are present within one's own body and within the physical universe. In this manner the aspirant becomes acquainted with the Tree at work within himself. The active side of the Tree stimulates action and feeling and the passive side restrains feeling, thereby leading to reflective thought. In Kabbalah this method of study is called, study of Action, Devotion and Contemplation.

The next two Sefirot are Hod and Nezah. They represent the passive and active side—theory and practice. The theoretical that is Hod refers to learning, monitoring and feedback. Like Vedānta, it consists of the study of Texts, Kabbalistic diagrams etc. Just as the Guru takes a *Mahāvākya* (e.g. tat tvam asi) and analyses it, so does the spiritual guide analyse Hebrew words and parables or a principle rooted in the Sefirah. On the other hand, Nezah refers to the active side, expressed by ritual, prayer, etc. The teacher (Maggid in Hebrew) stands at Tiferet as a watcher. His relationship is the relationship Moses had with the Slave-minded Israelites. All Paths both from above and below pass through him to the aspirant. A stage, however, is reached when the student himself attains the level of Tiferet. He becomes his own guide. Here he comes in contact with the Soul-triad. (Hesed, Gevurah and Tiferet). Thus Justice, Tolerance and Mercy come into play, together with their respective disciplines. The aspirant experiences severity from the left and Mercy from the right, resulting in proper emotional balance. But all this takes considerable time and effort. The aspirant develops his potential naturally and gradually. Only the best, the select, can reach the uppermost triad. This is the triad of Binah and Hokhmah, representing tradition and revelation, together with non-Sefirah of knowledge, DAAT. This is the triad that is in direct contact with the Divine. To the chosen few who attain this triad are attributed the biblical prophecies, the great Kabbalistic schemes of the universe. But as in other traditions, there are some chosen ones who may experience this stage spontaneously, as an act of Grace, "as a state of profound awe in which they are filled and surrounded by golden light and a sense of unity and peace. The Kabbalist seeks this act of *Yehud* or Unity consciously, with others or alone, under the wings of the tradition where Knowledge allows and aids the knower and known to be one."[53]

All the major mystical traditions caution against pitfalls on the Path to unity. The dangers of gaining supernatural powers through ego-motivated concentration on particular psychic centres are to be guarded against as they prove to be serious obstacles in the Path of unification. All major traditions forbid the turning of spiritual knowledge into magical power.

PATH OF DEVOTION :

The Ten Commandments form the very core of Jewish life. For the mystic they carry considerable significance inasmuch as he equates each one of them to a Sefirah on the Tree of Life. The first two commandments are contained in the *Shema*, a very important instrument through which the mystic contacts God. Moses received the Ten Commandments from God on Mt. Sinai. This is again significant because Mt. Sinai itself is symbolical of 'Ascent.' In mysticism, mere conformity is not enough. The soul has to ascend if it seeks spiritual perfection.

The Ten Commandments and the corresponding Sefirot are as follows:

1. Thou shalt have no other Gods before me. — KETER
2. Thou shall not make any graven image. — HOKHMAH
3. Thou shalt not take the name of the Lord thy God in vain. — BINAH
4. Remember the Sabbath day to keep it Holy. — HESED
5. Honour thy father and mother. — GEVURAH
6. Thou shalt not kill. — TIFERET
7. Thou shalt not commit adultery. — NEZAH
8. Thou shalt not steal. — HOD
9. Thou shalt not bear false witness against thy neighbour. — YESOD
10. Thou shall not covet. — MALKHUT

The way of devotion begins with the observance of the Ten Commandments. The Kabbalist interprets these commands to include love and fear of God. The Ten Commandments thus embody the very path leading to God. Each Commandment, as we have seen, is represented by a Sefirah on the Tree of Life. The first three Sefirot viz., Keter, Hokhmah and Binah, form a triad which is termed Supernal or Divine triad. At the emotional level are the next two Sefirot, Hesed and Gevurah. They speak of devotion at the emotional level. Tiferet (Beauty) which is the next Sefirah corresponds to the Commandment, Thou shalt not kill. This in Kabbalistic terminology is interpreted as a direction to desist from killing the self, which is tantamount to killing spiritual growth. Nezah (Eternity) corresponding to the prohibition of adultery, enjoins the eschewing of adultery inasmuch as the power seeking thus generated adulterates spiritual life, whereas theft (Hod) is the misuse of acquired knowledge to steal unfair advantage.

Yesod, (Foundation) — one must not delude oneself or others through the Yesodic ego. And finally, all is God's kingdom, Malkhut. Thou shalt not covet — not covet — anything in this world. In the words of Īśa Upaniṣad : "Do not covet for whose is wealth."[54]

Everything emanates from God. It is for this reason that the devout Jew recites prayers of thanks on all occasions. For instance, "Blessed art thou, O Lord, our God, King of the Universe, who bringest forth bread from the earth." There are such prayers for practically all occasions. A prayer is said on meeting a wise man or on seeing lightning or sea. All these prayers are not treated as lip-service by the devotee. They are repeated because he is aware that everything emanates from the Divine. Such prayers recited not mechanically, but with a heart full of devotion create in the devotee an awareness of the Divine in whatever he sees or does.

CONTEMPLATION

While the way of devotion is one of the ways (something akin to Bhakti of Hinduism), there is also the method of contemplation. Devotion and contemplation do not exclude one another. They can at best be said to be complementary. If the following simple prayer is contemplated upon word by word its full implication comes into consciousness, suffusing it : "Blessed art thou, O Lord, our God, King of the universe by whose words all things exist." This is a prayer that is uttered prior to eating certain food. Contemplation, for instance, on the meaning of each word of the prayer is used in the study of metaphysics. Metaphysics here constitutes the reaction between the Sefirot and their sub-systems. But there is a marked difference between the Kabbalistic and Hindu approach to metaphysics. The Hindu schools, as we have already seen in the foregoing chapters, have elaborate and intricate systems of philosophy. Moreover, there is always an attempt to define these ideas and render them thinkable. Long and successive generations of seers have devoted their lives to this task. Despite such Herculean efforts many concepts still remain so abstract that only the most rigorous disciplines (Yoga, etc.) can help in extracting the meaning of these concepts.

But when we come to a system like the Kabbalah we are up against a wall, because the Kabbalist goes to work in quite a different way. He does not endeavour to raise the mind up and give it the wings of metaphysics, with the result that he, rarely, if ever, climbs into the rarefied air of abstract reality. On the other hand he formulates a concrete symbol that the eye can see. This is done with a view to reduce the abstract reality to a concrete symbol. But as in the case of the Hindu tradition, in this case, too, the untrained human mind is unable to grasp it.

A great many objects like the Cross in Christiandom, or the phallic symbol, are used as objects of meditation. The uninitiated use them in more or less a routine manner. All that they do is to infuse into them certain thoughts which perhaps invoke certain associated ideas and activate certain feelings. To the initiate, the symbol comes up alive and discloses a meaning that is not apparent to the uninitiate. The ten Sefirot represent to the Kabbalist a transition from the Divine to the spiritual, from the spiritual to the moral, and from the moral to physical reality. We have discussed this in detail, while commenting on Equilibrium in the foregoing pages.

Were we to examine similar positions in Hindu mysticism, we would come across a transition from the primordial state to the Earth and back to the primordial, The Divine being can be comprehended, though not entirely, through speculation. Speculation shows that the universe is composed in a certain proportion. The panchīkṛta principle is one such example. At the time of creation the five elements (Ether, air, fire, water and earth) remain in an uncompounded state. The Pañcadaśī says :

"By dividing each element into two equal parts and subdividing the first half of each element into four equal parts and then adding to the other half of each element one subdivision of each of the remaining four, each element becomes five in one."[55]

It is the preponderance of a particular element that determines the nature of that element. We find this view also in Plato's Timaeus, wherein he deals with the proportion in which the universe is built. To illustrate we quote :

"Wherefore also God in the beginning of creation made the body of the universe to consist of fire and earth. But two things cannot be rightly put together without a third; there must be some bond of union between them. And the fairest bond is that which makes the most complete fusion of itself and the things which it combines; and proportion is best adapted to effect such a union . . . . If the universal frame had been created a surface only and having no depth, a single mean would have sufficed to bind together itself and the other terms; but now, as the world must be solid, and solid bodies are always compacted not by one mean but by two, God placed water and air in the mean between fire and earth, and made them to have the same proportion so far as possible (as fire is to air so is air to water and as air is to water so is water to earth), and thus be bound and put together a visible and tangible heaven."[56]

We observe that Hindu and Greek traditions, separated both by geography and history, express identical concepts of the creation of the universe. The emanation theory of the Kabbalah is not far different.

The unanswered question has always been : The transformation of the Infinite, the Absolute, into the finite world. The Kabbalist, as we have seen above, attempts to explain it by means of the Tree of Life, (Azilut, Emanation). The Advaitist attributes the multiplicity to Ignorance. The mind of man, he says, so to say, limits consciousness, so that man experiences only the finite. Remove Ignorance, and you experience the Absolute Truth. The Advaitist will add, you are the Truth. You are Brahman. Finally the problem reduces itself to the position where a counter question is asked : The Absolute, by its very definition, is beyond time, space and causation. When, therefore, we assume that we know it, we are limiting it by time, space and causation. We thus run into a contradiction in terms. The question, how does the Infinite become finite remains unanswered. We will not discuss it

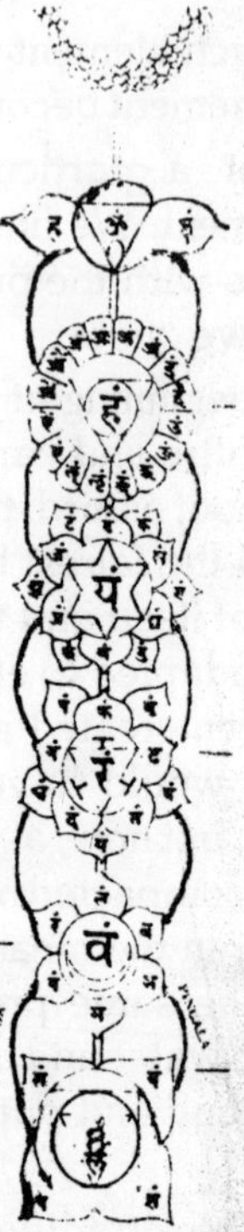

—Sahasrara Chakra (Thousand Petal Lotus)

Ajna Chakra —

Hakini Devi, Sambu, Itara Linga and Tricona, Mahat. The Sukshma Prakriti called Hiranya Garba. Mind, Letters Ham and Ksham.

Visudha Chakra

Sakini Devi, Sabda Tatwa, Hearing (sensation). Ether principle. Mouth (action). 16 letters. 16 petals. Bija Ha.

Anahata Chakra —

Kakini Devi. Isha. Bana Linga Trikona. Bija Yam. Air principle. Sparsatatwa, Feel and touch. 12 letters, 12 petals.

—Manipura Chakra

Lakini Devi. Rudra on a bull. Rupa (form and colour). 10 letters. 10 petals. Bija Mantra Ram. Fire principle.

Swadhishatana

Chakra —

Rakini Devi, Vishnu, Varuna Rasa' (sense), Hand (action), 6 petals, 6 letters, Bija Vam, Water Principle.

—Mooladhara

Chakra

Dakini Devi, Brahma,

Indra Devata, Earth principle. Gandha Tatwa. Smell. (sensation). Feet (organ of action). 4 petals. 4 letters. Swayambu Linga. Blia Lam. Kundalini.

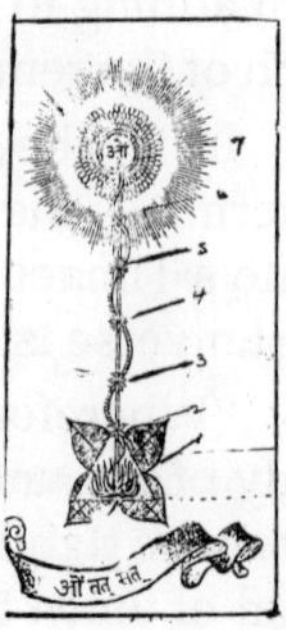

From the Complete illustrated Book of Yoga, Swami Vishnudevananda, Pocket Books, New York.

From Raja-Yoga, Swami Vivekananda, Advaita Ashrama, Almora, Fourth Edition.

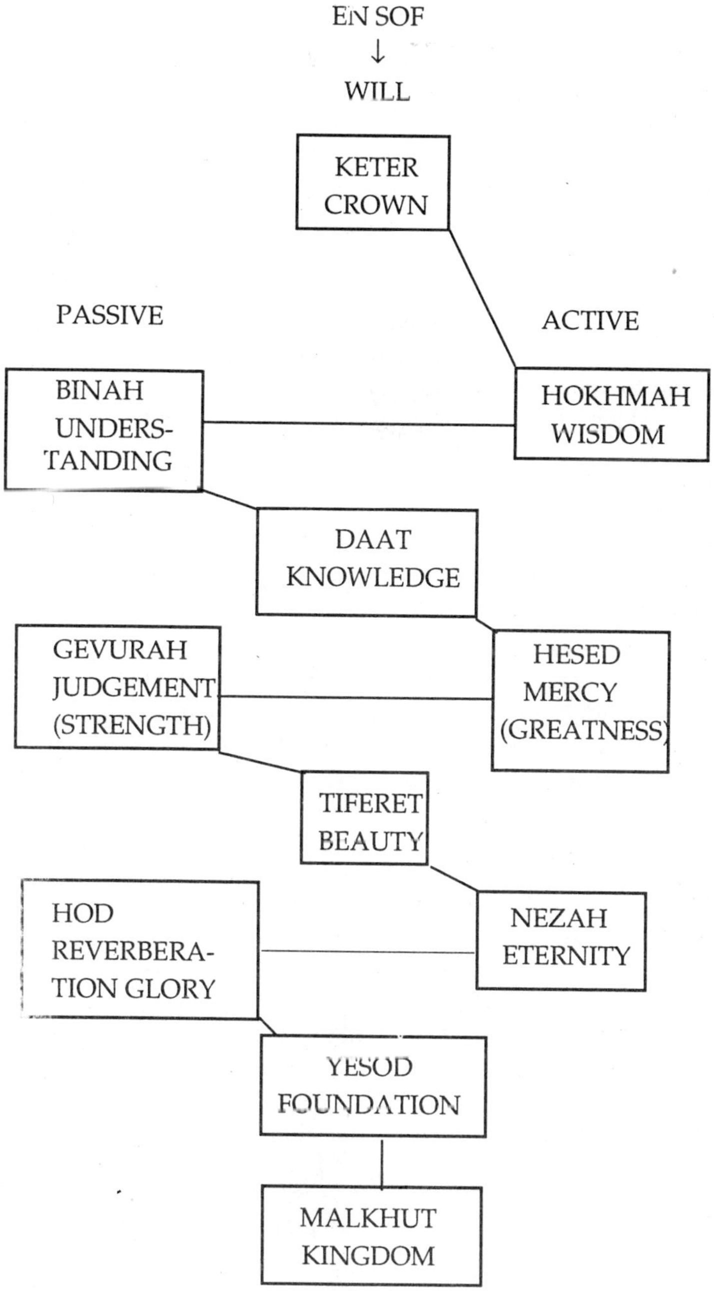
EN SOF
↓
WILL
KETER
CROWN
PASSIVE
ACTIVE
BINAH
UNDERS-
TANDING
HOKHMAH
WISDOM
DAAT
KNOWLEDGE
GEVURAH
JUDGEMENT
(STRENGTH)
HESED
MERCY
(GREATNESS)
TIFERET
BEAUTY
HOD
REVERBERA-
TION GLORY
NEZAH
ETERNITY
YESOD
FOUNDATION
MALKHUT
KINGDOM

here as we have discussed it, from time to time, in the preceding chapters.

The question was raised here because the theory of emanation necessitated it. It was raised also to show that the ultimate basic experience of the Absolute is possible only when all divergences disappear. In other words, the experiencer, the experience and the experienced (knower, knowledge and the known) are one. We are thus reduced to the position where we find that the Absolute is unknowable speculatively. But the mystic who practises various disciplines will not admit this position because he claims to have reached the Absolute position.

If we compare the two diagrams (at pp. 196-197), one showing the chakras and the other, the Tree of Knowledge, we find a striking similarity. Even if the comparison does not prove that the two systems are on all fours, the similarity is striking. In both, the ultimate aim is to go back to the source. In Kabbalah once the process of emanation is complete (i.e. descent), the tendency is to rise again and go back to the source. The start is made from *Malkhut*. The aspirant goes up 'level by level.' The word 'level' is not used in the ordinary sense of the word. G. Scholem writes :

"True, the Zohar frequently refers to the Sefirot as stages, but they are plainly regarded not as the steps of a ladder between God and the world, but as various phases in the manifestation of the Divinity which proceed from and succeed each other."[57]

If we examine the Yogic diagram, we find that the various chakras are also phases. The main purpose of the Yoga is to draw the energy from the *Mūladhārā* to *Sahasrārā*. Even if there is a difference in the method, the ultimate purpose is the same. In mysticism, no matter to what tradition it belongs, the human body, especially the nervous system, plays a very important part. The Chakras, for instance, are none else but astral nerve centres, which in turn also correspond to the five elements. It is for this reason, when Kuṇḍalini Śakti rests or is active *only* in the lower centres, man has *only* Finite experience. In a similar way the seven lower Sefirot from Hesed to Malkhut are legitimate objects of human contemplation and, therefore, of finite experience like the Sahasrārā Chakra (Thousand petalled Lotus), Keter too, is too elevated for human 'thought' to reach. Actually when the Kuṇḍalini Śakti is aroused and moves upwards she withdraws into herself the moving powers of her creation and unites with pure consciousness (called Śiva), in the Sahasrārā Chakra. The third triad consisting of Binah, Hokhmah and the non-Sefirah, DAAT, is in contact with the Divine. It is, therefore, attained only by the select.

It is not surprising, therefore, that the latter Kabbalists (Hassidic) came quite close to Advaita in their thinking. Like the Christian mystics, they drew some censure from their co-religionists. But then this should not be surprising because mysticism in all traditions has at some time or another drawn censure. The mystic is almost an outsider as far as his co-religionists are concerned. All mysticism is concerned with its accounting for the multiplicity and diversity of things in the world as we experience it. The Kabbalists were conscious about this and in trying to explain multiplicity and diversity they came close to Advaita. For this we must turn our attention to the 16th century Kabbalist, Isaac Luria. Scholem has come to the conclusion :

"How can there be a world if God is every-where? If God is 'all in all' how can there be things which are not God? How can God create out of nothing if there is no nothing?"[58]

Isaac Luria gives an answer which an Advaitist would have given centuries ago. The answer has the making of the ingredients of Advaita. We quote :

"God withdrew from Himself into Himself in order to leave room for the world. In the Zoharic scheme the Ten *Sefirot* are emanations of God. In the Lurianic Kabbalah the first impulse, as it were, in God's unfolding is this withdrawal and the Ten *Sefirot* only emerge after this withdrawal."[59]

This theory was known as *Tzimtzum*. It received many different interpretations among the Kabbalists. The most prominent interpretation came from the Hasidism movement of the 18th century.[60]

"In the 18th Century Hasidic movement, and particularly in the branch of it known as *Habad* (founded by R. Schneor Zalman of Liady), it is interpreted in such a way that the doctrine of God's unity means not alone that there is only one God and that God is unique, but that there *is* only God. In this philosophy God is all. There are no creatures from His point of view, as it were, only the One. All the multiplicity of things we observe in the universe as well as we ourselves are due to the screening of the divine light. *Tzimtzum* does not, in fact, really take place. Its meaning is rather that the Divine Light is progressively concealed so that creatures eventually enjoy existence from their point of view; but not from God's. This is acosmism with a vengeance and would seem to be a surrender to Far Eastern monistic views on the nature of Ultimate Reality."[61]

The book goes on to say :

"A possible term for the Hasidic view is *Panentheism* — all is *in* God. The 'all' is not identified *with* God in such a way that it would be meaningless to speak of the possibility of God without the 'all.' It is rather that the 'all' is in God."[62]

By whatever 'ism,' it was called, one thing was clear : It was Advaita pure and simple. It was no doubt open to attack from the logicians. How can it make sense to say that from God's point of view there are neither creatures nor universe, and yet to hold that from our point of view they do exist? In answer, to add the word 'really' exist, smacks of play on words. The Habad thinkers eventually resorted to the idea of sublime mystery and felt that it was beyond human understanding. The Hasidic thinkers were not prepared to bring in 'Iśvara,' though they had by a devious route brought in both 'Māyā' and 'Ignorance.' They did not admit that, as in the Monistic scheme, the world of senses is an illusion. The world is real enough from the point of view of creatures.

Whatever the merits of this argument, one thing stands out that there was a uniqueness and dynamism in the Kabbalah and Hasidic Panentheism.

DEVEKUT AND KAVVANAH

These are very important concepts in Jewish mysticism. The former, Devekut, is that state which results in a sense of beatitude and intimate union. But where Jewish mysticism is concerned it is well to remember that when we talk of union, we do not mean that the soul and God become one. Such a concept is foreign to Jewish mysticism. Though the distance between the soul and God, or creature and creator is diminished, it is not entirely wiped out. The mystic never claims that the distance is obscured. In the Kabbalistic consciousness the main path travelled by the mystic consists in the strict observance of the Commandments. But intrinsically they were not connected, because in the final analysis, the ascent of the soul took place through concentrated thought and meditation. Prayer plays a paramount role in Kabbalah. Prayer, of course, does not mean the mechanical repetition of words. But this does not also mean that the practical Commandments were excluded. Their *exclusive* use demanded certain translation into action which is time consuming and leaves no time for meditation and concentration of thought. No doubt each Commandment has its mystical import on the Tree of Life. But prayer reinforces mystical thought. Prayer can be turned inwards into mystical meditation. Scholem writes :

"The greatest Kabbalists were all great masters of prayer, nor would it be easy to imagine the Kabbalah's speculative development without such permanent roots in the experience of mystical prayer."[63]

As in the Hindu tradition, *mantra* meditation is not uncommon in Jewish mysticism. In fact books written on Jewish mysticism, by Jews, even use the word 'mantra.' As in the Hindu tradition, words or verses from the Bible are repeated a certain number of times. As in Hindu mysticism, the cautionary instructions given to the neophyte were similar to those given by a Guru to his disciple. One must be careful, however, not to take these images too seriously. As one advances, the images become more explicit and can take the form of vision. The neophyte meditator may be tempted to place great significance on these visions, and think that he is actually experiencing prophecy or the like.

"In the Kabbalah literature, there are warnings, even to advanced meditators, not to give credence to visions. Even the most impressive visions can be spurious and come from the Other Side .... Therefore, when a person experiences images or visions they should be taken as aesthetic experiences and nothing more. At the most, they should be taken as the first hints of a spiritual experience."[64]

The Kabbalists prescribed several methods of meditation. Some of the topics in the book Jewish Meditation by Kaplan referred to above, lists :

(1) Nothingness.

(2) Conversing with God.

(3) The Way of Prayer.

(4) Unification.

Meditation on 'Nothingness' has been practised by advanced disciples in all the major mystical traditions. Like all advanced techniques, it is not to be taken lightly. A guide or a Guru is a 'must,' otherwise one is likely to be "swallowed up in the 'nothingness' of meditation."[65]

But how does one set about meditating on 'nothingness'? If one were to meditate on 'space' or 'blackness' one would not be meditating on nothingness. After all 'space' is space and 'Blackness' is blackness. Says Kaplan :

"It is taught that nothing is what you see behind your head. Of course, sight does not extend behind the head. Therefore, what you see behind the head is *nothing*. In other words you see *nothingness.*"[66]

The practice perhaps has its origin in the Bible where such a technique was used as a precursor of prophecy :

"Then the spirit took me up, and I heard behind me a voice of a great rushing, saying, Blessed be the glory of the Lord from his place."[67]

"And thine ears shall hear a word behind thee".[68]

Meditation on 'Nothingness' was likely to be traumatic, resulting in such acute sensitiveness as to make the slightest sensation overwhelming. Once the mind is cleared of all thoughts, the softest voice or sound may be magnified into an earth-quake. The visions of Ezekiel were striking examples of this. The Kabbalists have found considerable mystical material in Ezekiel. The Zohar teaches that a prophet has to pass through three great barriers before reaching God or the realm of the Divine. These are wind, cloud and fire. In the visions of Ezekiel we read :

"And I looked, and behold, a whirlwind came of the north, a cloud and a fire."[69]

The Hebrew word for 'wind' is '*ruah.*' The word also means 'spirit.' The interpretation of the above vision of Ezekiel would be 'stormy spirit.' When the mind becomes literally a vacuum, there is great agitation in the mind — the first step through which the mystic has to pass. The second step is blurred by a cloud. The mystic experiences an opaqueness, in which he is left bewildered as he can hardly see anything. The prophet falters at this stage. If he lacks the will he will even give up. This is the juncture at which mystics in all traditions falter. The Sufis have composed great poems on this theme (The Conference of the Birds)."[70] The 'fire infolding' is the final step — the final barrier. If the cloud blurs sensation, fire has the opposite effect of intensifying sensation. Unlike Hindu mysticism, throughout the Bible fire is used as a metaphor for dread, in the sense that it burns. Once the mystic gets past this barrier he is face to face with God.

This method of meditating on 'Nothingness' can also be used to get in touch with the innermost self. No tradition had dealt so extensively with the problem of self as the Hindu tradition. It has examined it from different angles. We have dealt with this in the preceding chapters. When we come to Jewish mysticism we find that it has not lagged behind the other traditions. We will only deal with one approach. In Hebrew the word for 'I' is *'ani.'* It is significant that in the event of the letters being rearranged, we have the word 'ayn' or 'ayin,' which means 'nothingness.' In other words the 'me' the 'I' within is 'nothingness.' Kaplan says that since there is nothing in the human mind that can relate to God as He actually is, 'nothingness' is the closest perception of God that can be obtained.

In classical Kabbalah, the highest spiritual levels are referred to as Ayin — literally nothingness. There are four universes :

(1) *Azilut* (nearness) the universe of the Sefirot.

(2) *Beriah* (creation) the universe of the Throne.

(3) *Yezirah* (formation) the universe of angels.

(4) *Asiyah* (making) the universe of forms.

Keeping this kabbalistic division in mind the following quotation will show how the universe of Sefirot is Nothingness :

"Thus, the Universe of Beriyah literally refers to the level that is called 'creation.' Creation, however, is defined as bringing forth 'Something from Nothing.' The level above Beriyah, from which it emanates, must, therefore, be considered 'Nothing.' It is in this context that the universe of Azilut is often referred to as 'Nothingness'."[71]

That is, the universe of Sefirot is nothingness. But, sometimes nothingness is used to denote Keter (Crown) the highest of the

Sefirot in Azilut. As Hokhmah (Wisdom) emanates from Keter (Crown) it is also referred to as Nothingness. Then what is the difference between Azilut and the Sefirot ? The difference is that Azilut is nothingness in general, in a conceptional sense ; Keter (Crown) is nothingness in *also* a spiritual sense. Similarly, *En Sof* is also Nothingness, but it is the ultimate Nothingness, that ultimate level in nothingness to which one ascends.

AMIDAH

This is a silent prayer said standing up with the feet close together. This has great Kabbalistic and mystical significance. The first paragraph of this silent prayer is very important inasmuch as it puts the worshipper in harmony with God. The prayer begins :

"Blessed art thou, O, Lord, Our God, and God of our fathers, God of Abraham, God of Isaac and God of Jacob, the great, mighty and revered God, the most high God, who bestowest loving kindnesses and possessest all things; who rememberest the pious deeds of the patriarchs, and in love wilt bring a redeemer to their children's children for thy name's sake."[72]

Kaplan writes

"When one says that word 'blessed' (*barukh*) at the beginning and end of the first paragraph one should bend the knees. When one says the next word, 'are you (art thou, *attah*) one should bow down from the waist.' This bowing is repeated again at the beginning and end of Modim, which is the next-to-last section of the Amidah."

"Bowing is integral to getting oneself into the meditative state. According to the Talmud, one bows down fairly quickly, but then comes up very slowly, 'like a snake'. "[73]

Also :

"Bowing in the Amidah also has another important connotation. The Talmud states that one of the reasons why the Amidah has eighteen blessings is that they parallel the eighteen vertebrae of the spine and neck. The nineteenth blessing, which was added later, parallels the coccyx the small bone at the base of the spine. This brings to mind the concept of *Kuṇḍalini* energy that is discussed in Eastern teachings. "[74]

We quote two more paragraphs from the same book :

"The *Kuṇḍalini* energy is also seen as taking the form of a serpent. In Jewish tradition, however, the serpent is seen as the enemy of mankind. The serpent is the tempter, who tries to use sexual energy to draw humans away from God. The Talmud, therefore, teaches that if one does not bow during Amidah, then one ' s spine turns into a snake. In contrast, the posture in *Kuṇḍalini* meditation requires that the spine be kept perfectly straight and erect. If a person worships in this manner, without bowing, then his spine will become infused with the *Kuṇḍalini* energy, which is the serpent.

"Bowing may be a way of overcoming this energy of the serpent. The concept of *Kuṇḍalini* is to bring energy up from the sexual area to the rest of the body. Bowing has the opposite connotation, namely that of bringing energy down from the head to the body. Therefore, when we bow, we lower the head toward the body. Only after we have bowed and infused the body with spiritual energy, can we rise and lift energy from the spine to the head, 'rising like a snake'. "[75]

Expressions like 'blessed' have a special significance in Judaism. When it is said : 'Blessed, art thou, O Lord,' we are saying that His immanent presence is the source of all blessing. This can only mean that God is very close to us.

The Amidah is about two thousand five hundred years old. Kuṇḍalini Yogạ may be even older. All this goes to show that similar methods of ascent existed thousands of years ago. Perhaps they were contemporaneous.

UNIFICATION

Unification is the goal of all initial theory and practices. Unification as we have repeatedly stated in the preceding pages, has a different connotation in Hindu, Buddhist, Christian and Kabbalistic mysticism. We have defined its characteristics in each of the traditions. In Kabbalah unification is brought about by bringing together of the 'component parts' of the body and psyche, and harmonising them with the higher worlds. For this rigid disciplines, deligent work and a devout attitude are necessary, although, as one rises up through the various levels of the psyche, Grace sometimes descends to meet the aspirant and grant *Yeziratic* or psychological insights and *Beriatic* or spiritual insights and experience. Action, devotion and contemplation form the

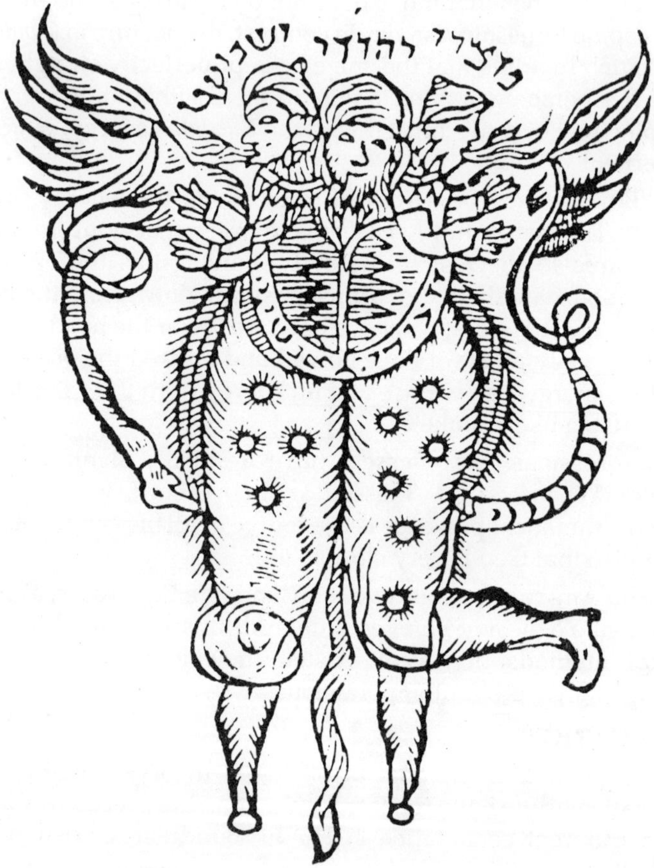

From KABBALAH by Z'ev ben Shimon Halevi, Publisher Thames and Hudson, page 92.

basis of these disciplines. The ultimate aim of this development is to unite the Worlds, to bring about a unity in the four levels that exist in every human being. In Kabbalah this 'unity' is referred to as joining that which is above to that which is below. 'As above, so below' is a fundamental principle with mysticism. It means that the soul and God are one and the same.

The diagram[76] at p. 206 shows the union of Christianity, Judaism and Islam.

In the diagram the three Hebrew words read from the right to the left are as follows :

Nosri The followers of Jesus of Nazareth, Christians.

Yehudi Followers of Judaism, Jews.

Ishmael Followers of Islam, Muslims.

Halevi writes :

"The work of Unification must involve contact with other spiritual traditions. At this level the outer forms of worship become less important : mystics meet in a spiritual World that is above form. A Jewish Kabbalist may converse with a Muslim Sufi or a Christian contemplative and discover the same reality beneath differing theories and practices. This unity at the spiritual level does not mean that the outer form of a tradition is redundant — each religion has its role to play — but that all human beings are made in the same Divine image."[77]

In this regard the diagram (p. 206) showing the union of Christianity, Judaism and Islam as figured by Rabbi Jacob Emden of Altona, Germany, 18th century, makes interesting reading. In the higher reaches of mysticism at the time of union the outward forms of worship melt away. The different theories and practices as between one tradition and another disappear, showing the mystic, that beneath all these theories and practices, exists one Reality. The fact that the mystic is a Hindu, or Jew, or Christian or Muslim ceases to have meaning at this point of time. The methods and means he used to reach unification are like scaffoldings, to be dismantled after they have served their purpose. Distinctions disappear. They existed because of the conditioning the mystic received from his tradition. The effects of this conditioning are, however, inescapable at the lower reaches.

SHEMA

For the Jew, the Shema is the symbol of unification. Taken from the Old Testament (Deuteronomy 6 : 4), it runs as under :

"Hear, O Israel, the Lord is our God, the Lord is One."

(*Shema yisrael, adonoy elohenu adonoy echad*).

This sentence occupies a central place in Jewish religious and Kabbalistic thought. The Shema as a mystical formula exercised tremendous influence on the methods used in the Kabbalah. The meditator was instructed to utter the words with a particular emphasis. The final word One-*Echad*, was pronounced with a special emphasis.

"It is to be said audibly, they ordained, the ear hearing what the lips utter; and its last word *echad* (One) was to be pronounced with special emphasis. All thoughts other than God's Unity must be shut out. It must be spoken with entire collection and concentration of heart and mind, the reading of the Shema may not be interrupted even to respond to the salutation of a king . . . . When men in prayer declare the Unity of the Holy Name in love and reverence, the walls of earth's darkness are cleft in twain, and the face of the Heavenly King is revealed lighting up the universe" (Zohar).[78]

The Shema is reminiscent of 'Aum' of the Hindu tradition. Both traditions require that the words be pronounced with a certain emphasis, with reverence and devotion, and both symbolise Unity. While the Hindu tradition derived the word from the Upaniṣads, the Jewish tradition got it from the Old Testament. From the outset the Kabbalists tried to prove that this formula referred only to the manifestation of the ten *Sefirot*, which were nothing other than the effective Unity of God.

Like Advaita, the Shema excludes dualism. At that point in the history of the world, Zoroaster exercised tremendous influence on the Semetic religions. It regarded the universe as the area of perpetual conflict between the principles of Good and Evil. Light and Darkness. This was a purely dualistic conception, in complete contradiction to the concept of One. Historically, the influence of Zoroaster on Judaism cannot be ruled out, but it is not necessary to go into that aspect of the question. Suffice it to say that even if the question of Light and Darkness comes up in

Judaism, the supremacy of the One is maintained. The One shapes Light and Darkness. The Old Testament is categorical on this point :

"I am the Lord, and there is none else. I form the light, and create darkness. I make peace and create evil. I the Lord to all these things."[79]

And,

"In the Jewish view, the universe, with all its conflicting forces, is marvellously harmonised in its totality; and, in the sum, evil is overruled and made a new source of strength for the victory of the good."[80]

Light and Darkness are not, therefore, two independent concepts, each having a power of its own, but both are the creation of God — One. To deem them to be independent would be tantamount to blasphemy.

Another concept that is abhorrent to Jewish mysticism is Pantheism. We have already discussed it above. Jewish mysticism holds that though God pervades the universe, He transcends it.

Let us analyse in brief the Shema from the Kabbalistic view point. Let us take the word 'ISRAEL' Jacob wrestles with a Heavenly messenger. The fight is, of course, symbolic and it only portrays the inner conflict, in which Jacob over-powers his baser passions.

"And he said: 'Let me go, for the day breaketh. And he said, 'I will not let thee go, except thou bless me.' And he said unto him, 'What is thy name?' And he said: 'Jacob.' And he said 'Thy name shall be called no more Jacob, but Israel; for thou hast striven with God and with men, and hast prevailed.' And Jacob asked him, and said: 'Tell me, I pray thee, thy name.' And he said, 'Wherefore is it that thou dost ask after my name?' And he blessed him there. And Jacob called the name of the place 'Peniel' : 'For I have seen God face to face, and my life is preserved'. "[81]

In the Torah the name Israel is taken to mean one who has contended with the Divine. The wrestling of Jacob is, as we said, symbolic. Kaplan interprets this as under :

"A number of commentaries see Jacob's experience as having taken place in a meditative state. Jacob did not physically wrestle with an angel, but he perceived a spiritual being while meditating. The name Israel that Jacob received would then pertain to his entering into a spiritual state and contending with his experiences there. It is precisely when one is in a meditative state that one has contact with the spiritual on an intimate level. The Shema addresses itself to such a seeker and calls him by the name Israel. The Shema is addressing the 'Israel' in each one of us."[82]

The following words of the Shema are : Adonoy (Our God), (*Adonoy Elohenu*). Here the Shema declares man's closeness to God — so close is God to us that we call him 'Ours.'

The Shema ends with 'Adonoy is One' (*Adonoy Echad*).

"We see in God the most absolute Unity imaginable, the Oneness that unifies all creation.

"The more we realise this, the more we begin to see that on an ultimate level there is no plurality. If there is no plurality, then we are also one with God. When saying the word 'One' (*Echad*) in the Shema, one can realise this in a deep sense."[83]

The Shema, as we said above, demonstrated the essential unity of God. This led the Kabbalists to speculate on the words YHVH Elohim, YHVH[84] and the letters of *Echad* (One).

G. Scholem writes

"According to the manuals of even the oldest schools of the Kabbalah, the mystical meditation, which seeks to penetrate the words in their Kabbalistic sense, passes through the entire world of the *Sefirot*, 'from bottom to top and top to bottom.' Not any single aspect, however important of this world, but the whole of it, is said to be concentrated in this formula."[85]

The Kabbalists were preoccupied with the Hebrew alphabet and numerals (please see the Alphabet Table at p. 211). There are no separate numerals, but each letter of the alphabet stands for a numeral. For instance, the first letter *Aleph* is equivalent to One. The last letter *Tau* is equivalent to 400. If we take the word *Echad* the Hebrew word for One, we find that its total numerical value is 13. The letters constituting the word *Echad* are Aleph + Heth + Daleth 1+ 8 + 4 = 13.

HEBREW ALPHABET

With their numerical values.

HEBREW ALPHABET.

Sign	Name	Transliteration	Numerical Value
א	Aleph	A	1
ב	Beth	B	2
ג	Gimel	G	3
ד	Daleth	D	4
ה	Hé	H	5
ו	'Vau	V	6
ז	Zayin	Z	7
ח	Heth	H	8
ט	Teth	T	9
י	Yod	Y	10
כ	Kaph	K	20
ל	Lamed	L	30
מ	Mim	M	40
נ.ן	Nun	N	50
ס	Samekh	S	60
ע	Ayin	I	70
פ	Pé	P	80
צ	Tzaddi	Z	90
ק	Kuf	Q	100
ר	Resh	R	200
ש	Shin	Sh	300
ת	Tau	Th	400

The Hebrew word for Love is *Ahavah*. It is constituted by the letters Aleph He Beth He 1 + 5 + 2 + 5 = 13. The numerical value of both One and Love is 13. It is love that breaks down barriers and unifies opposites. If we take the first word, 'Shema,' we notice that in Hebrew it is spelt as *shin, mem* and *ayin*. In the *Sefer Yezirah Shin* and *mem* are described as mother letters. The *Shin* is pronounced as 'Sh' or 'S' depending on where a diacritical point is placed on the right or left of the letter. It thus has a sound which comes closest to 'White noise.' White noise is defined as sound that "contains every possible wave length, and is usually heard as a hissing sound. On an oscilloscope, the '*S*' sound would appear as a totally chaotic jumble with no structure whatsoever."[86]

Harmonic sound is the opposite of white noise. "This is a hum, like the sound of a tuning fork. On an oscilloscope, this would appear as a perfect wavy line : The epitome of order and regularity. This is the sound of mem."[87]

Thus the sound of '*shin*' stands for a chaotic state of consciousness — a level of consciousness that exists in normal everyday life. '*Mem*' on the other hand, stands for *cool* and harmonic state. In the Hindu tradition, the word 'AUM' occupies a very similar place in meditation. It will be observed that 'Aum' too has the '*mem*' sound at the end — a sound that is conducive to harmony.

What conclusion do we draw from the foregoing discussion? First, that unity is of the essence of the Kabbalah. This comes very close to the views held by the Hindu mystics, particularly to Advaita. Another very important area in which Kabbalah comes close to the Hindu tradition is in the fact that it subscribes to the idea of reincarnation. In both Christianity and Christian mysticism the concept of reincarnation is unthinkable. Halevi quotes from the Zohar :

"Every soul is subject to the trial of transmigration . . . . An individual does not know that he is called for assessment before entering this world as well as after leaving it. He does not know how many transformations and esoteric trials he has to pass through . . . . and that souls revolve like a stone shot from a sling."[88]

The word for reincarnation in Hebrew is *Gilgulim* (Turnings). Halevi comments :

"Our free will, leading to wilful, will-less or willing actions generates what in India is called Karma, and in Kabbalah reward and punishment," ('unto the third and fourth generation').[89]

A comparison of the writings of Jewish mystics, with the mystical literature of other traditions, shows a striking restraint on the part of the former. Autobiographical descriptions of mystical experiences is the glory of mystical literature. These autobiographical descriptions not only form part of the great literature of the world, but also afford material for psychological study of mysticism. Hindu, Christian and Sufi traditions have produced considerable literature of this kind. But the Kabbalists were no friends of mystical autobiographies. Their descriptions are impersonal, something like those of the Upaniṣadic seers, completely objective. They are deeply averse to allowing their own personality to intrude into the picture. There may be many reasons for this barren attitude. G. Scholem hazards a guess that it may be due to sense of incongruity between mystical experience and the idea of God, which stresses the aspects of Creator, King and Law giver. Be that as it may, the absence of such autobiographical descriptions is a great obstacle in the way of psychological understanding of the Kabbalah.

Another very important difference between the Kabbalah and other non-Jewish forms of mysticism, is the masculine character of the Kabbalah. Feminine influence is non-existent. Hindu, Islamic and Christian traditions have had feminine representatives who brought glory to their traditions. Social status can hardly be the reason for this absence. One can hardly conceive of Catholic mysticism without its great women mystics. The only consolation Jewish mysticism derived from this absence was freedom from the tendency toward hysterical extravagance sometimes found in the outpourings of the feminine mystics.

Finally, when we examine the problem of the Messiah, the Kabbalah gives a startlingly different answer from that given by Judaism. "Such a person," writes Halevi, "is said to be present in every generation, so that the usual conception of the Messiah as having been, or being yet to come, takes on the dimension of the Divine, which is, 'I Was, I Am and I Will Be'."[90]

REFERENCES

1. Schoken Books, New York, 1967, pp. 5-6.
2. Ibid, pp. 10-11.
3. Ibid, p. 206.
4. *Note* : Brahman, for instance, is neuter in Sanskrit.
5. The Age of Faith, Simon and Schuster, New York, 1950, p. 416.
6. *Note* : There were three successive temples in Jerusalem, all on the same site. The first temple was begun in the fourth year of Solomon's reign and was completed in seven years and six months. After an existence of four hundred and ten years it was burned down by Nebuchadnezzar of Babylonia in 586 before the common era. The second temple was begun fifty years after the destruction of the first and was completed within twenty years

(516) by the exiles who returned to Judea. The third temple, referred to as that of Herod the Great, was begun twenty years before the common era and was destroyed after ninety years of existence by the Roman soldiers in the year 70. The remains of the third temple disappeared. Part of the wall enclosing Herod's temple is still standing in the old section of Jerusalem. This wall is known as Western Wall (*Kothel ma'aravi*). It is popularly known as the 'Wailing Wall.'

7. *Note* : The author of The Cloud specifically warns against the misuse of such powers.
8. Quoted by Evelyn Underhill, in Mysticism, Methuen and Co. Ltd., London, 1967, pp. 100-101, from "The Three-fold Life of Man," Cap. VI, 71.
9. Ibid, p. 101.
10. The Mystical Quabalah, Ernest Benn Ltd., London, 1966.
11. Yathorṇābhiḥ sṛjate gṛhṇate ca
    yathā pṛthivyām oṣadhayaḥ sambhavanti
    Yathā sataḥ Puruṣāt Keśalomāni
    tathā kṣarāt sambhavatīha viśvam.
    (Muṇḍ. 1.1.7)
12. See p. 159.
13. Encyclopaedia Judaica, p. 564.
14. Kabbalah, Thames and Hudson, 1979, p. 5.
15. Zohar, Vol. I, Tr. by Harry Sperling & Maurice Simon, The Soncino Press, New York, 1984, p. 387.
16. Ibid, pp. 379-380.
17. Ibid, p. 380 — *Beth* — Second letter of the Hebrew Alphabet. *Bereshith* = in the beginning.
18. Encyclopaedia Judaica, p. 560.
19. Ibid, *pp. 560.*
20. Chānd. VI. 2.2.
21. Chānd. VI.2.3.
22. Bṛ. III.ix. 28.7.
23. See Vedānta Sāra of Sadānanda, Advaita Ashrama, Calcutta, 1987, p. 21.
24. Encyclopaedia Judaica, p. 562.
25. Invocation : Īśa.
26. Answer to Job, Bollingen Series, Princeton University Press, 1973, p. xi-xii.

27. Ibid, p. Xiii.
28. Collected Works, Routledge and Kegan Paul, London, Part 1.79, Vol. 9.
29. Gershom Scholem, On The Kabbalah and Its Symbolism, Routledge and Kegan Paul, London, 1965, p. 100.
30. Encyclopaedia Judaica, p. 584.
31. Genesis, 1 : 3 to 8.
32. Zohar, Vol. II, p. 398.
33. Genesis, 2 : 17.
34. Genesis, 3 : 5.
35. Genesis, 3 : 24.
36. Encyclopaedia Judaica, p. 585.
37. This contraction is technically called "*Sumsum*." The primordial space that came into being as a result of the contraction is called *Tehiru* originally, a Zoharic term meaning 'splendour.' It is the Aramaic form of the Hebrew Zohar.
38. Gershom Scholem, Sabbatai Sevi, The Mystical Messiah, Bollingen Series, XCIII, Princeton University Press, 1975, Tr. R.J. Zwi Werblowsky, pp. 300-301.
39. Kabbalah, Thames and Hudson, p. 5.
40. The Black Arts, G.P. Putnam's Sons, New York, 1967, p. 90.
41. The Kabbalah Unveiled, Routledge and Kegan Paul Ltd., London, 1968, p. 18.
42. The Zohar, Vol. V, The Somcino Press, New York, p. 396.
43. NOTE : The immanence and omnipresence of God among men is signified by the term Shekhinah. Some modern writers also equate it with the last Sefirah — Malkhut. Where men gather in worship, or judges sit in court to dispense justice, or where even one man studies the Torah, Shekhinah is present. Bridal mysticism, so familiar in Hindu mysticism (Mira, the Alvars) is also associated with the Shekhinah.
44. Law of Moses.

    Pentateuch is a Greek word meaning the five books of Moses : Genesis, Exodus, Leviticus, Numbers, Deuteronomy.
45. The Zohar, Vol. V, p. 395
46. The Kabbalah Unveiled, Routledge and Kegan Paul Ltd., London, 1968, p. 16.
47. Kabbalah, Thames Hudson, London, pp. 5-6.
48. Ibid, p. 6.
49. Isaiah 43 : 7.

50. Z'ev ben Shimon Halevi, Kabbalah, Thames and Hudson, London, pp. 8-9.
51. Ibid, p. 9.
52. Ibid, pp. 19-20.
53. Ibid, p. 24.
54. mā gṛdhaḥ kasyasviddhanam (Īśa 1).
55. Pañcadaśī — 1.27.
56. The Dialogues of Plato, Vol. II, p. 15.
57. Major Trends in Jewish Mysticism, Schoken Books, New York, 1967, p. 209.
58. Ibid, pp. 260-261.
59. Louis Jacobs, Jewish Theology, Darton, Longman and Todd, London, 1973, p. 32.
60. *Note* : *HASIDISM* :

    Hasidism denotes godliness, goodness. Modern Hasidism owes its origin to Rabbi Israel Baal Shemtov (1700-1760). He was born in the Ukraine. He taught that devotion was the main ingredient that brought an aspirant in contact with God. Like the Upaniṣads, he too preached that scholarship and learning were not necessary for this purpose, but the aspirant had to be optimistic and keep away from grief and sadness. Thus music and dance formed an integral and essential part of Hasidism. Omnipresence and immanence of God was the central teaching. Divine light pervaded all things, with the result that there was no place which was void of God. Therefore, there was actual good in all things. The essence of Hasidism was a passionate devotion to God. Ecstatic prayer, singing and dancing infused fresh vitality not only in Judaism but also in Jewish mysticism.

    The Hasidism emphasis on joy and dance was prompted by the fact that presence of God cannot rest where there is sadness and grief and despair. The generality of religious people associate solemnity with matters spiritual. The Hasidic attitude appeared strange and even frivolous. In fact a great authority, Scholem, took the movement to task.

    We find several mystics in our land who dance and sing in mystical ecstasy in their attempt to reach God. Tukaram, Mira and Chaitanya Mahaprabhu, despite their tribulations, sang their way to God.
61. Louis Jacobs, Jewish Theology, Darton, Longman and Todd, London, 1973, p. 34.
62. Ibid, p. 35.

63. Encyclopaedia Judaica, p. 628.
64. Arysh Kaplan, Jewish Meditation, Schoeken Books, New York, 1985, p. 61.
65. Ibid, p. 83.
66. Ibid, pp. 84-85.
67. Ezekiel, 3 : 12.
68. Isaiah, 30 : 21.
69. Ezekiel, I : 4.
70. Farid-ud-Din Attar, Mantiq-ut-Tayr (Colloquy of the Birds), Humphrey Milford, Oxford University Press, New York, 1924.
71. Aryeh Kaplan, Meditation and Kabbalah, Samuel Weiser, York Beach, Maine, 1986, p. 299.
72. Authorised Daily Prayer Book of the United Hebrew Congregation of the British Commonwealth of Nations, p. 46.
73. Kaplan, Jewish Meditation, p. 104.
74. Ibid, p. 120.
75. Ibid, p. 121.
76. Diagram figures by Rabbi Jacob Emden of Altone, Germany, 18th C.
77. Kabbalah, p. 92.
78. The Pentateuch and Haftorah, Ed. Dr. J.H. Hertz, Late Chief Rabbi of the British Empire, Soncing Press, London, 1973, p. 922.
79. Isaiah, 45 : 7.
80. Op. cit. 920.
81. Genesis, XXXII : 27-31. (Pentateuch and Haftorahs).
82. Jewish Meditation, Schocken Books, New York, 1985, p. 125.
83. Ibid, p. 126.
84. YHVH = Yod Hé Vau Hé. It is never pronounced. The Divine Name is spoken of as Tetragrammaton, which is a Greek word meaning 'The Name of four letters.' It is pronounced as '*Adonoy*.' It gives expression to the fact that He was, He is, He ever will be. Here, too, the words must not be understood in the philosophical sense of mere 'being' but as active manifestation of Divine existence.

(See Exodus III.15. Also Foot Note The Pentateuch and Haftorahs, pp. 215 216).

Note: 'Jehovah' is a misreading by non-Jews, who are unaware that the vowel points of the four-letter name belong to the word *Adonoy* which is used as a substitute.

85. On The Kabbalah and Its Symbolism, Routledge and Kegan Paul, London, 1965, p. 131.
86. Jewish Meditation, p. 129.
87. Ibid, p. 129.
88. Kabbalah, p. 29, quoted by author from Zohar, Spain, 13th century.
89. Ibid, p. 29. Also see Exodus 20 : 5.
90. Ibid, p. 30.

CHAPTER V

Conclusions

In the preceding chapters we have attempted to explore the mystical traditions of the three great religions of the world viz., Hindu (which includes Buddhist), Christian and Jewish (Kabbalistic). Among the many facts that have emerged from this exploration, one of the most significant is that the observer is himself a part of the content of consciousness. This view is supported not only by the mystical traditions but also by New Physics (Quantum mechanics).

The mention of quantum mechanics brings us within hailing distances of our own times, which gives us the determination to keep hold of a proper perspective. Most writers are historians of sorts. They may be political or military historians. But their task is different from that of a historian of ideas. The former are not expected to include active participation in the events they chronicle. On the other hand the historian of ideas, like the one writing on Mysticism or Aesthetics, is in a situation where his readers can fairly hope that he knows whereof he talks, as one who has taken some part, howsoever modest, in the concepts and ideas of which he writes. It is, therefore, not easy to write on a subject like mysticism, without at some time or the other having been touched by what Wordsworth called 'Intimations of Immortality.'

Another very significant fact that emerged was that, on account of the three widely differing traditions the key terms sometimes shifted senses according to the movement of the dialectic. But this was inevitable. No matter to what tradition the key terms belonged — Hindu, Christian or Jewish — they would at all times fall short of the ideal terms. In fact it is essential to the notion of Reality that its description should fall short of it, otherwise the description itself would be the Reality. The Ideal, as we have tried to show while quoting Plato can never be described as it is. Reality or Brahman or En Sof or the Absolute is like absolute Beauty, not seen with eyes, but grasped when the mystic identifies himself with it. This identification can take place through recollection (*anamnesis*). The mystic would term this 'recollection,' meditation.

After exploring the three traditions, we have reached a stage where we may assert that for the mystic to claim to have experience of Absolute Perfection while still retaining his limitations as a finite being, has in it nothing impossible, nothing contradictory. Again, we must remind ourselves that properly to understand mysticism we must in some degree be mystics ourselves.

In describing a region of consciousness so vast and inclusive, that even the most detailed description must needs seem but meagre and inadequate. If our definition of mystic experience, that it is the direct and immediate experience of Divine Perfection, is correct, then it should not be difficult to accept that the suddenness and completeness of the transfiguration of consciousness is quite in accordance with the nature of things, that is, there is validity in the mysticism's claim to have experience of Absolute Perfection while still retaining his finite status.

This transition, however, is possible only in the traditions of the most developed religions of the world, where it has been prepared for subconsciously, by the long religious history of the races. Where other factors, like solitude and silence are freely available, such a transition from the phenomenal to the noumenal, takes place with greater suddenness. It was for this reason that in the midst of the solitude and silence afforded by the great forests of India, the Upaniṣads, which contain the profoundest metaphysical and mystical religion in the world were given birth to. Similarly, the peaceful and secluded atmosphere of the monasteries of the middle ages in Europe produced some of the greatest mystics in the world.

Another fact that emerged from our exploration is the ineffability of the mystical experience. Despite this handicap, mystics in all ages have not refrained from recording their mystical experiences— in words and in action. The purpose of this was to share their experiences with others, which, in turn, gave birth to great cultures and religions, like Hinduism. The teachings and principles of religion invariably begin with an experience of God : The Upaniṣads in Hinduism, the Bible in Judaism and Christianity, the Koran in Islam, and the other great scriptures of the world are the fruits of such mystical experiences. Ineffability, therefore, far from being a hindrance, not only gave birth to the great religions of the world, but also produced some of the greatest and finest classical and spiritual literature.

The mystics' constant reiteration of words and expressions like 'beyond the understanding,' 'subler than the subtle,' 'beyond logic' and so on, will have to be judged within the framework they are used. For the mystic words like 'understanding,' 'intellect,' 'logic,' 'reason' are synonymous. We have noticed that these words are used interchangeably. These words, and some others like them, indicate that ineffability is due to the incapacity of the understanding or intellect to cope with the mystical experience. The mystical experience is such that it can be directly experienced, but cannot be abstracted into concepts. That is to say, it cannot be conceptualised.

In any theory of language, every word (except proper names), stands for a concept. It, therefore, follows that where concepts are not possible, expression in words is not possible. Ineffability in the case of Śa ṅkara's monism could be explained more easily than it could be explained in respect of other forms of mysticism. Where there is undifferentiated unity, the experience is devoid of all empirical content. It is, so to say without 'form' or 'void.' There are no distinguishable characteristics which can form the basis of concepts. Hence no words can be employed in regard to them.

If we examine the full implications of these remarks, it becomes problematic whether such a theory would be acceptable or not. Apparently the discussion leads us to an impasse. On the face of it, it would appear that the difficulty in expressing is due not so much to an emotional block, but to a logical difficulty. In the circumstances the word 'ineffable' or 'ineffability' should be used sparingly, because, there is a risk that the reader will take it literally, that is, he would be led to believe that an experience of 'undifferentiated unity' only may be properly called 'mystical.' This form may be the highest type of mysticism, but it does not follow from this that there are no other forms of mysticism. The preceding chapters have endeavoured to show this. We can only observe here that statements like 'It is so-and-so' 'It is not so-and-so' are not paradoxical. It is not the words in which the utterance is couched that is paradoxical, but the experience itself is paradoxical. In the circumstances the mystic retracts a statement as soon as he has made it. When he says "It is so and so," he realises that it is incorrect. So he says "It is not so and so." Having uttered such contradictory language, he blames language for its inability to express his experience, without realising that he has actually described an experience which by its very nature is paradoxical.

This would be one way of explaining the paradoxicality of the language. It would be the psychological way of explaining a spiritual experience. Moreover, it would be wrong to assume that the mystical experience ends abruptly. In fact in the Hindu tradition the view is that once realisation takes place, the mystic does not slide back. With the Hindu mystic the *ideal pattern* remains even after the clear manifestation has faded away. In this regard the Christian view is just the contrary : The mystic has to be on his guard lest he fall back into sin.

It has, therefore, to be admitted that the mystic cannot report his experience as it has occurred to him. Some part of it has to be an interpretation of his experience. This interpretation is naturally extrinsic to the experience and constitutes extraneous material. Insofar as the mystic adds non-experienced data to his description, he is falsifying his account. But when it is admitted that there is genuine mystical experience, it will also have to be admitted that this addition is an unpremeditated act, that is, the mystic does not deliberately add this material.

In Zen Buddhism there is a saying that the Buddha, wishing to entice the blind, playfully let words escape his golden mouth. The saying goes on to add that since then, Heaven and Earth are filled with entangling briars. Zen Buddhism is replete with paradoxes illustrating the relationship between experience and the words in which it is the duty of the knower to hand on his experience. The preceding chapters have shown that despite heavy odds the mystics have handed on their experiences.

Such words, recorded in the great scriptures of the world have inspired one man to become a mystic, and another, theologian. In other words, the former gives up the words in an attempt to know God directly, the latter devotes himself to an intensive analysis of words in an effort to know *about* God indirectly through discursive reasoning. The famous and oft-repeated utterance about he who knows does not speak and he who speaks does not know, taken literally is false, because most of those who knew have spoken, and at least some speakers have known. These latter were aware that their words were inadequate to match the Reality they have known.

In spiritual matters knowledge is dependent upon being, that is to say, words have different meanings for people on different levels of being. The unenlightened, for instance, are likely to interpret utterances for their own selfish ends.

We would make nonsense of our scriptures if the mystics, because of the ineffability of their experience, remained mum. The mystic must speak and indirectly hint at the nature of intuitively known Reality. Even if words cause confusion and create entanglements their absence will lead to total darkness.

Like 'ineffability' another word that has been the source of considerable confusion in mysticism is the word 'union.' We have shown how this word in the three traditions has different meanings. Generally speaking the monist would understand by 'union,' a sense of distinctionless unity whereas the devotional mystic would describe it as identity-in-difference. The Christian, Jewish, Viśiṣṭādvaitist would fall in this category. In other words for the latter, a mystic on reaching realisation does cease to exist as a limited and selfish individual, but at the same time he still exists in the sense that he has attained the state of boundless consciousness. The mystic is not blotted out, which is what would happen if there was annihilation. The identity persists in and through the difference. In Judaism and Christianity an unbridgeable gulf exists between man and God. Mansur paid with his life for uttering 'I am God, I am God.' Even Eckhart, a great exponent of undifferentiated unity wrote :

"Does she find herself or not? . . . . God has left her one little point from which to get back to herself . . . . and know herself creature."[1] What is meant is that 'one little point' is the point at which the 'I' though purified, still remains its individual self. The 'little point' shows the 'difference.' Here we have an advocate of undifferentiated unity, in the tradition of Śaṅkara, expressing in terms of 'identity in difference.'

No matter what interpretations are placed on terms like 'ineffability,' 'union' and so on, mysticism is the intuitive experience of direct union with the Supreme Being, on this earth while one is in his mortal body. The 'union' may be an undifferentiated unity or identity-in-difference. We hold that the Advaitic realisation is the highest form of spiritual realisation : Dvaitā, Viśiṣṭādvaita and Advaita are not contradictory, but complementary. If they are treated as three stages, the Advaitic experience could be attained. In fact most great mystics (Rāmakṛṣṇa for instance) after their Advaitic experience continued to live on the relative plane, so that they could be of use to other aspirants.

Let us now briefly examine the traditions we have discussed in the preceding chapters for their points of divergence and convergence. The Hindu tradition, with the exception of the early materialist schools, both Vedic and non-Vedic, propounded theories that laid the foundation for a way of life, with enlightenment and liberation as the end in view. Besides, these systems placed considerable reliance on the scriptures. In fact all the traditions placed their foundation in their respective scriptures.

With enlightenment and liberation being the chief aims of all theories, it was not surprising that the great mystics, seers and philosophers were preoccupied with topics like the source of knowledge, criteria of truth and error. Serious arguments to support their theories are clearly discernible in their theories of knowledge or epistemology. Even a cursory glance at the Indian philosophical systems shows that the Indian philosophers were serious thinkers. In general it could be said that the philosophers and mystics view human beings as having a destiny which transcended both change and time. Though religiously oriented,

Hindu mysticism as a whole had an ambivalent attitude to belief in the existence of God.

If we take Śaṅkara, we find him rejecting sense perception as a source of knowledge. Both Rāmānuja and Madhva accept it. In Śaṅkara we have, what Dr. S.G. Mudgal aptly termed a two tier system. While the empirical world was an appearance in relation to Brahman, it was real enough at the level of practical life. This latter could be termed scientific knowledge. Perception for Śaṅkara belonged to the sphere of Appearance, because it implied a perceiver-perceived, subject-object distinction. This was the level where the One *appeared* as many.

Śaṅkara, Rāmānuja and Madhva discussed in their epistemology the ways of arriving at knowledge. This led to the corollary; what was the relation of enlightenment and liberation to the problem of error. When we declare that we have obtained knowledge and that we believe it to be what it is, the possibility of an error cannot be ruled out. How then do we distinguish between truth and error ? Various ways were suggested. We refer to Śaṅkara's view. Śaṅkara imputes error to interpretation. A vital word where mysticism is concerned. Interpretation is nothing but our judgement about a particular datum. We recall here the oft-repeated example of the coiled rope and snake. The error is corrigible. When the rope is mistaken for a snake there is an error in our interpretation. We can make a correct interpretation by replacing the first experience with another experience, by viewing the coiled rope as a coiled rope. While the first experience could be contradicted, the second one cannot be contradicted. It follows, therefore, that absence of contradiction is the manifestation of truth. Śaṅkara would say that Truth is self-manifesting. But he would not stop with this. He would add that truth can be veiled. So when there is erroneous judgement of perception, it has to be substituted by an experience which unveils the truth. In our illustration the rope is now seen as a rope. Now nothing can contradict it. For Śaṅkara, seeing the rope as a rope is a mystical experience. All that the mystic has to do is to avoid mixing up the rope with the snake. In other words to 'know' it, "He who knows Brahman, becomes Brahman."[2]

Therefore, the key to Reality is the self. Evidently such a oneness is ineffable. It has to be apprehended intuitively. There can be no error at the level where subject-object distinctions disappear. The hierarchical vision of Advaita is built on four levels represented by the four stages described in the Māṇḍūkya Upaniṣad, viz., waking (*viśva*), dream (*taijasa*), sleep (*suṣupti*) and finally (*turīya*).

"The Self is possessed of four quarters."[3]

The initiate is expected to examine each of these states, both psychologically and spiritually. When viewed introspectively in this manner they disclose their macrocosmic and microcosmic implications, which finally lead to *turīya* or the fourth state. A similar form of meditation is also to be found in the Kabbalah where instead of four levels we have ten levels.

These three states are also identified with AUM, Turīya being identified with the *soundless* stage. In either case when the first three stages are sublated, the Turīya stage is attained, in which all the previous stages are sublated. It does not exist in Christian mysticism. No hierarchical system was erected by it. The Vedāntists and to a certain extent the Kabbalists had some help from the scriptures, which the Christian mystics did not have. To build a hierarchical system of meditation co-operation is of prime importance. The Hindu tradition was unique in this respect. It built up systems of meditation which have no parallel in the world. As for Judaism its mystical tradition thrives only in a crisis. And there was no dearth of crisis in its history. In Christianity on the other hand mysticism was not looked upon with favour, with the result that a lot of it developed in a clandestine atmosphere which was not conducive to the erection of a structure which could be used as a model for meditation. Even if in the ultimate stage, everything, even the way falls away, the structure is necessary to reach the ultimate stage.

Rāmānuja's attitude to Realisation differs from that of Śaṅkara and to a lesser degree from Madhva. It would not be far wrong to say that Rāmānuja and Madhva are fellow theists. Rāmānuja, like Śaṅkara, accepts the scriptures as the final authority, as infallible, and indestructible. He resolved the tension between knowledge and action with Vedic ritualists on one hand, and Vedāntic monist on the other by independently synthesising knowledge and action. What is significant in Rāmānuja is that he holds *all* scriptures as being of equal importance, implying that

Śaṅkara was selective in his resort to the scriptures. Thus for Rāmānuja it was enough to take the statements made about the Being in their direct sense. For him, therefore, Mahāvākyas like *tat tvam asi* (That Thou Art) and other important texts have to be interpreted with reference to their contexts, that is, in relation to what has been previously mentioned. Rāmānuja in this sense can be called a religious realist. For Rāmānuja no less than Śaṅkara, realisation is the ultimate end, but ritual is a necessary part of it, insofar as it prepares the aspirant for the final stage by purifying his mind. This purification aids in the steadfast meditation on the being of Brahman. Even if this reminds us of Śaṅkara's attitude to works, it must be borne in mind that Rāmānuja does not separate action and knowledge in the sharp manner in which Śaṅkara does. For Rāmānuja the ritual part is a life long exercise.

This is a very important difference between the mysticisms of the two great mystics. For Śaṅkara action is superseded once knowledge is obtained. The crutches of action/ritual are to be discarded. Ritual is like a good farmer preparing the soil. Once the fruit (knowledge) springs up everything else loses its importance. For Rāmānuja, control of mind, senses, etc. is a continuing process, a process that helps to perfect the knowledge already attained. In other words there have to be repeated note of knowledge which can only be achieved by concentrating the mind on the Supreme Being uninterruptedly. It is this uninterrupted process of bringing action — knowledge in an interrelation in devotion, that gives rise to the concept of grace, which forms the very foundation of Rāmānuja's mysticism. This concept is almost totally absent in Śaṅkara. In fact it is not a concept that can easily go with Advaita. We have discussed this concept in several contexts in the preceding chapters. Suffice it to say that for Rāmānuja, devotion itself was a sort of knowledge. Continuous devotion, therefore, brought about the descent of Grace which is another name for the Supreme Being. If the descent of Grace is the descent of the Supreme Being, then it follows that the Supreme Being is both the means and the end of all religious practice.

Madhva too regards the scriptures as the source of revelation, but his use of the scriptures is definitely more sophisticated. When doubt arises reason should be employed. Perception was basic to knowledge, but in the final analysis the inner witness was the chief arbiter. The scriptures, however, have a self validating character. Like Rāmānuja he held that the existence of the Supreme Being had to be accepted on the basis of the revelation of the scriptures. In this regard Judaism, too, accepts the existence of God on the basis of the Old Testament.

For Madhva the greatest mystical experience was to see the Supreme Being. He held the immediate vision of the Supreme Being to be of paramount importance. Besides he held this experience to be far superior to that gained through a medial method. Intuition thus played a very vital role in his system. He never made devotional dependence on the Supreme Being redundant. Only for him the immediate experience was of a superior kind. The usual preparation of hearing, reflecting and meditating were not to be neglected. In this regard we could hazard a guess that though the End realised by devotion and meditation is the same as that attained directly, for Madhva, the two experiences were not on equal footing. Despite all this, the overall picture of Madhva's system shows that the essence of his mysticism lay in the devotional attachment to the Lord. If immediate mystical experience was of the essence then the hierarchical structure he raised would hardly be necessary. Besides, the distinction he draws between Lord's independent being (*svatantra*) and the other beings (*paratantra*) would necessitate the devotional scheme.

What conclusions can we draw from the above discussion? That there is common concern for the Perfection of Brahman. At the same time this common concern is the cause of division among the Vedāntists. The divergence between the monistic position on one hand and the theistic position on the other, is epistemological, ontological and soteriological. But despite all these differences, all the three positions are mystical, in that they expound doctrines that are purported to lead the aspirant to liberation. Talking of the other traditions, Rāmānuja's doctrines would appeal the most to the Christian mystic. The Kabbalist would come close to Advaita. The En Sof of Kabbalah would come closest to Śaṅkara's Brahman. With Madhva's emphasis on Images, Kabbalah would hardly have any common ground with Dvaitā.

To revert, in Vedānta, Brahman is seen as a transcendent perfection. Śaṅkara, Rāmānuja and Madhva all agree on this. But where there is transcendence there is immanence. It is this immanental dimension that is the cause of divergence among the Vedāntists. The immanental aspect of Brahman's transcendence involves relationship with the universe. It is in the interpretation of this aspect the Vedāntists differ; which brings about a difference between their forms of mysticism.

Śaṅkara's Advaita identifies the Ātman with Brahman, the two being one, separated by Ignorance. The monist thus takes his stand on the absolute oneness of selfhood. Such a position is abhorrent to the theist who while extolling the Supreme Person and Lord, stops short. In the ultimate state of release, all that the soul attracts is qualities that are similar to Brahman. The distance between Brahman and the soul is thus maintained. This is a position again that comes close to Christian and Jewish mysticism, both of whom along with the Hindu theists desire to safeguard the perfection of God which is threatened when the soul identifies itself with Brahman, that is, when there is absolute unity, or pure unitary consciousness. Incidentally it may be observed that Christian mysticism gives a very important place to Grace and devotional prayers. But it does not give the same measure of importance that the Hindu theists give. To the latter, these are not provisional states but they have ultimate reality. The dualist, for instance, never identifies himself with the Supreme Person, nor does the Christian mystic. The author of The Cloud says that God is my being. Never, I am God.

The mystical position changes when we come to Buddhism. For Buddha metaphysical discussions were futile. Brahman or Ātman held no reality for him. What was real was *nirvāṇa*, which was nothing but the subjective state of enlightenment. It was, therefore, not surprising that Buddha was accused of being an atheist.

For him everything is flux. Events take place, one succeeding another. *Sarvaṃ duḥkhaṃ, sarvam anityaṃ*. The world of forms, things, events is *cittamātra* or mind only or *vijñaptimātra*, representation only. If we examine the Eastern traditions carefully, we discover similar views expressed in all of them. Back of them all is cosmic consciousness. The final emphasis is always placed on the non-reality of the material world.

We will not enter further into a discussion on this, because we have discussed them before. One thing, however, stands out loud and clear, and that is, that the final thrust of Hindu and even Buddhist mysticism is towards monism. The Vedic search was always for the one reality. The spiritual search was converted into a psychological one, when the seers studied the waking, dream and deep dream states. But always the thrust was towards monism. Even New Physics supported this thrust. Giving a survey of the various doctrinal positions, R.T. Vyas writes :

"Yājñavalkya's theory of *Advaita,* supported as it was by comprehensive analysis of consciousness, braced by Śaṅkara's dialectics, exercised great influence on Indian philosophical thought to the extent that all great *Ācāryas,* . . . . accepted Advaita to be the fundamental Upaniṣadic teaching. Differences in their doctrine are mainly regarding its type, interpretation and modality."[4]

The holistic tendency is inherent in nature. Till the dawn of modern physics, science and mysticism tended to go their antagonistic way. But today, the physicists tend to think in mystical terms. One important reason for this is that both physics and mysticism have ineffability as one of their chief characteristics. Hitherto mind-matter, God-man formed an ontological dualism. Modern physics ruled it out of court as out-moded. The universe could not more be described *per se.* It had become imperative to include man as part of this description. As we said at the outset, the observer and the observed can no more be separated. In fact what the physicists write is more like Advaita than physics. Only the language they use is mathematics. The mystic used poetry and music. We quote one example from The Eye of Shiva :

"It is highly symbolic that such an eminent physicist as Erwin Schrodinger should lend his powerful voice to a persuasive defence of Eastern monism as against Western monotheism, in the light of the fundamental Oneness displayed at the microcosmic level of physics where all phenomena are interrelated and cannot be viewed as autonomous and isolated events or processes. He points out that the plurality perceived by us is an illusion, quoting Vedāntic philosophy and its famous analogy of the universe assimilated to a many-faceted crystal which shows multitudes of pictures of what is a single realty, without multiplying it."[5]

Q of unity of Vedanta

Where do we go from here? The existence of God cannot be proved. Both philosophy and theology are unable to prove it. All that can be said is that it is one of the mysteries that cannot be fathomed. Are we, for that reason, going to abandon it, leave it alone? The answer is 'NO.' The answer lies in the mystical glimpses, intuition of the great seers of all traditions. It has been admitted that both philosophy and theology do not possess the infrastructure to encompass the mystical experience. All that mysticism will demand from these two disciplines is sympathy and co-operation. Philosophy will have to make a concession in its logical approach and theology will have to forego, at least in part, its insistence on definite beliefs. It will have to abandon its stand that (at least in Christian theology to some extent Jewish also) salvation is a sort of perennial fixity. Besides, philosophy, which exclusively concerns itself with thinking, will have to step down and add a philosophy of feeling by introducing more discipline in it. As for theology, it will have to view the mystical experience, more from the psychological, than from the moral or theological point of view. For this the mystical experience will have to be evaluated both intellectually and aesthetically. The Beautiful has always excited the mystic. It is this reaction to Beauty that has given birth to Art, music, poetry. The artist in the widest sense of the word, contemplates God with his whole being, that is, all his faculties come into play in the process of such contemplation. Such contemplation also brings the artist into union with God. Aesthetics, therefore, play a very important role in mysticism.

The mystical experience is an aesthetic experience. The Hindu mystic experiences joy, happiness and bliss. In the Jewish Hasidic tradition, joy and happiness form an integral part of the experience. Any negative emotion like sadness, sorrow are frowned upon. Besides, Beauty constitutes one of the ten Sefirot on the Tree of Life. But the Christian looks upon Beauty with suspicion, because of the ugly emotions associated with it in our mundane life. This is unfortunate. The Beautiful, whether in spirituality or Art has always a mystical element in it. The misunderstanding arises because, writes Alan Watts, "Of that trinity of virtues, the Good, the Beautiful and the True, the Beautiful has always been somewhat problematic for Christian thought, since it has felt that so many things are beautiful which are neither true nor good. The restoration of Beauty to its proper place in our image of God is one of the more important results of an incarnational mysticism, for Beauty is at once the most spiritual and the most material of the three virtues."[6]

Watts adds

"To Christians infected with Gnosticism, beauty is suspect just because it is associated with matter and especially with woman, the symbol of Mother Earth."[7]

For the Hindu mystic, the prerequisites for the aesthetic experience and the mystical experience are the same, identity of subject-object, even of cause and effect. Ananda K. Coomaraswamy citing from *Sāhitya Darpaṇa* of Viśvanātha writes :

"What then are *rasa* and *rasāsvādana*, beauty and aesthetic emotion? The nature of this experience is discussed by Viśvanātha in the *Sāhitya Darpaṇa* : 'It is pure, indivisible, self-manifested, compounded equally of joy and consciousness, free of admixture with any other perception, the very twin brother of mystic experience (*Brahmāsvādana sahodaraḥ*), and the very life of it is supersensuous (*lokottara*) wonder.' Further, 'It is enjoyed by those who are competent thereto, in identity, just as the form of God is itself the joy with which it is recognised'. "[8]

From what we have discussed in the foregoing chapters, it is clear that in the higher reaches in both the aesthetic experience and the mystical experience, the intellect must be transcended. The mystic claims that at this level, to associate the intellect in an attempt to know God, is futile. The mystic is not an artist, who merely delights. He has also to enlighten. Blake wanted us to cleanse The Doors of Perception, so that everything may appear as it is, infinite.

A mystic who continues to sit under a tree or on the top of a mountain meditating even after he has achieved Salvation, indifferent to the world, has perhaps missed the point. No doubt, mysticism is a flight of the alone to the alone. The Buddha or The Christ or Moses or Tukaram, meditated *alone*. They were realised souls. But did they, therefore, continue to sit in meditation contented with their realised state? No. They all moved out of their solitude and became active in the world. The individualism of the search for salvation lasts so long as salvation is not attained. The moment it is attained, the mystic returns to active life in the world. Whether it was Śaṅkara or Rāmānuja or Madhva or Moses or Christ or Tukaram or Rāmadāsa or Jñāneśvara or Rāmakṛṣṇa, all returned to carry on work in the world. This was the reason Rāmakṛṣṇa is said to have kept himself at the 'Sixth plexus' of Tantra, that is on the threshold of relative consciousness (*bhavamukha*) which is the boundary between the Absolute and the Relative. For the Hindu mystic this return is inevitable. It is the best way of spending the unspent portion of his Karma. Even Plato's liberated 'Prisoner' returns to the cave to tell the inmates, that the substance is outside the cave and is not a shadow. 'Barechested and barefooted he stands in the market place, he touches a log and lo! It sprouts' (Zen).

Mysticism is not marginal in the life of the mystic. It permeates his whole life. It is for this reason that the mystic feels himself in tune with not only the Infinite but also with the whole universe. He does not, he cannot, remain in isolation, cut off from the outer world. He comes down from the heights of his mystical experience, in some cases to communicate his experience to others in an esoteric report, as in the case of the Vedic and Upaniṣadic seers, where the experience was communicated to a circle of disciples. Some communicated it in the form of written accounts, giving it the form of instruction or confession. The Buddha is the classic example of one who communicated it in an *exoteric* manner by spurning the peace and blessedness of Nirvāṇa, going among the people to preach his saving doctrine. Plato, Plotinus were politically active. Lao-tzu, modelled a state on mystic lines. In our times we have the example of Dag Hammarskjold, who tried to serve the world through the United Nations. He left a mystical diary, with a note to the Swedish Permanent Under Secretary for Foreign Affairs, Leif Belfrage. He wrote to him *inter alia* :

"If you find them worth publishing, you have my permission to do so—as a sort of 'White Book' concerning my negotiation with myself— and with God."[9]

Hammarskjold is an illuminating example of a great mystic who entered world politics. He writes in his diary :

"In our age, the road to holiness necessarily passes through the world of action."[10]

We have another classic example of Martin Buber. He says, there is no independent "I" but only the "I" existing and known in objective relation to something other than itself, an "It" or as encountered by and encompassed by the other, the "Thou." He writes :

> "The primary word I—Thou can only be spoken with the whole thing.
>
> The primarily word I—It can never be spoken with the whole being".[11]

The mystic never loses sight of the fact that ultimately, the level he has reached is not an achievement, but grace. At all the high points of mysticism there follows a breakthrough of the experience of the grace, irrespective of the tradition to which the mystic belongs. To receive grace there has to be self surrender. The words 'I am nothing,' 'I am nobody' uttered by weakminded people are of no avail. They are, to say the least, fake. The mystic is a strong minded person, whose self surrender is somewhat in the nature of Hanumān's surrender to Rāma, whom Hanumān instals in his heart. When man places himself in this frame of mind, he realises that not only is he seeking God, but God is seeking him.

It is our thesis that there are several kinds of relationships with God. Strict empiricism is only one of the several modes of relationship with reality, but a life based solely upon this mode is likely to be anaemic to the core. Reality is both revealed and hidden (*deus revelatus* and *deus absconditus*). The mystic experiences both these forms of Reality. In some traditions, particularly Hindu tradition, the mystic can experience *deus revelatus* even in an image. To him, as for a devotee, the image is not an image. For him, it is a consecrated image in which by virtue of being consecrated, the image which would otherwise be a lifeless stone, is imbued with life by the condescension of the Deity in it. This is true of images and icons both in the Eastern and Western traditions. The Deity controls the mystic as a Thou.

But then the true mystic is not satisfied with this level of contact. Over and above this personal God, is the Brahman, the *En Sof* or what Eckhart called *Gottheit*, the Deity in the absolute mysterium, ineffable, unfathomable and unknowable. It is described aptly in the Old Testament : "And He said : 'Thou canst not see my face, for man cannot see me, and live', "[12] or, "If the splendour of a thousand suns were to rise up simultaneously in the sky, that would be like the splendour of that Mighty Being."[13] This is the ineffable. The mystic who dares to penetrate into this secret is 'Shattered' by it. But a mystic who did not enter this secret is no mystic. Mysticism is not static or theoretical. It is something practical.

If there are several modes, it is because Reality has several dimensions within Itself. The Upaniṣads repeat this Truth again and again. Even the Bhagavad Gītā is a reiteration of the first two verses of the Iśāvāsyopaniṣad. We have analysed these thoughts in our chapter on the four Upaniṣads. The gist of these two verses is : Everything in the universe abides in the Supreme Being (Īśa vāsyam idaṁ sarvaṁ).

If this is the case nothing belongs to us. We should do our duty and live out the allotted span of our life.

These two verses reflect the call of ultimate reality heard in the recesses of noble seers. But to understand their import, just as fully to understand mysticism, man needs in some measure to be a mystic himself. After all we are not dealing here with an experience common to humanity.

The mysticism of the various traditions dealt with by us, relates the good life to truth, goodness and beauty. The differences are superficial and qualitative. This is mainly due to the conditioning each mystic receives from his tradition. But, no matter what the differences, the final unifying vision is that of the Real, whether reached by a strict concatenation of logical judgments or by adherence of rigorous disciplines and control of desire, sense, emotions and will. Imperfections due to partial human judgment have no place in it. In other words, the core of mysticism remains unchanged. The mystical consciousness is thus not just a change in the threshold of ordinary consciousness. Drugs or even certain injections or environment could bring about a hightened sense of consciousness. This could hardly be the consciousness to which the Upaniṣads or the Bhagavad Gītā or The Cloud or Kabbalah refer.

In mysticism there are no relative values. Relative values are part and parcel of everyday consciousness. For the mystic the values are absolute. Another name for relative values would be 'responses.' Our limited consciousness conditions them. Absolute values cannot be so conditioned. It is for this reason that great mystics like Śaṅkara, or Rāmānuja, or Madhva, or Rāmakṛṣṇa, or Christ, or Moses are able to establish immediate contact with deeper values. On the other hand the average man gropes in the dark.

In this book we have tried to show that for the mystic ultimately even the anthropomorphically described God becomes a nameless Ultimate Reality about which no attributes can be predicated. Even if the mystic begins with a concept of God, he ends with the experience of the Ultimate Reality.

So when the question is raised : Is God dead? A counter question can be asked, Is the concept of God dead or the experience of God? Even if the philosophical foundation has been removed from the concept of God, over the years, can we say the same thing about the experience to which the concept of God points? Were this experience to die, man would be as good as dead. Technology has turned him into practically, a thing. Besides, man is no more interested in answers to questions he raised before. Greater than the nuclear danger is this danger which springs from man's disinterestedness. But mysticism can turn him away from this apathy. Both the concept and the experience will have to survive—*it will survive*. In the words of Evelyn Underhill :

> "To be a mystic is simply to participate here and now in that real and eternal life; in the fullest, deepest sense which is possible to man. It is to share, as a free and conscious agent—not a servant; but a son—in the joyous travail of the Universe : its mighty onward sweep through pain and glory towards its home in God."[14]

REFERENCES

1. Quoted by W.T. Stance, Mysticism and Philosophy, Macmillan, London, 1972, p. 244.
   'She' refers to soul.
2. Muṇḍ. III.ii.9.
3. Mā. 2.

4. The Ten Classical Upaniṣads, Vol. I, Ed. P.B. Gajendragadkar, Bharatiya Vidya Bhavan, Bombay, 1981, p. 255.
5. Amoury de Riencourt, William Morrow and Co. Inc., New York, 1981, pp. 167-8. Riencourt quotes from Schrodinger's My View of the World, p. 18.
6. Behold the Spirit, Vintage Books, New York, 1972, p. 154.
7. Ibid, p. 155.
8. The Dance of Śiva, Essays on Indian Art and Culture, Dover Publications Inc., New York, 1985, p. 35.

   Note: Raso vai Saḥ, Rasam hi eva ayam labdherā, ānandī bhavati.
9. Markings, translated. Leif Sjoberg and W.H. Auden, Faber and Faber, London, 1964, p. 7.
10. Ibid, p. 23.
11. I and Thou, Trs. Ronald Gregor Smith, T. and T. Clark, Edinburg, Second Edition, p. 3.
12. Exodus, XXXIII : 20.
13. B.G., XI : 12.
14. Mysticism, Methuen & Co. Ltd., London, 1967, p. 447.

APPENDIX ONE

Psychedelic Experience

Our age may be called the psychedelic age. At no time in the history of the world did psychedelic culture play such an important and prominent (also disastrous) a part as it plays today. Aldous Huxley wrote in his famous essay, 'Drugs : That shape man's mind' :

"In the course of history many more people have died for drink and their dope, than have died for their religion or their country. The craving for ethyl alcohol and the opiates has been stronger, in these millions, than the love of God, of home, of children, even of life. Their cry was not for liberty or death, it was for death preceded by enslavement. There is a paradox here, and a mystery. Why should such multitude of men and women, be so ready to sacrifice themselves for a cause so utterly hopeless and in ways so painful and so profoundly humiliating?"[1]

The above quotation sums up the drug scene today. At the same time it asks questions to which there are no simple or single answers. One of the earliest known of the substances, *Soma* of the Vedic hymns, was an object of worship. Ṛg Veda IX is replete with references to *Soma*. We have drunk *Soma*, we have become immortal, we have arrived at the light, we have reached the Gods, what power has malevolence over us now, what can perfidy of mortals do to us, O, Immortal? This is the burden of the hymns. Suffice it to say that "the plant occupied an integral part in the myth and ritual structure of the Vedic religion, was regarded as divinity, and was itself ritually consumed to bring the worshipper to a state of divine exhilaration and incarnation."[2] The following thesis advanced by De Felice and quoted by the authors of

Varieties of Psychedelic Experience, make interesting reading, He quotes from De Felice's book Poisons Sacre's[3] :

"De Felice advanced the thesis that one of the earliest known of the substances, the *Soma* of the Vedic hymns, may have been indirectly responsible for the development of Haṭha Yoga. The *Soma* appears to have been some kind of a creeping plant which the Āryan invaders brought down with them from Central Asia about 1500 B.C. .... According to de Felice as the Āryans moved deeper into India the Gods proved more difficult to find as the *Soma* plant, like fine wine, would not travel. The exercises of the Haṭha Yoga school, he suggests, may have been created as an attempt to fill the 'Somatic' gap and achieve that physiological state of being conducive to religious states of consciousness, similar to those brought on by the ingestion of the sacred food. The larger implication of this thesis is that "vegetable-provoked mysticism", was the result of early man having, "come upon his first instances of consciousness change through his random eating of herbs and vegetables."[4] Of course this ingenious thesis cannot move beyond the sphere of conjecture.

We do not propose to give an historical account of psychedelic drugs. That would be beside the point—What we propose to do, however, is to show that it is amazing that claims of religious and mystic efficacy should be made for psychedelic drugs. It would indeed be a supreme irony of history of religion and mysticism should it be proved that a mere swallowing of a pill should induce states of exalted consciousness which the most ardent and adept seeker tries, very often in vain, to attain through a lifetime of disciplines and exercises. What is more amazing is the claim that drugs are a key to mystical illumination. Of course there is also a camp which holds that drugs produce conditions which mimic schizophrenia and distort the mind. There is also a section of writers who claim that the mystic is a schizophrenic. These controversies do not concern us directly. But what does concern us is the reference to the mystic as a schizophrenic. Such an accusation, for instance, was levelled against St. Teresa of Avila. We hold that whatever the mystic is or is not, he is definitely not a schizophrenic.

SCHIZOPHRENIA AND MYSTICISM

It is not our intention to go into the clinical and pathological details about schizophrenia. To all outward appearances, as we stated above, the mystic and the schizophrenic share the same flight from the social world. Mysticism and schizophrenia have often been linked together in psychedelic literature. If we were to define schizophrenia in simple terms we would say that it is a condition in which the individual experiences himself and the world about him, in a manner distinctly different from that of most members of society. The schizophrenic's conception of time, space and the relationship between social situations and inner feelings are often not those shared by the social world. The apparent similarities between the schizophrenic and mystical experience are :

(a) They both experience a dichotomy between two levels of experience—the outer or social as opposed to inner or personal.

(b) They experience pain and terror as they 'enter' the inner world. (In the case of the mystic the pain and terror are caused by the Dark Night of the Soul.) These, as we said at the outset, are apparent similarities. In point of fact it is observed that among the most important differences, the schizophrenic's inability to control his inner experience is of paramount importance. For the schizophrenic the difference between the social world and inner world is completely blurred. The schizophrenic cannot, in fact he is unable to come to terms with himself. The mystic on the other hand is in complete command of himself. He is in full control of his inner experience. It is for this reason that the mystic does not break with social reality which the schizophrenic does. This becomes clear when we seek the reason for this state of affairs.

The mystic is prepared for the experience. He goes through disciplines which, so to say, build his 'spiritual' muscles, which in turn help him to withstand his inner experience. These disciplines help the mystic to purify his self. A short quotation from Underhill will show what we mean :

"So too Al Ghazzali, the Persian contemplative says of the period immediately following his acceptance of the principles of

Sufism and consequent renunciation of property. 'I went to Syria where I remained more than two years; without any other object than that of living in seclusion and solitude, conquering my desires, struggling with my passions, striving to purify my soul, to perfect my character, and to prepare my heart to meditate upon God'."[5] Evidently, the schizophrenic undergoes no such training. When thrown into the 'inner World' he is overwhelmed with no means of dealing with his experience and no conviction that he will survive it. Those who, through ignorance, compare the mystic to a schizophrenic, completely lose sight of this important and vital aspect of mysticism.

The second important difference is that the mystic *temporarily* frees himself from the customs and habits so necessary to live in a society. Once the state of total freedom has been achieved the mystic is able once again to involve himself in social activities. A life lived completely in the inner world would ultimately lead to physical death. In writing about his confrontation with the unconscious, C.G. Jung stressed the importance of his external life in protecting him from the too sudden exposure to the inner world of the unconscious. The importance of the following quotation lies in the fact that it is from no less a person than Jung. If we have quoted at some length it is because it throws light on the issue of how important it is to return to the social world, and the disastrous consequences that ensure on failure to do so. Jung writes :

"Particularly at this time, when I was working on the fantasies, I needed a point of support in 'this world', and I may say my family and my professional work were that to me. It was most essential for me to have a normal life in the real world as a counterpoise to that strange inner world. My family and my profession remained the base to which I could always return, assuring me that I was an actually existing ordinary person. The unconscious contents could have driven me out of my wits. But my family, and the knowledge : I have a medical diploma from a Swiss University, I must help my patients, I have a wife and five children, I live at 228 Seestrasse in Kusnacht—these were actualities which made demands upon me and proved to me again and again that I really existed, and that I was not a blank page whirling about in the winds of the spirit, like Nietzsche. Nietzsche had lost the ground under his feet because he possessed nothing more than the inner world of his thoughts—which incidentally possessed him more than he it. He was uprooted and hovered above the earth and therefore he succumbed to exaggeration and irreality."[6]

In the passage above Dr. Jung in a masterly fashion warns us about the exclusive use of the inner world. Such a state, as illustrated by the case of Nietzsche, is pathological. For the mystic the inner world is not a refuge. For the schizophrenic, it is a refuge, because be is not able to function in the social world. The inner experiences of the mystic are consciously chosen over a period of time and developed within the cultural context. On the other hand the experiences of the schizophrenic come on suddenly and occur in the denial of his social functioning. The mystic's experience prepares him for a lifelong movement between inner experience and social functioning. In the case of the mystic there is integration : the outer and inner may be joined. When these are separated you have the schizophrenic. It is apparent from this short discussion that dismissing the mystic by calling him a schizophrenic is not only not borne out by facts but totally unjustifiable.

We do not, however, completely rule out the possibility of mysticism induced by certain drugs. Mysticism is not a subject that can be put to empirical tests in the laboratory. However, a cursory view of the Hindu scriptures as noticed in the Ṛg veda shows that *Soma* was used and worshipped for reasons that transcended their use as stimulants. Practically all the ancient civilizations of the world have used drugs. Looking at the drug scene today it would appear that such uses lead to abuse and trouble when the technique of using them is separated from their religious and cultural associations. In general, we have become more awed than aided by our experience with many drugs. Here undoubtedly are agents that reveal previously hidden consciousness and modes of thought, but revelation, although perhaps instructive is not tantamount to understanding. For that we must employ our mental faculties in the undrugged state. This is the lesson of civilization.

REFERENCES

1. Collected Essays, Bantam Books, New York, 1960, p. 336.
2. R.E.L. Masters and Jean Houston, The Varieties of Psychedelic Experience, A Delta Book, New York, 1966, 9th Printing, p. 250.
3. Ivresses Divines : Editions Albin, Paris, 1936.
4. Op. cit., pp. 249/250.
5. Mysticism, Methuen Co. Ltd., U.K. 1969, p. 226. The unknown author of Theologia Germanica says : "Christ's soul must needs descend into hell, before it ascended into heaven. So must also the soul of man."

   Stuart and Watkins, London, 1974, p. 50.
6. Memories, Dreams, Reflections, Collins, 1974, p. 214.

APPENDIX TWO

Modern Physics and Mysticism—The Quantum Factor

The title may sound strange. Physics and mysticism, it may be argued, make strange bedfellows. That such an accusation is not sustainable will be borne out by what follows. The Christian, Judaic and Muslim traditions all propose a rational deity who is the creator but distinct from the physical universe. Such a belief was implicit in the work of Newton and his contemporaries during the rise of modern science in the Seventeenth century. This theistic dimension has long since disappeared, but its implications for the natural order of the physical world still remain unchanged. In recent years there has been a growing interest among certain physicists and cosmologists concerning the nature of the laws of physics.

If, therefore, we are to consider the relationship of mysticism (particularly the Eastern variety) to modern physics, then a reference to Quantum Mechanics and Relativity is absolutely necessary. It is through these that we can come to cosmology, which in turn brings us to Mysticism.

The changes in our world view brought about by modern physics have been widely discussed both by philosophers and physicists. But what passes notice is that these discussions drift towards views held by Eastern philosophers and mystics. When we say Eastern philosophies or mysticism we include, Hinduism, Buddhism and Taoism. No doubt these philosophies and mysticism comprise of systems with subtle and sometimes major differences, but their basic views are the same. In fact, it can be stated without hesitation that modern physics seems to lead to the view that there is considerable similarity, between its view and that held by mystics belonging to all major traditions of the world.

A brief comparison between the Eastern world view and the world view emerging from modern physics will demonstrate what we are trying to say. It should be remembered that the world view that dominated classical physics from the second half of the seventeenth century to the end of the 19th century was purely mechanistic. Such a mechanistic view could only be based on dualism between spirit and matter, it permitted scientists to look upon matter as dead and completely different from themselves. The material world was therefore looked upon as an assembly of multitude of different objects, assembled, so to say, into a huge machine.

In sharp contrast to this mechanistic view, the Eastern mystic looked upon all things and phenomena as interrelated, connected and, therefore, they constituted for him manifestations of the same ultimate reality. Man's mind is so constituted that he classifies, categorises; but the Eastern mystic views this tendency of perceiving things as separate and to experience ourselves as separate egos, as an illusion. Though such a tendency may enable man to cope with everyday life, it is not a fundamental feature of reality. For Eastern mysticism, any such objects have a fluid and ever changing character.

The Eastern view is thus dynamic. By this is meant that the cosmos is at one and the same time alive, organic, spiritual and material, forever in motion, but one inseparable reality.

QUANTUM MECHANICS

To understand the position above, we will go back to Quantum Mechanics. From times immemorial atoms were looked upon as hard and solid particles. This turned out to be a totally incorrect concept. Not only atoms were not hard and solid particles, but they were vast regions of empty spaces. In these vast empty spaces moved extremely small particles. These were called electrons. These moved around the nucleus. But with the dawn of quantum mechanics (theoretical foundation of atomic physics) even the electrons, protons and neutrons in the nucleus (known as subatomic particles) were nothing like the solid objects of classical physics. They were almost abstract entities. They appeared sometimes as particles and sometimes as waves depending on how you viewed them. Matter thus had a dual aspect which proved to be quite baffling. Dr. R. Puligandla writes :

"Having generalized the uncertainty principle into the doctrine of complementary, Bohr has untiringly argued in the last forty years through critical analysis of ingenious experimental situations that complementarity is an inescapable feature of nature. According to the doctrine of complementarity, wave-particle dualism is ultimate; there can be no single experimental set-up in which both particle and wave aspects of a micro-physical system can be detected; an arrangement for observing the manifestations of one aspect automatically eliminates the possibility of observing those of the other."[1]

We give one more quotation from Paul Davies (a professor of theoretical physics at the University of New Castle Upon Tyne, whose books and articles attempt to establish a relationship between science and religion). He writes :

"Uncertainty is the fundamental ingredient of the quantum theory. It leads directly to the consequence of unpredictability. Does every event have a cause? Few would deny it.

"Most scientists, under the leadership of the Danish physicist Niels Bohr, accepted that atomic uncertainty is truly intrinsic to nature : the rules of clockwork might apply to familiar objects such as snooker balls, but when it comes to atoms, the rules are those of roulette. A dissenting, albeit distinguished, voice was that of Albert Einstein, 'God does not play dice,' he declared."[2]

This duality puzzled physists, "How can the mind be both thought and neural impulses? How can a novel be both a story and a collection of words? Wave-particle duality is another software-hardware dichotomy. The particles aspect is the hardware face of atoms—little balls rattling about. The wave aspect corresponds to software, or mind, or information, for the quantum wave is not like any other sort of wave anybody has ever encountered. It is not a wave of any substance or physical stuff, but a wave of knowledge or information. It is a wave that tells us what can be known about the atom, not a wave of the atom itself."[3]

The seeming contradiction between the two (particles-waves) was finally solved. This solution came like a blow to the very foundation of the mechanistic world view, that is, to the concept of the reality of matter. It was found that at the subatomic level, matter does not exist with certainty at definite places, but rather shows tendencies to exist. These tendencies are known as probabilities in quantum mechanics. The corresponding mathematical quantities take the form of waves. This is the reason why at one and the same time, particles can be waves. Of course these waves are not waves like the waves of the sea or like sound waves. They are known as 'probability waves,' abstract mathematical quantities possessing all the characteristic properties of waves which are related to the probabilities of finding the particles at certain points in space at particular times.

What does all this add up to? It adds up to the conclusion that at the level of the atom, what classical physics took to be solid material objects dissolve into wavelike patterns of probabilities.

When we say that solid material objects dissolve into probabilities we run into a paradox. Such a statement can be interpreted to mean that the world is made up of probabilities. What is actually meant is that these are not probabilities of things, but probabilities of co-relations. This is because a close study of the process of observation in atomic physics reveals that as isolated entities subatomic particles have no meaning. These particles, therefore, can only be understood when viewed as correlations between the preparations of an experiment and the subsequent measurement.

Reduced to physico-philosophical terminology, we can say that quantum mechanics reveals that basically there is oneness in the universe. In other words, it is not possible to break the world into independently existing units. If we go deep into matter, if we pierce matter, we discover that nature does not reveal independent building blocks, but what we see is a complicated web and fabric with one part related to the other. Werner Heisenberg writes :

"The world thus appears as a complicated tissue of events, in which connections of different kinds alternate or overlap or combine and thereby, determine the texture of the whole."[4]

Words like these show that the Eastern mystic experiences the world in almost an identical manner. His expression of the experience, too, is significantly identical. Lama Angārika Govinda writes :

"The Buddhist does not believe in an independent or separately existing external world, into whose dynamic forces he could insert himself. The external world and his inner world are for him only the two sides of the same fabric, in which the threads of all forces and of all events, of all forms of consciousness and of their objects, are woven into an inseparable net of endless, mutually conditioned relations.

"The word *'Tantra'* is related to the concept of weaving and its derivatives (thread, web, fabric, etc.) hinting at the interwovenness of things and actions, the interdependence of all that exists, the continuity in the interaction of cause and effect, as well as in spiritual and traditional development, which like a thread weaves its way through the fabric of history and of individual lives."[5]

The quotation above brings out a very important point. It shows that just as in quantum mechanics, so also in Eastern mysticism, the interconnectedness of the universe invariably includes the human observer and his consciousness in an essential way. In atomic physics when we speak about nature, we have at the same time to speak about ourselves. Heisenberg says :

"Natural science does not simply describe and explain nature, it is a part of the interplay between nature and ourselves."[6]

In modern physics, the physicist cannot play the role of a detached observer. He has to become part and parcel of the world he observes. The word 'observer' has been replaced by 'participator.' Sacred knowledge, whether of the Upaniṣads or of Buddhist texts or Taoist texts cannot be obtained merely by observation. What is necessary is active participation with one's whole being, just as in quantum, so also in the Eastern mystical traditions, the notion of participation is central to the issue.

Lama Angārika Govinda says

"The abstractness of philosophical concepts and conclusions requires to be constantly corrected by direct experience, by the practise of meditation and the contingencies of daily life . . . . This cannot be achieved through building up convictions, ideals, and aims based on reasoning, but only through conscious penetration of those layers of our mind which cannot be reached or influenced by logical arguments and discursive thought."[7]

So, the fact that matter at the atomic level appears as particles and as waves also, goes to show that there is an essential interconnectedness of all phenomena. One more thing is noticed at this stage. We notice that particles restricted in a confined state tend to move around. The more one confines a particle, the faster it moves around. We have a very striking passage from Swami Vivekānanda. He writes :

"Everything that we perceive around us is struggling towards freedom, from the atom to the man, from the insentient, life-less particle of matter to the highest existence on earth, the human soul. The whole universe is in fact the result of the struggle for freedom. In all combinations every particle is trying to go on its own way, to fly from the other particles; but the others are holding it in check. Our earth is trying to fly away from the Sun, and the Moon from the Earth. Everything has a tendency to infinite dispersion."[8]

Matter is never quiescent, but always in a state of motion, modern physics thus pictures matter not at all as inert, but as being in a continuous dancing and vibrating motion, whose rhythmic patterns are determined by the molecular atomic and nuclear structures. Compare this with the following from a Taoist text :

"The stillness in stillness is not the real stillness. Only when there is stillness in movement can the spiritual rhythm appear which pervades heaven and earth."[9]

We will not go into the theories of quantum mechanics or relativity further. Suffice it to say that the Eastern mystics did not know anything about these theories. Somehow or the other they sensed the whole thing in their mystical moments. Their theories exhibit the main features of the Eastern world view.

What, therefore, is the upshot of the discussion above? In the words of Amaury de Riencourt : "Nature itself exhibits a *holistic* tendency to form wholes that are greater than the sum of the parts we obtain when we break them up—a fact that was apprehended by the East thousands of years ago."[10]

When this monist vision of the world is taken, the opposition between subject—object melts away, leaving behind only Ultimate Reality.

In fine, the basic theories of modern physics actually exhibit the main features of the Eastern world view. Quantum mechanics, as we have briefly discussed above, has abolished the notion of fundamentally separated objects. It has replaced the concept of the observer by that of the participator and has found it necessary to include the human consciousness in the description of the world. It is not unlikely that at some future date these similarities will become more and more apparent, as physics progresses in its explanation of the subnuclear world.

REFERENCES

1. Quantum Theory, An Examination of the Copenhagen Interpretation, Sterling Publishers Pvt. Ltd., New Delhi, 1977, p. 1.
2. Paul Davies, God and the New Physics, Penguin Books, 1986, p. 102.
3. Ibid, p. 107.
4. Physics and Philosophy, Allen and Unwin, London, 1963, p. 96.
5. Foundations of Tibetan Mysticism, Rider and Co., London, 1959, p. 93.
6. Op. cit., p. 75.
7. Op. cit., p. 91.
8. The Complete Works of Swami Vivekānanda, Mayavati Memorial Ed. Vol. 1, Advaita Ashrama, Calcutta, 1965, p. 108.
9. Quoted by N.W. Ross, Three Ways of Asian Wisdom, Simon and Schuster, New York, 1968, p. 144.
10. The Eye of Shiva, William Morrow & Co. Inc., New York, 1981, p. 170.

Bibliography

Aurobindo : *Essays on the Gītā*, Sri Aurobindo Ashram, Pondicherry, 1986.

The Upaniṣads, Sri Aurobindo Ashram, Pondicherry, 1985.

Selections from Sri Aurobindo's Sāvitri, Sri Aurobindo Ashram Trust, Edited, Mary Aldridge, 1975.

Broad, C.D. : *Religion, Philosophy and Psychical Research*, Routledge and Kegan Paul Ltd., London, 1953.

Buber, Martin : *I and Thou*, Second Edition, T. and T. Clark, Edinburgh, U.K.

Capra, Fritjof : *The Tao of Physics*, Fontana Collins, England, 1976.

Cavandish, Richard : *The Black Arts*, G.P. Putnam Sons, New York, 1967.

Chaudhary, Pravas Jivan : *Philosophy and Phenomenological Research*, Quarterly, Vol. 20, No. 2, Buffalo, New York.

Chinmayānanda, Swami : *Talks on Śaṅkara's Vivekachūḍāmaṇi*, Central Chinmaya Mission Trust, Bombay, 1981.

Sri Śaṅkarācārya's Bhaja Govindam, Central Chinmaya Mission Trust, Bombay, 1965.

Coomaraswamy, Ananda K. : *The Dance of Śiva*, Essays on Indian Art and Culture, Dover Publications, New York, 1985.

Dasgupta, Surendranath : *Hindu Mysticism*, Motilal Banarasidass, Delhi, 1983.

Davies, Paul. : *God and the New Physics*, Penguin Book, London, 1986.

Descartes, Renée. : *Discourses on Method*, Penguin, London, 1960.

Deussen, Paul : *The Philosophy of the Upaniṣads*, Dover Publication, Inc., New York, 1966.

Sixty Upaniṣads of the Veda, Volumes I—II, Trs. from German by V.M. Bedekar and G.B. Palsule, Motilal Banarsidass, Delhi, 1980.

Durant, Will : *Caesar and Christ*, Simon and Schuster, New York, 1950.

The Age of Faith, Simon and Schuster, New York, 1950.

Eliade, Mircea :*Yoga, Immortality and Freedom*, Bollingen Series, Princeton University Press, New York, 1973.

Encyclopaedia Judaica, 1986.

Fromm, Erich :*You Shall Be As Gods*, Fawcett Premier, New York, 1986.

Gajendragadkar, P.B. : *The Ten Classical Upaniṣads*, Volume One, Īśa and Kena, Bharatiya Vidya Bhavan, Bombay, 1981.

Govinda, Lama Angarika : *Foundations of Tibetan Mysticism*, Rider and Co., London, 1959.

Halevi, Ziev Ben Shimon : *Kabbalah*, Thames and Hudson, U.K., 1979.

Hammarskjold, Dag : *Markings*, Tr. Leifsjoberg and W.H. Auden, Faber and Faber, London, 1965.

Hocking, William Ernest : *Types of Philosophy*, Charles Scribners Sons, New York, 1930.

Hume, Robert Ernest : *The Thirteen Principal Upaniṣads*, Humphrey Milford, Oxford University Press, London, 1934.

Hume, David : *A Treatise of Human Nature*, Edited Selby Giggs, Clarendon Press, 1955.

Huxley, Aldous : *Ends and Means*, Chatto and Windus, 1957.

Collected Essays, Bantam Books, New York, 1960.

The Perennial Philosophy, Chatto and Windus, London, 1946.

Jacobs, Louis : *Jewish Theology,* Darton Longman and Todd, London, 1973.

James, William : *The Varieties of Religious Experience,* The Modern Library, New York, 1929.

Johnston, William : *The Mysticism of the Cloud of Unknowing,* Anthony Clarke, U.K., 1987.

Jung, C.G. : *The Basic Writings of C.G. Jung,* Ed. Violet Staub de Laszla, The Modern Library, New York, 1959.

Answer to Job, Bollingen Series, Princeton University Press, 1973.

Collected Works, Routledge and Kegan Paul, Volume Nine, London.

Memories, Dreams, Reflections, Collins, The Fontana Library, London, 1974.

Psychology and the Occult, Bollingen Series, Princeton University Press, U.S.A., 1977.

Kant, Immanuel : *The Critique of Pure Reason,* Ed. Norman K. Smith, London, MacMillan, 1930.

The Critique of Practical Reason, Tr. Thomas Kingshil Abbot, Longman, 1967.

Kaplan, Aryeh : *Jewish Meditation,* Schocken Books, New York, 1985.

Meditation and Kabbalah, Samuel Weiser, U.S.A., 1985.

Kolhatkar, K.K. : *Bharatiya Manas-shastra Athava Patanjala Yoga-Darshan* (Marathi), Keshava Bhikaji Dhaavale, 1955.

Lebail, Patrick : *Six Upaniṣads Majeures,* Le Courrier du Livre, Paris, 1971.

Mahadeyan, T.M.P. : *Time and Timeless,* Upaniṣad Vihar, Madras, 1953.

Mohapatra, A.R. : *Idea of the Inexpressible,* Cosmo Paperbacks, New Delhi, 1984.

Mudgal, S.G. : *Advaita of Śaṅkara, A Reappraisal,* Motilal Banarsidass, Delhi, 1975.

Mueller, Max : *The Upaniṣads,* Part II, Motilal Banarsidass, Delhi, 1969.

Plato : *The Dialogues of Plato*, Tr. B. Jowett, Volumes 1—2, Random House, New York, 18th Printing.

Potter, Karl H. : *Encyclopaedia of Indian Philosophy, Advaita Vedānta upto Śaṁkara and His Pupils*, Edited Potter, Motilal Banarsidass, Delhi, 1981.

Pratt, James Bisset : *The Religious Consciousness*, The MacMillan Co., New York, 1951.

Puligandla, R. : *Quantum Theory, An Examination of the Copenhagen Interpretation*, Sterling Publishing Private Ltd., New Delhi, 1977.

Radhakrishnan, S. : *Indian Philosophy*, Volumes 1-2, Blackie and Son Publishers Private Ltd., Bombay, 1977.

The Bhagavad Gītā George Allen and Unwin Ltd., London, 1967.

The Hindu View of Life, Blackie and Son Publishers Private Ltd., Bombay, 1983.

The Idealist View of Life, Mandala Books, Unwin Paperbacks, London, 1980.

Brahma Sūtra, George Allen and Unwin Ltd., U.K., 1960.

Ranade, R.D. : *Mysticism in Maharashtra (Indian Mysticism)*, Motilal Banarsidass, Delhi, 1982.

Vendānta, The Culmination of Indian Thought, Bharatiya Vidya Bhavan, Bombay, 1970.

A Constructive Survey of Upaniṣadic Philosophy, Bharatiya Vidya Bhavan, 1986.

Ranganathānanda, Swami : *The Message of the Upaniṣads*, Bharatiya Vidya Bhavan, Bombay, 1968.

Eternal Values of a Changing Society, Volume One : *Philosophy and Spirituality*, Bharatiya Vidya Bhavan, Bombay, 1980.

Reincourt, Amaury de : *The Eye of Śiva*, Eastern Mysticism and Science, William Marrow and Co. Inc., New York, 1981.

Ross, Nancy Wilson : *Three Ways of Asian Wisdom*, A Clarion Book, Simon and Schuster, U.S.A., 1966.

Russell, Bertrand : *A History of Western Philosophy,* Unwin Paperbacks, London, 1987.

Sadānanda : *Vedānta-Sāra,* Advaita Ashrama, Calcutta, 1987.

Scholem, Gershom : *Major Trends in Jewish Mysticism,* Schoken Books, New York, 1967.

On The Kabbalah and Its Symbolism, Routledge and Kegan Paul, London, 1965, Tr. Ralph Manheim.

Scholem, Gershom : *Sabbatai Sevi, The Mystical Messiah,* Tr. R.J. Zwi Werblowsky, Bollingen Series, xciii Princeton University Press, 1975.

Sharma, B.N.K. : *Philosophy of Madhvācārya,* Motilal Banarsidass, 1986.

Sri Madhva's Techings In His Own Words, Bharatiya Vidya Bhavan, Bombay, 1979.

Srinivasachari, P.N. : *The Philosophy of Viśiṣṭādvaita,* Adyar Library and Research Centre, Madras, 1978.

Stace, W.T. : *Mysticism and Philosophy,* MacMillan, London, 1971.

Time and Eternity, Princeton University, New York, 1952.

The Teachings of the Mystics, A Mentor Book, New York, 1960.

Suzuki, Daisetz Teitaro : *The Lankavatara Sutra,* Routlege and Kegan Paul, London, 1978.

Teachings of the Compassionate Buddha, Ed., E.A. Burlt, New American Library, Mentor Books, New York, 1955.

Thera, Nyanaponika : *The Heart of Buddhist Meditation,* Rider and Co., London, 1969.

Toynbee, Arnold : *Man's Concern with Death,* Robin Denniston Publishers, Arnold Toynbee and Others.

Underhill, Evelyn : *Mysticism, A Study in the Nature and Development of Man's Spiritual Consciousness,* Methuen and Co. Ltd., London, 1967.

Varieties of Psychedelic Experience, Ed. R.E.L. Masters and Jean Houston, Delta Book, New York, 1966.

Vishnudevananda, Swami : *The Complete Illustrated Book of Yoga,* Pocket Books, New York, 1972.

Vivekānanda, Swami : *Rāja-Yoga,* Advaita Ashrama, Almora, 1930.

Complete Works, Volumes 1 and 4, Mayavati Memorial Edition, Advaita Ashrama, Calcutta, 9th Edition, 1966.

Watts, Allan : *The Supreme Identity,* Vintage Book, New York, 1972.

Behold The Spirit, (A Study in the Necessity of Mystical Religion), Vintage Book, New York, 1972.

Psychotherapy, East and West, Jonathan Cape, London, 1972.

Whitehead, Alfred North : *Science and the Modern World,* A Mentor Book, New York, 14th Printing.

Winkworth, Susanna (Translator) : *Theologia Germanica,* Stuart and Watkins, London, 1966.

Zaehner, R.C. : *Hindu and Muslim Mysticism,* Schocken Books, New York, 1969.

The Zohar, Tr. Harry Sperling and Maurice Simon, Volumes 1-5, Soncino Press, New York, 1984.

Glossary

Absolute :	The ultimate underlying reality, world ground, that being which depends on nothing else for its existence and activity, but upon which all other things depend for their existence and activity.
Advaita :	Variously defined as non-dualism, the doctrine that posits the Ultimate Reality, as one and undifferentiated; non-dual absolute. Received its clearest statement in Śaṅkara.
Alef :	First letter of the Hebrew alphabet.
Agnosticism :	The thesis that it is impossible to know whether God exists or not.
Amidah :	The central prayer of Jewish liturgy, the word meaning 'standing' since the prayer is said standing, facing towards Jerusalem. It consists of nineteen benedictions.
Anthropocentric :	Referring to the view which maintains that man is the centre and ultimate goal of the universe.
Anthropomorphic :	The representation of God as having human form, attributes etc.
Archetype :	An important concept in Jungian psychology. Jung believed that all human beings share a common set of deep seated motivational and behaviour patterns carried over from generation to generation and part of our evolutionary heritage.

Ātman :	The true Self, often coupled with Brahman. The two are intimately entwined. May be used as synonyms. Subjectively known as self, objectively as Brahman.
Avidyā :	Ignorance, Individual ignorance, often used as a synonym for ajñāna. Has been the subject of endless speculation.
Avatār :	Manifestation of God on earth.
Beth :	Second letter of the Hebrew alphabet.
Bhakti :	The path of devotion as opposed to the path of knowledge.
Big Bang :	A theory that suggests that there was a time called the "Big Bang" when the universe was infinitesimally small and infinitely dense. One may say that time had a beginning at the Big Bang.
Bodhisattva :	A Buddha to be, anyone who has passed arahantship or perfect being.
Brahman :	The supreme reality conceived as one and undifferentiated, static and dynamic, yet beyond definition. It is neti neti.
Chakras :	Literally wheel. Mystically, in tāntric yoga, centres of the body. In the human body, along the central spinal canal, (called sushumnā) six main chakras (centres of consciousness) are located. These chakras, and a seventh centre in the cerebrum, are sometimes called 'lotuses' in yogic language, because they are said to open like lotus blossoms and resemble them in shape.
Cogito ergo sum :	I think, therefore, I am.
Empiricism :	Referring to knowledge founded on experience, observation, facts, concrete situations and real events.
En Sof :	That of which nothing can be predicated and yet must be postulated; absolute perfection; God who is called En Sof in respect of himself

is called Ayin in respect of first self revelation.

Epistemology : Theory of knowledge; that branch of philosophy which asks the question 'Where does knowledge come from.' 'How is it formulated, expressed and communicated?'

Eschatological : The doctrine of the last or final things, as death, judgement, state after death.

Gnosticism : Gnosis is a Greek word meaning knowledge, Gnostic Knowledge was open only to the initiate, and not to the laymen. Gnosticism teaches a single, unknowable divine God, in his most formidable and unknowable form, beyond the grasp of any, but the initiates.

Hasidism : A mystical mass movement founded in the late 18th century by Israel Baal Shem Tov.

Husserl : German philosopher, set off the study of phenomenology into pure non-empirical science. (See Phenomenology)

Idealism : A name given to philosophical theories, that have in common the view that what would normally be called 'external world' is somehow created by the mind.

Illusion : A mistake in perception caused by insufficient information or by conflicting cues being provided. For example, snake-rope.

Immanent : Indwelling, as distinct from the transcendental.

Intuition : A form of uninferred or immediate knowledge.

Israel : In the Torah the name Israel is taken to mean one who has contended with the Divine

Jñāna : Knowledge of Ultimate Reality, the transcendental realisation that ātman and Brahman are one.

Kabbalah : The 'received tradition' of Jewish Mysticism. The main text of the Kabbalah is the Zohar. The Kabbalah teaches that, the creation of the

	world took place through a series of emanations from En Sof.
Kuṇḍalini :	Literally 'coiled up' like a serpent; the spiritual energy dormant in human beings at the base of the spine. When this energy awakens and passess through Centres of Consciousness in the central spiral canal it manifests itself in mystic experiences.
Lebensanschauung :	The basing of religious life on the emotional side of man's nature.
Mahāvākya :	A terse Vedāntic formula or mantra, stating the oneness of the individual with Brahman (tat tvam asi) that thou art of (aham brahmansmi) I am Brahman.
Narcissism :	Excessive love for oneself.
Neo-Platonism :	A modern term for the recasting of Plato's philosophy as first completed by Plotinus.
Occult Power :	Psychic power, siddhi, these powers obstruct spiritual progress. The aspirant should not succumb to them.
Ontology :	The branch of metaphysical inquiry concerned with the study of existence itself. That branch of philosophy which asks the question "What does 'to be' 'to exist' mean?" It inquires about the reality status of a thing.
Panentheism :	All is in God.
Pantheism :	The doctrine that the Divine is all inclusive and that man and nature are not independent of God, but are modes or elements of his being.
Pentateuch :	The first five books of the Old Testament, Genesis, Exodus, Leviticus, Numbers and Deuteronomy.
Phenomenology :	The study of consciousness by introspection and subjective inspection of metal states. (See Husserl)

Prarabdha Karma : That portion of stored up karma from past lives which has begun to bear fruit in present life, in which it must be exhausted.

Quantum : The indivisible unit in which waves may be emitted or absorbed.

Quantum Mechanics : A system of mechanics used to explain the behaviour of atoms, molecules and elementary particles.

Sahasrārā : The seventh and the highest centre of yogic consciousness. It is symbolically referred to in tāntric terminology as thousand petalled lotus.

Saṁsāra : The doctrine, characteristic of all Indian religions, of an endless cycle of death and rebirth.

Scepticism : In a general sense and with a small 's,' the philosophical attitude that maintains that sure knowledge of how things really are may be sought but cannot be found.

Scepticism : With a capital 'S' is the name attached to a particular school of ancient Greek philosophy.

Soteriological : Man's efforts and energy should be directed towards transcending the consequences of his own actions.

Substratum : The basis of unity, uniformity of different objects and diverse properties of an individual singular object, thing and their sum total.

Sublime : An aesthetic category expressing the essence of phenomena, events and processes of great social significance. The idealist theories attribute it to the subject or to ideas of divine infinity, eternity etc.

Talmud : The written interpretation and development of the Hebrew scriptures.

Teleological : A thesis that assumes the existence of a superintelligent creation. A doctrine that everything in the world has been designed by God to be of service to man. The theory or study of purposiveness in nature. It underlies the theological proof of God's existence.

Theism : A religious philosophy which acknowledges the existence of a personal God as a supernatural being, endowed with reason and will and mysteriously influencing all the material and spiritual processes.

Theology : The study of God, systems of dogmas in a given religion.

Torah : The teachings of Moses. Five books of the Old Testament. See Pentateuch.

Transcendent : A term denoting that which is beyond consciousness and cognition, as opposed to the immanent. Beyond experience.

Turīya : The superconscious; the 'Fourth,' in relation to the three ordinary states of consciousness—waking, dreaming and dreamless sleep—which it transcends.

Weltanschauung : A general view of the world.

Zen Buddhism : A trend in Buddhism. It preaches sudden awakening, the comprehension of truth.

Zohar : It is the fundamental book of Jewish Kabbalah. It is the premier text book of Jewish mysticism. It is a commentary on the Pentateuch. It comprises treatises, texts, extracts or fragments of texts belonging to different periods, but all resembling in their method of mystical interpretation of the Torah and their anonymity.

Index

F

G

H

N

O

P

T